W9-AFI-222

NAKED HEART

NAKED HEART

A SOLDIER'S JOURNEY TO THE FRONT

by Harold Pagliaro

THOMAS JEFFERSON UNIVERSITY PRESS
Kirksville, Missouri
1996

Copyright © 1996 Thomas Jefferson University Press.
All rights reserved.
Printed in the United States of America.

03 02 01 00 99   5 4 3 2

Library of Congress Cataloging-in-Publication Data

Pagliaro, Harold E.
   Naked heart : a soldier's journey to the front / by Harold Pagliaro.
     p.   cm.
   Includes index.
   ISBN 0-943549-41-8 (alk. paper)
   1. Pagliaro, Harold E.   2. World War, 1939–1945—Personal narratives,
American.   3. Soldiers—United States—Biography.   4. United States.
Army—Biography.   I. Title.
D811.P2678   1996
940.54'8173—dc20   96-18820
                                                      CIP

Published by Thomas Jefferson University Press at Truman State University in
Kirksville, Missouri 63501 (*http://www2.truman.edu/tjup*).

No part of this work may be reproduced or transmitted in any format by any
means, electronic or mechanical, including photocopying and recording, or by
any information storage or retrieval system, without permission in writing
from the publisher.

The paper in this publication meets or exceeds the minimum requirements of
the American National Standard—Permanence of Paper for Printed Library
Materials, ANSI Z39.48 (1984).

To Judith

Contents

Preface

THE INCIDENTS IN THIS book are real. They make up the story of my life in the Army during World War II. In 1990, I found out that my mother had saved over two hundred letters I'd written home during that time. Before then I didn't know they existed. When I read them, I couldn't believe how little they said of my real feelings during those bad days, especially my weeks at the front. The pale letters, misleading as they are, made me remember how much I hid from my family and from myself when I wrote home. I was a kid of eighteen when I was drafted. When I turned nineteen, I was taken from the infantry division I'd trained with and sent into combat as a lone replacement. There, I fought side by side with men I didn't know. My story has many strands, but a lot of it turns on what it's like to be sent to the front at nineteen to fight among strangers. Thousands like me, boys just becoming men, went up to the lines without friends, taking the ultimate risk alone.

As I write, I hope I can recapture some of the uncertainty and naivete of my Army days. I was an idealistic kid, sometimes shrewd in sizing up people and situations, and in the long run tough, but I was immature. With many others, I became skeptical about how the Army used us, and yet mute and cooperative in the face of death. I'll do my best to show you the vulnerable young man, not the wily survivor, telling it as I lived it then. It is in some ways my special story. But it's also the story of countless frontline replacements.

Until the spring of 1942, nobody had talked much about drafting eighteen- and nineteen-year-olds. The Selective Service Act of 1940 called for all males between twenty-one and thirty-five to register at their local draft boards, which were manned by civilian volunteers who exempted men with dependents from military service; also exempted were men who had jobs essential to the war effort or to national health, safety, and welfare. When the Act was changed, shortly after America declared war in December 1941, it prepared the way for the President to call for registration of all men between eighteen and sixty-four, but it limited military service to those between twenty and forty-four. It wasn't until May 23, 1942, that the *New York Times* reported on its front page, "President Roosevelt ordered today the registration on June 30 of every male resident of the United States, Alaska, Hawaii, and Puerto Rico who will attain the age of eighteen or nineteen before June 30." The report goes on to say that the President may soon ask Congress "to remove the prewar restrictions exempting youths of eighteen and nineteen from compulsory military service."

Before this report was printed in the *New York Times,* the matter of drafting eighteen-year-olds had been settled in discussions between the Roosevelt administration and the Pentagon. But the issues involved were complicated, and they've never been completely resolved in the American conscience. All agreed that the military needed more men. The question was where to get them. Should married men be drafted? Should married men with children be drafted? Many believed that drafting men in either group was a danger to American family stability—exactly what the war was all about, they said. The newspapers were full of such arguments.

The alternative was to draft eighteen- and nineteen-year-olds. But there were arguments against this idea, too. Again the newspapers reported opposition. For example, on October 16,

1942, the *New York Times* printed a letter written by seven eminent psychiatrists who argued against drafting the younger men for combat on the grounds that they were not mature enough and would be permanently damaged by the experience.

The choice was a tough one—draft fathers and break up a generation of young families or draft eighteen-year-olds and send them to the front before they were grown up.

The American public was uncomfortable. Most agreed that the country needed these youngsters to increase the size of the Armed Services. But many were doubtful about drafting them for combat duty. Aware of the country's doubts, President Roosevelt tried to soften things. On June 10, he was reported in the back pages of the *New York Times* as saying no decision had been made on plans to draft the eighteen- to nineteen-year-old group. Obviously he was giving people time to get used to the idea.

Mrs. Roosevelt also tried to help. She was reported in the *Times* of June 9 as saying, "... the draft boards ought to be very careful to determine whether the boys are mature"; but she also said she saw no difference between drafting men at lower ages and at twenty-one. Her caution to the draft boards—which was right on the money—coupled with her acceptance of the draft for younger men, was intended to calm things. Her advice may have helped the nation's conscience for a time, but what draft board could follow it when each was soon given a stiff quota to fill?

Despite their willingness to lower the draft age, top brass were also divided, though not about sending the youngsters to the front. They were worried about another matter. Some, afraid the war would drag on for years, were against drafting all eighteen- and nineteen-year-olds, because no young men could then go on to college, and the military would lose its steady supply of highly trained personnel—men would be drafted straight out of high school. Others thought the war would end soon, especially with the huge increase in the armed forces made possible by the addition of eighteen- and nineteen-year-olds, and they weren't worried about the loss of highly educated recruits. The two sides decided on a compromise. They would establish programs to encourage qualified men to combine military service with college work, usually in engineering. The best known of these were the Navy's V-12 and the Army's ASTP. The Navy V-12 Program invited young civilians who scored high on a Navy IQ test to enlist as midshipmen and to go to college, working both for an engineering degree and a commission as ensign. The Army used its standard IQ test, taken by all recruits, as a way of finding new draftees eligible for the Army Specialized Training Program (ASTP); once in the Program, these men were given 13 weeks of infantry basic training—everyone in the ASTP was in the infantry—and then they were assigned to a college to study a subject the Army chose, usually engineering.

But the ASTP lasted hardly more than a year, from late 1942 until early 1944, both because support for it among the generals was halfhearted to begin with and because the anticipation of D-Day—June 1944—pointed to the need for additional ground troops. After March 1944, a few men in the ASTP were assigned to college and medical school, but thousands were sent to two infantry divisions, the 87th and the 104th, which did not see combat until the Battle of the Bulge. Then they were ripped apart.

Rumor had it that the brass never intended to commit these divisions, long held in reserve, because their ranks were untypical—filled with men who were very young and very promising for the professional life of the nation. Maybe these men should have been spread out among many divisions and not concentrated in just two.

There's yet another clue that the Army was ambivalent about eighteen-year-olds at the front. It was the policy that you could not be sent overseas and into a combat zone except as part of a unit with which you'd done extensive training. That way you'd know the people around you, and they'd know you; you'd be an integral part of the outfit you fought with, not only tactically, but emotionally.

Yet the Army drew the line abruptly. Once you turned nineteen, they could send you out by yourself, as a solo replacement, to a unit at the front, where you'd fight among strangers who didn't know you and who didn't want to know you—they had other things on their mind. In following this policy, the Army sent up men many thought too young for battle. It also placed them where they could not share in the outfit's esprit de corps, the sense of belonging that alone makes the repeated exposure to death bearable.

When in 1970 the nation gave the vote to eighteen-year-olds, it was in a way trying to legislate the maturity of these young people—a maturity in which it did not and does not believe. The legislation was a belated gesture, meant to correct, but actually acknowledging, the injustice we were again committing—sending our youth to war, this time to Vietnam. Not that drafting the very young is worse than drafting young fathers. The choice continues to be a tough one. There are ways to avoid it, but until we recognize what it means to kill or be killed, day in and day out, we'll never find one.

*

The few letters I quote are verbatim letters I wrote home during my Army days. The names of most of the people in my story are fictitious, but both they and the events in which I locate them are real. Though I treat most of them kindly, I thought they and their families might not want to be identified publicly. Members of my family have been given their true names. So have these others who figure only fleetingly in the narrative—Vice-Admiral Ben

Moreell, Madeleine Carroll, Edith E. Martin, Red Skelton, Art Smith, Melvin Douglas, Major General Richard J. Marshall, and Burt Lancaster.

Acknowledgments

I WISH TO THANK Avery Rome for her several suggestions about chapter 7, Frederic W. Hills for his helpful advice about narrative voice, and most of all, my wife, Judith Egan, who willingly read, discussed, and advised me about the book from the beginning.

Chapter One

The Army Gets Me

November 10, 1943
Dear Folks,
Arrived at Penn St OK-Stop-stomach settling-Stop-
Love, Harry

My stomach was slightly upset the morning I left for the Army. My mother and father and my younger brothers, Robert and Edward, said a simple good-bye after breakfast. Then I took a bus and subway from our house in the east Bronx, which was about halfway between the Zoo and Pelham Bay, to 34th Street. Just before I left Penn Station, I sent my first message home—on November 10, 1943—by postcard, pretending it was a telegram.

The long train carrying me from New York City to Camp Upton on the Long Island Railroad, in a slow, rocking motion, was a real introduction into Army life. Its shabby cars were packed. I sat next to a dirty window, feeling alone, vacantly watching the world pass by. It was a gray November day. Against the barren sky, I saw leafless scrub oak and very low sandhills, mile after mile. We were moving through the eastern part of Long Island. I looked out at the monotonous landscape and then at the men, taking them in and turning away, over and over until late in the trip.

The mood of that massed humanity was strange to me. I know there were others on the train as young as I, and in fact I was soon to meet them at Upton. But all the faces I saw in that worn, dirty car looked completed, each having taken on the shape of its own maturity. Mine hadn't. Not only did the faces of these men seem set for life; they themselves were focused on the present moment as if they'd been riding to an Army post forever. Some played poker or rummy, others shot craps, and yet others kept telling dirty jokes, in groups of four or five, sitting two by two on facing seats, sometimes with a fifth man standing over them in the aisle. All the games were marked by well-known calls to the Universe—"Beat that, Motherfucker," "Baby needs a pair of shoes." And all the bad jokes were followed by raw laughter coming from cheerless mouths.

I saw the men around me in a wise-guy role as Watcher and Judge, expecting to recognize their essential natures rather than the flesh and blood people they were. Not that I couldn't tell a phony from a decent human being when I was young. But what I wanted on that long ride into Army life was a way to reassure myself that I still had a grip on things, when I knew in my gut that I'd lost whatever independence people have in civilian life, that I'd left behind the ones I loved and who loved me, and that I might be dead soon. I kept trying to size up the men around me so I could get on top of things. Part of me knew there was nothing I could do except to wait for whatever happened. But another part of me kept trying to figure out what was going on. So I looked at my fellow recruits, and I decided they were blind—unmindful of where they were and where they were going.

That day, on the last forty-mile leg of the trip to Camp Upton, I tuned out my fellow recruits, and I began to do what I often did when I rode the subway in New York or the Norfolk and Western Railroad to and from Virginia—I listened for music to the unlikely rhythm of the train's clickety-clack, imagining the words and melody of a song as if they were really being played and sung. It almost always worked for me.

> I walk alone,
> And to tell you the truth I am lonely;
> I don't mind being lonely,

When my heart tells me you
Are lonely too.
I walk alone,
For to tell you the truth I would rather;
There are dreams I must gather....

Alone, I gazed out the window, letting the music take me
away. The train moved along slowly, grudging the effort. It was a
long trip, moving me from one world to another. Like millions of
people across the earth, I had been taken by the war. Many were
worse off, but that didn't make me feel any better. In fact, when-
ever I thought about things beyond my own life, I came up with
images of confusion and death. In Africa, England, Italy, France,
Russia, Germany, Burma, India, and a thousand islands in the
Pacific, frightened people were killing each other. The whole
world had been drawn into destruction as a way of life. I remem-
bered August 1939, when England and France had gone to war
with Germany. I was fourteen. The night after I heard the news, I
dreamt half awake of exploding artillery shells that broke across
the skies, lighting them in deep shadowed blazes of fire and shak-
ing them with thunder. I remember the dream, as intense as hal-
lucination, the live painting of a world gone mad.

The troop train slowed down for a curve. With the change of
speed, the clickety-clack changed. The wheels and track lost their
music and their power to evoke reverie. I heard the locomotive
sound its forlorn whistle four times as we approached a crossing.
Once over it, we were inside Camp Upton. Two-story barracks,
painted white, their long axes perpendicular to straight roadways,
stretched in files in all directions as far as the eye could see. All the
buildings and all the spaces around them were uniform.

When we got off the train, we were counted off by noncom-
missioned officers (noncoms) and made to stand in four rows of
about fifteen men each. The man in charge of my group was a

big, red-faced sergeant with a beer belly. He was very serious, and his voice was loud. A short man, a corporal, was with him.

"All right you men, stand in straight lines facing me. Okay, break it off here. You others, form a second line behind the first. And you, form a third line, and a fourth. Okay, okay, straighten it up. Straighten it up. You call those lines! Pull in there."

He kept working on our lines by adjusting our positions with his hands and shouting. It was several minutes before he was satisfied.

Then he said, "Watch Corporal Hinksey when I give him the command 'Right face.' Right FACE!" We watched the corporal pivot on his right heel and on his left toe at the same time, executing the command. We'd all seen snappy drill in the movies, but doing it was unreal.

"All of you together, pick up your gear, NOW! Then follow my command. Right FACE!"

We did our best to turn by the numbers, in unison. The sergeant, more or less satisfied, said, "When I give the command 'ForWARD MARCH!" everybody start moving on the left foot and get your pace from me and the corporal. ForWARD MARCH!"

The sergeant marched us to our barracks, a few hundred yards away, shouting, "Left, right, left, right, left, right," with each footfall, until we were moving pretty well together. Then he began skipping a beat, grunting, "Hut, hut, hut," each time our left feet hit the ground. He enjoyed the rhythmic cooperation until we got near our quarters. Then, without warning this time, he gave the command, "PlaTOON HALT!" The end of our short march was ragged. We didn't all stop at the same time. The sergeant's gloomy face made it clear he wanted more precision, but he didn't say anything. He just counted us off for the second floor of the barracks. When we went inside, he and the corporal assigned us to bunks.

The next hour passed quickly. The sergeant showed us how to make our beds and then told us where to stow our gear for the night.

"When you finish," he said, "stand at ease in front of your bunk, and I'll see what kind of job you did. Then we'll go to chow. When you go through the chow line, ask for as much food as you want, but don't leave anything on your tray. No waste! No waste!"

After the sergeant inspected our beds, straightening a blanket and retucking a corner here and there, we lined up outside the barracks, and he marched to the mess hall. His last words before we went in to eat were, "Remember, don't leave anything on your trays!"

Upton's Army mess hall was huge. Thousands of men ate there three times a day, moving through the feeder lines, sitting and eating quickly—shouting to be heard above the sounds of metal ladles, spatulas, trays, and eating utensils, scraping and banging—and then moving down a line of garbage cans to separate the refuse—paper napkins in one can, bones in another, fruit skins in a third. The vast hall was an orderly tumult. The odors of the food we ate—beef stew, mashed potatoes, string beans, and coffee—floated distinctly above the heavy smell of former meals. I was hungry and enjoyed the food. Not like home, but it was zesty. No waste on my plate.

At my table nobody found time to talk. It was a couple of days before we started wondering about ourselves out loud. When we finished our food, we walked back to the barracks as we were told to do—on our own. Once upstairs, some of the older men, who couldn't have been more than twenty-three or twenty-four, began to play cards. The rest of us just rested on our bunks, waiting for the Army to give us a command. This was the first minute of free time we'd had since we got off the train. I wondered what the long night would be like. I'd been alone before, but not with the same prospect ahead of me.

A little after 9:30, the sergeant came out of his private room at one end of the barracks.

"Men, get a good night's sleep. Reveille is at 5:45 A.M. Bounce right out of bed, wash up, and we'll go to chow as soon as we're called. Right after you eat, you'll be issued uniforms. In the afternoon and for the next three or four days you'll get needles against all the diseases known to man, and you'll take tests to help the Army decide what basic training you'll get—infantry, artillery, radio and communications, and so on. Is that clear? Okay, into the sack, and no talking after lights out."

In a little while the lights were switched off. It was very quiet, and the darkness was deep, holding me endlessly far from everything I knew. Though once in a while I heard a man turning, the dark silence was heavy. I was alone, wide awake, thinking about the strange place I was in, and about tomorrow and all the unknown days to follow. Where would I end up? The world didn't have much shape just then. I was afraid.

My mind turned to home, the people and things I knew and loved. I was less than a hundred miles from the place in New York where I'd grown up, a solid brick house surrounded by virgin woods, and beyond them, commercial truck farms, until just a few years before the war. A thousand memories drew me to my mother and father, Grandma Pagliaro, and my brothers, especially Robert, who was about two years younger. Edward and I weren't as close—he was almost seven years younger. Robert and I shared a room for as long as I can remember. Our close past and my parents' expectations made me feel responsible for him. I was always his protector. Even while I waited for the draft to pull me out of college, I worried about his military service as much as I did my own.

When the family lived in Virginia, where my father spent three years, 1940 to 1943, supervising the construction of a dry dock in the Norfolk Navy Yard, Robert and I were closer than ever, because at first we had no other friends there. We fished and crabbed and played together, and we always talked before going to sleep.

We made friends in Portsmouth through a girl, Helen, who lived a couple of blocks from us. The three of us went to school on the bus together and got to know each other. After the second term started, she invited us to a Valentine's Day party at her house, and we were thereafter accepted by the local Virginians. We had friends again.

Helen knew I was crazy about her. She was really good-looking. But I think it was her happiness that got me. She spoke in an eager, soft voice that made you know everything was just right. One day at the swimming pool, she let me know she liked me too. After that she was my girl until I left for college.

I thought we'd stay in touch, but she acted as if my going were the end of things between us. She didn't write for a month, and when she did she let me know she was dating somebody else. I'd heard from her only a few times in the ten months since I'd left Virginia. I knew it was dumb, but I couldn't stop longing for her.

A choking noise nearby brought me back to the dark Upton barracks. The guy in the next bed was sobbing. I didn't even remember his face. He was trying to muffle the sounds, which came out like whimpering gasps. It was awful. If it had been Robert, I would have jumped out of bed and comforted him. But what could I do for a stranger? Maybe I'd hurt his feelings? Besides, I wasn't feeling so good myself. I listened to him cry until he quieted down. Then after a while he began to breathe deep and loud.

I thought I'd be awake all night, but I gradually relaxed, and just before I drifted off, I mentally heard a ridiculous sentence that made itself sound important: "Robert needs you, and you need Helen." As if I didn't know. It took a while, but finally I went under and slept like a rock.

Early next morning, we were all startled out of sleep by the immense voice of the beer-bellied barracks sergeant coming through a loudspeaker. It wasn't yet dawn, but the lights were blazing from the ceiling.

"Drop your cocks and grab your socks! Drop your cocks and grab your socks! Drop your cocks and grab your socks!"

He repeated the order more than a dozen times, as perplexed slow-risers struggled to their feet. What the hell was he doing? Where was the sound of the bugler playing reveille? Though the sergeant's repeated cry cut a sure path to my adolescent heart, with its vulgar, cruel, comic undertones, I was shocked, and in a way, I couldn't handle it. That was also true of other language I first heard at Camp Upton. Though I had done some cursing as a boy, and I have a Rabelaisian side of my own, it took me a while to neutralize graphic Army metaphors like "Snap shit" for "Hurry up," "Fart sack" for "Bed," and "Chicken shit" for "Army regulations, hyper-enforced." It also took me a while to accept "Fuckin'" as the most nearly universal modifier in the language.

As the sergeant bellowed, we got up, made our beds, washed and dressed, then "fell in" (lined up outside the barracks) for roll call. I looked at the kid who was sobbing the night before, but I couldn't catch his eye. He didn't want to be recognized. In a while, we all marched in the dark to the mess hall for breakfast. At first the woodsy smell of the chilly autumn air made me sad for home, but as we got near the kitchen, the odor of bacon and coffee made me think of food. I really put it away. Again the din of men shouting at each other to be heard. Again the smell of the new meal, especially the bacon, floated above more settled odors. I just ate and took it all in. I didn't want to talk. I emptied my tray and walked back to the barracks on my own.

As the sergeant promised, GI clothing was issued soon after breakfast. Underwear, socks, pants, and shoes all fit very well, especially the shoes, which were the most comfortable I've ever worn. Shirts, field and dress jackets, however, were tents—large enough in the shoulders and short enough, but far too roomy in the waist. I looked like Mr. Five-by-Five throughout basic training, unless I wore my overcoat, which was a 37 regular and very tight. When I got to the supply room, they were out of my size, 39 short—and out of 40s and 38s too.

Life at Upton provided a few light moments. Sometimes we found relief in a noncom with a sense of humor or in an officer who didn't look down his nose at the enlisted men. But it was generally an intense introduction to the impersonality of Army life, which aimed at reducing unique beings to a mass of undifferentiated soldiers who took orders blindly. We were uniformed; tested; indoctrinated; marched; yelled at; inspected as to the cleanliness of our bodies, our gear, and our quarters; restricted to a tight schedule; confined to the post even during off-duty hours; and taught that our opinions would not be heard, much less tolerated, even in the shape of a facial expression. We were also examined naked, in large groups, without privacy, made to pull back the foreskin and milk, then to bend over and spread our buttocks, for signs of venereal disease and piles.

We hated these public inspections. They were a brutal example of the Army's class system, which divided personnel between officers, who enjoyed the status and privileges of gentlemen, and enlisted men, whose minds and bodies were no longer their own. Officers were not subjected to the indignity of mass physical inspections, but "the men" were. A lot of things the Army did seemed just about unbearable. But humanity can often triumph over the most insidious human planning. Amidst all this wearing force of reduced dignity and regimentation, we were saved by our energy and love of life.

I never got to know anybody well at Upton. I got a chance to talk to the guy in the next bed, the one who had a hard time the first night. But we never got close. He had just finished high school in Brooklyn, and he would have looked for a job if the Army hadn't gotten him. That's really all I found out. After a couple of days, I talked a little to others at meals and while we stood in line, waiting to get a needle or waiting for the chow line to move. But nothing came of it. We were kept too busy, and we were reminded every day that we'd soon be shipped out to some faraway place for basic training. I guess we all understood that we needed to be settled in a permanent camp before we made friends. Besides, Army life was new and strange. We were in many ways naked in each other's company. Few of us had the confidence for friendship.

A side of barracks life that I never got used to was the loss of privacy. The Army had appropriated our bodies, and it was obliged to accommodate our bodily functions. It did so in its own way. We slept in large barracks at Upton, with about thirty double bunks to the room. So sixty men or so, some restless and noisy, others still and quiet, slept together. If someone had a nightmare—and more than a few did in those early days away from home—the whole barracks might be disturbed. Some snored loud in their sleep. They were awakened or turned over, but it was impossible to get them to stop snoring once and for all. So we had to get used to their noise.

But for me the worst part of barracks life was the latrine. I had no trouble showering with dozens of others. I had done the same thing in school gyms for years. And urinating into a long trough, elbow to elbow with a dozen others, was not too bad, though not exactly to my taste. But there was worse. The toilet bowls in Army barracks were not enclosed. I was never able to use these open seats with others around. Many men had the same trouble. But there were enough who seemed not to mind such exposure. In fact, some held forth *ex cathedra* as they defecated, expecting and usually securing an audience, which paid close attention as the lingering squatter dictated practical wisdom or told dirty stories. At first I ran the risk of constipation. After a while, my body took over, waking me up in the middle of the night so I could relieve myself, quietly and in private, and get back into a deep sleep as if there had been no interruption.

The day before we were scheduled to take the intelligence test that would help the Army to decide the kind of basic training we'd be assigned to, I went up to the barracks sergeant. I wanted to tell him I'd already taken the Navy's equivalent exam, while I was at Columbia College, and I'd been assured the Army would honor the results, which were good. I had the test score with me, on the official card the Navy sent right after I failed their physical exam.

"If your score was so good, Kid, how come the Navy didn't take you?" the sergeant asked. "What were they supposed to do with you guys, keep you in college to study engineering or something?"

"Yes, Sergeant, that's right."

"Then what happened? How the hell could you flunk their physical and then get grabbed by the Army?"

"I was a quarter of an inch too short," I said.

His eyes opened. He was surprised, but he believed me. And he was a little embarrassed, too.

"Don't worry, Kid," he said. "I saw you stripped. You must go a lean, hard 160. You'll put on even more muscle in basic and knock 'em dead."

He sounded sympathetic. I decided to repeat my question. "Sergeant, will the Army accept the score I made on the Navy test?"

His expression grew heavy. "Soldier, the Navy's score will be respected, but you have to take the Army test anyway, because nobody gets excused."

His tone and face told me I was to leave his answer unquestioned. I didn't say anything, but I knew I'd never get used to this way of thinking. As it turned out, I tested well enough to qualify for the Army Specialized Training Program (ASTP). I also did well enough on the communications hearing test to be asked to train as a radioman, but I decided against the offer, preferring basic infantry training and the return to college in the ASTP.

After the tests and inoculations were ended, days at Upton were filled with lectures and films, calisthenics, "policing" the grounds (Army talk for picking up cigarette butts and other litter), short walks in ranks, and cleaning the barracks. A rumor circulated—it turned out to be true—that the Upton administration was ordered to keep us at the induction center until the ASTP basic training battalion in Fort Benning, Georgia, was ready to receive us. We were going to get standard infantry training, but we would not be mixed with regular troops.

During the days of waiting to be sent to Benning, the ASTP-ers got to know each other a little. The ones I spoke to seemed okay, but I didn't make friends with any of them. When we reached Benning, we were assigned to different companies, and I never saw them again. I got to know a few men well during basic training, but I never felt drawn to the ASTP as a group. Without thinking about it, I wanted friends who were interesting and compatible. Not everybody with a high IQ was likable.

Two men stand out in my mind from these first Army days at Upton, very different from the others there, and different from me. But I felt a real kinship with their vitality. They were both about thirty years old. Neither was willing to make the best of being drafted, which they regarded as an unfair intrusion into their lives. They said openly that they'd find a way of getting themselves discharged. Michael Prohaska and Frank Nardelli were physically strong and energetic men who made their livings at manual labor. Both were married, both missed their wives, both revered their mothers, and both caught my attention in the huge PX (the Army term for Post Exchange, a general store where you could buy anything from razor blades to 3.2 beer, which you drank on the spot). There, Frank and Mike leered and grinned at the women who worked behind the counters, often with loud lip sucking and moans of desire. But they didn't focus their attention on a particular woman, and they managed to generate a sense of themselves as ridiculous rather than threatening. The other men, including me, paid more attention to them than the women did.

Seeing me take him in, Nardelli looked me up and down. Then he asked, "You miss screwing since you come to Upton?"

It was hard for me to answer the question. I said, "I've always missed it."

He smiled, showing a kind face. Then he said, "Well, maybe you're better off than me. Anyhow, Kid, why don't you look at the women? You like it, they like it."

Prohaska, who overheard the conversation, said, "Yeah, Kid, you like it, they like it. And it don't hurt nuttin."

Their robust vulgarity fascinated me. I'm sure I felt what they felt when I looked at the women, but I couldn't show my feelings. And I thought the women deserved better treatment than Frank and Mike gave them. Over the next three weeks, it became clear that I was both right and wrong about the women. Most of them paid no attention to the two hardy bulls, but a few began to talk easily to them, as if they found them acceptable. I don't think Mike made out, but I think Frank did.

Besides their activity as lovers, they waged war against Army life. They must have talked things over, because they put on the same kind of show, making ridiculous displays of their military ineptitude. We did no close-order drilling at Upton, but we did "fall in"—that is, align ourselves in ranks to establish a formation of men, after which we were given simple orders, which we were expected to execute with snap, all of us at the same time. We got the idea pretty quickly, and we became willing robots, turning right or left, or marching in unison, in response to orders that were delivered by the person in charge, in that coughing-bark of command unique to the military. It took no time to recognize that "tenHUT" (long vowel on the "ten," followed by a sharp, stressed cough-bark on the "HUT") meant "attention" (a command telling us to come to the stiff stance called Attention). But Mike and Frank pretended not to understand. Mike would shout in Polish, "What did he say?" Or Frank would do the same in Italian. Or one of them would sit down when he heard the command. Or leave ranks, walking towards the barracks as if dismissed. They had a thousand routines, which no noncom's threat could get them to abandon. They were as good as Two Stooges, and I've always hoped the Army decided to return them to civilian life, though the odds are heavy against it.

I telephoned home a lot during those weeks. Calls were important to me, away from the family for the first time, though I had the excuse that my parents and brothers wanted to hear from me. They knew I'd been depressed ever since we moved back to our house in the Bronx, after three years in Virginia. My father's job in the Navy Yard ended within a few weeks of my graduation from high school, so that I began work as a pre-engineer at Columbia at about the time he returned to the company office in New York. Though I was good at math and science, I didn't want to be an engineer. But he insisted. He was an engineer, his father and his grandfather had been engineers, and that was the only work he imagined for me. But I wanted to imagine for myself. I did a lousy job during the two semesters I spent at college before the draft got me. Part of the reason was the engineering. Mostly, though, I was feeling lonely, away from Helen; she seemed to be doing just fine in Virginia without me. And then, of course, I was waiting for the Army to get me, and I knew Robert would soon follow.

So my mother and father wanted to know how I was making out. And my father, a little annoyed with me for failing the Navy physical, wanted to know whether I made it into the ASTP. Besides, everyone in the family, including me, was trying to size things up in a general way. It was not only that I'd be in the Army for a while. Robert's turn for service wasn't far off. So we had a lot to talk about. I wrote home, too, partly because my parents wanted letters and partly because I wanted to write. I was very lonely—lonely for home and for Helen, or for the Woman she represented.

It was raining when I boarded the troop train from Upton to Benning. Going to that unknown place far away, especially on a bleak day, made me tense and sad. When I saw things I'd seen before between New York and Virginia, I felt a little better, but the good feeling didn't last. I had a bad case of the blues. Though the next step in my life was only the long ride to Georgia and the start of basic training, it made for a separation from everything I knew. I told myself I was making things look worse than they would be. But the heavy sense of loss and uncertainty would not go away. I had no clear premonition, just an undefined dread.

Caught in that dark mood, I didn't even try to imagine where the war would finally take me. But if by some magic the future could then have been revealed to me, I would have known that ten months ahead, on another bleak day in the unseasonably cold autumn of 1944, I'd find myself on a bare hill in north-central France, three days before going to the front. There I was, dressed in the same uniform and speaking the same language as the men around me, but I recognized nobody I'd known for more than four days. I was alone in a gathering of about 650 men that made up most of the understaffed combat units of the

106th Cavalry Reconnaissance Group to which I had just been assigned—as solo replacement.

My new commanding officer, Colonel Carlton Nelson, thought it would be good to give the men in the Group encouragement and the sense of his presence on the eve of battle. Fixing the time and place, he ordered all the units in his command to rendezvous. Nelson stood on the crest of the hill and looked down on his men. He was about forty years old, of medium height and build. His dark brown hair was just beginning to gray. Before he began to speak, he strode back and forth along the crest line, with the thumbs of his hands hooked under his belt, which was loaded with .30 caliber carbine rounds. Two grenades were attached to his field jacket, ready to be armed and thrown. He opened his mouth and looked ready to speak, but said nothing. Then he moved a few paces toward us, lifting his right arm in our direction, as if to confer a blessing.

"Men, you're about to see action again. I've called you here to tell you how proud I am to be your leader. I'm proud of the courage you've shown in the face of the enemy. Our part in the breakthrough at Saint-Lô is one of the greatest moments of my life. Your brave deeds and those of our comrades no longer with us will live forever in my memory. I'm sure they were proud to give their lives for a cause they knew was just. General Anderson told me the other day that our small unit, the 106th Cavalry Group, was worth a whole division to him. I was very pleased to hear him confirm what I have long known to be true.

"When you return to the front, I want you to carry with you my heartfelt good wishes. There will of course be casualties. Some of us will be wounded. And I know some of us will not return. But we must remember that the enemy of our country stands between us and victory. Only by destroying him at whatever cost will we make America with all our loved ones safe.

"We must not spare ourselves in this last all-important phase of the battle for Europe. I'm counting on you to continue to bring honor to the 106th. And to you new men, I want to say a special word. You have the heavy responsibility of living up to the high standard of heroism set by those in the Group who have come before you. I'm sure you'll be unselfish and do your best not to let your comrades down. They have set the precedent for your behavior in the field. Follow their good example, and we cannot fail.

"Major Chalmers, please come forward with the citations."

The major marched up to the colonel, and they exchanged salutes. Then between them they performed the ritual of awarding the Silver Star to four enlisted men for gallantry in action. After that, Group was dismissed, and we all headed toward our vehicles for the return to quarters. I walked beside the only man I knew even slightly, Corporal Clewes, who had picked me up at the replacement depot a few days before and brought me to my new outfit, Troop A, 121st Squadron, 106th Cavalry Group, quartered in Raville, just behind the lines.

"Where'd these other units come from?" I asked, more for something to say than out of real curiosity.

"Little villages like Raville, close enough to be moved in quick, except Troop B," Clewes answered in his low voice. "They're the ones dug in on the hill in Parroy Forest."

"What about the colonel?"

Clewes smiled. "You won't see him where you're goin'. He ain't no John Wayne. The grenades are just for show. He's okay, I guess. Headquarters is in Luneville. That's where the colonel gives the orders from just now."

Chapter Two

Basic Training

LATE ON THE LONG TRAIN ride to Fort Benning, I turned my thoughts to home—my mother and father, Grandma Pagliaro, and Robert and Edward—and our house in New York, where I'd said good-bye before reporting for duty. Before 1940, when we left for Virginia, there was only a cinder road to take us from Pelham Parkway to the house. It was far from Manhattan. The brick walls were strong, and the world of woods and farms around it, a perfect setting. Robert and I loved it. Several other houses were located beyond the woods to the west, where our few friends lived—Kenneth Evans, Charlotte Walker, and Rose Moran. Our school was over a mile away, and we went there by bus. So I was used to playing with Robert most of the time, though we saw our friends on the other side of the woods pretty often.

As the train moved south, I looked out at the trees and buildings we rolled past slowly. The shuffling sounds of movement were far away and lazy. The wheels turned and the landscape changed in an uneventful motion picture that lulled me into reverie. Helen filled my mind, mostly in images that showed I liked her and she liked me—pieces of the broken past, precious and lost. I kept hoping she'd show a change of heart. Brooding about her was no way to start the next phase of Army life. But I kept remembering the first time she showed me she liked me. I needed a woman to love, and I needed a woman to love me, even more than I needed to go home. Night closed in, and the clickety-clack of the wheels echoed back the blues.

On the morning of December 4, 1941, we arrived at Fort Benning—a flat, barren-looking land of red clay. A corporal, who told us his name was Thaxter, counted us off in groups of twelve and assigned us to barracks.

"Just move in and pick your bunks, men. More troops are coming in from Chicago in a day or two. They'll take up the other twelve places. Corporal Stoddard is gonna be in charge of this hut, but he's on duty somewhere else today."

The living quarters for enlisted men were small, tar-paper-roofed, one-story buildings, an ugly black-brown. They were badly lighted huts that slept twenty-four men in double-tiered bunks. A potbellied stove, which could not be used at night because of the danger of fire, was their only source of heat. Winter nights in Georgia can be very cold. But the warning sign on the wall of every hut in the training battalion read loud and bold, THIS HUTMENT WILL BURN IN TWENTY MINUTES. And if it caught fire, it would be hot enough to roast you long before twenty minutes passed, with the dry old wooden walls and the tar paper. The sign was menacing. During the thirteen weeks of training, we were all careful with our cigarettes, and with the stove as well.

Most of us grabbed the lower beds, but four or five wanted the uppers. I got a lower, right next to the stove. We had just begun to stow gear in our footlockers when Thaxter returned and told six of us that we'd be on KP starting at 2:00 A.M. the next morning. I was one of the six.

"It'll be a short night, men, so hit the sack early. I'm coming to get you out at 1:30. Put everything you need close by so you don't waste time getting ready."

Thaxter was as good as his word. He roused us at the appointed hour, and we all jumped. I reached for the potbellied stove, hoping to warm my hands, but the rounded metal was already cold. The hut was damp and raw. I blew into my hands and slipped on my chilled clothes and shoes. With the others, I made a fast trip to the company latrine, about fifty yards down the clay road from our hut, and then we walked along the same road the remaining fifty yards to the kitchen.

Thaxter turned us over to a cook with three stripes and left. I was expecting the kind of propriety speech made by every supervisory noncom I'd come across, but the sergeant was sleepy and grumpy. All he said was, "This is your company kitchen; it serves only the 160 men in the outfit and any officers who want to eat here. Do as you're told right away." Then he gave us jobs.

We were in our own kitchen. No more meals for thousands. No lingering odor of former meals. After Upton, the arrangement seemed almost familial, and in some ways it was. One way or another, the cooks and the mess sergeant could recognize all of us within a couple of weeks. But it had its less happy side, too. Army cooks are touchy about their culinary turf. On the first night we found out that anyone on KP with his own ideas about how to work the kitchen had to scrap them. The cooks told you how to peel potatoes, how to break eggs by the dozens for scrambling, in what order to wash pots and which to dry and which to hang wet, how thick to slice the ham, and on and on. If you followed instructions, things were okay, but if you thwarted a cook's expectations, all hell broke lose. Despite supervision by the mess sergeant and the mess officer, cooks had broad discretion in the hour-by-hour operation of the kitchen, and they could make you happy or miserable. We followed orders.

My first KP assignment was long. Besides getting meals for the men in the company from Upton, we got separate batches of food ready to cook after the arrival of the men from Chicago. They were expected that day, but just when, nobody knew. As it turned out, they pulled in late that night, and those of us who had done KP from 2:00 A.M. until 5:00 P.M. were called back. What with two nights of short sleep, hard work, and the empty feeling that came from being far from home, I was light-headed. But this giddy sense of the insubstantial went away whenever a cook told me to do some new thing that made daydreaming impossible.

When we got back from our second tour of KP, the new men assigned to our hut had not yet settled down for the night. After they ate the meal we'd helped prepare, they were given instructions about the danger of fire and the next day's work. So they weren't in their bunks yet. We could tell from their accents that they were midwesterners, but there was no time for real talk before late lights out. I wondered about them for a while, and then my mind turned to home—and then to Helen. But not for long. Worn out by hours of work without rest, I fell into a deep sleep.

I was awakened next morning not by the sergeant's voice, but by the voice of Peter Moskovitch, of Gary, Indiana, mumbling as if to himself while he crumpled newspaper and piled kindling, before lighting our potbellied stove. "Cold as a witch's tit, Christ! Cold as a witch's tit! Cold as a witch's tit, by God! Cold as a witch's tit!"

His voice was deep, and he spoke in a fake moan, to his largely unknown audience, most of whom were still fast asleep. I watched and listened, getting out of bed to join him at the stove. Like all the dawns in Georgia that winter, this one was cold. The fire took quickly, and Moskovitch added soft coal from the bin and began to congratulate himself vigorously.

"Christ, can I build a fire. Feel that heat? Get close, you guys. Oh, God, can I build a fire."

Soon all twenty-four of us were out of bed, the dozen from Upton, and the second dozen from induction centers in the West. None of us was older than eighteen, most of us had been drafted from high school or college, and we were all feeling lonely. The

ASTP was the only part of the Army in which all the men were very young and all had the same educational background. At one level, we were members of a homogeneous family. That first morning we began to reveal ourselves to each other. No one displayed himself as much as Moskovitch, whose role suited him perfectly. But we all found a way of declaring ourselves. Before three days had passed, Peterson, tall, lean, blond, and blue-eyed, from Northfield, Minnesota, told us he liked to keep a stock of food and candy on hand so that he could eat whenever he chose. Though his habit of storing edibles seemed generous, it turned out he was a hoarder who resented being asked for even the loan of an item. Boris Osterberg, from Manhattan, pockmarked and plain, told us with an amiable candor that he was the ugliest guy in his high school, turned down by all the girls, so in desperation, he lived his sex life on the subways of New York, leaning against women who would not otherwise let him near them. Alfy Pollack, from Brooklyn, fat and sad-looking, said his parents were bakers, who would send him homemade bread every week. He promised to share it with us, and he did.

The rest of us came on less directly, revealing ourselves more slowly. But our first item of business was getting ourselves known to each other. Without knowing it, we made a plan to become a community in which we could each find a place. And we grew so close over the weeks of basic training that it seemed we'd been chosen by some divine power to complement each other— O'Brien, from Salina, Kansas; Melton, from Peekskill, New York; Norton, from Denver; Oliver, from the Bronx; Marlowe, from Cheyenne; Pinkton, from Wichita Falls; and many others. So naturally ordained did our community seem that it was hard to believe that everyone in the hut had a last name that started with one of four letters—M, N, O, or P.

We spent the first week of basic getting ready for what was to follow—receiving instruction in the use of weapons and in tactics, and building our strength and endurance for long marches and for survival in the field. Officers and noncoms checked the fit of our shoes and socks—you can't march very far with blisters. They also showed us how to lace our leggings so they gave us support without cramping our calves. Then we were issued rifles, and taught to disassemble, clean, and reassemble them. They weighed fourteen pounds, about one-fourth the weight of the equipment each man carried on the march. Sixty pounds is a heavy load. In addition, we were instructed in how to space our use of the quart of water we carried in our canteens. We were even told how to rest during the ten-minute breaks we'd get after every fifty minutes of hiking. And we were shown films about how to avoid getting syphilis or gonorrhea from a prostitute and films about why we were at war. We didn't doubt the truth the films were driving at, but we thought they were funny because they were pitched to morons.

Toward the end of the first week, the company commander, Captain Porter, a tall, slim, dark, forty-year-old southerner, with a firm, soft voice, told us we'd be taking a ten-mile hike the next day, with rifles, steel helmets, and light packs. It sounded like the beginning of real training. While we walked back to barracks, we heard several noncoms talking, including our own platoon sergeant, Marciano.

"Ten miles is too far the first hike," he said.

Corporal Thaxter, a squad leader, agreed. "Yeah, these kids...." He cut himself short, realizing we could hear him.

"You're right, it's too far the first time. They should build up slow," said Marciano, trying to cover Thaxter's blunder. "They'll get blisters, and it'll be a mess around here for a week. What the hell has Harris got in his head?" Major Harris commanded our battalion, the essentially independent training unit in which our company was one of four.

Back in the hut, we talked over what we'd heard. O'Brien, one of the country boys, from Kansas, said, "I think we could do ten miles standing on our heads."

We all agreed with O'Brien, yet there was something in Marciano's voice that told us he knew what he was talking about. So when we were given the word at roll call next morning that the length of the hike had been changed to seven-and-a-half miles—three hours at two-and-a-half miles an hour—our disappointment was mixed with the sense that the change was a good one.

After breakfast, Marciano gathered us in an informal group before we went into the barracks to load up for the hike. "Men, check your socks for a smooth fit. No lumps, no creases. They seem like nothing at first, but two miles out they'll start to burn and cut. Fill your canteens. Check your slings so the rifle feels good on your shoulder. As soon as we leave the company area, you'll hear Captain Carter give the order, 'Rout Step.' That means you don't have to stay in step. Keep up with the others, but you can set your own stride, short, long, whatever feels good, and you can talk."

At eight o'clock our company of two hundred eager ASTPers began the march down the red dusty street. The sky was a clear blue, and the air was pleasantly cool. We soon left the two rows of blackened huts behind and marched past the latrine and past the mess hall to the open road. We were headed for the countryside.

When we heard Captain Carter's soft, penetrant voice say, "Rout Step," we adjusted our strides and looked around at each other and at the low, scrubby greens that lined each side of the rough road for a hundred yards, right up to the woods that seemed to stretch beyond for miles on our left and right. I breathed the fresh air. The dank smell of dew-dampened ashes, cold in the potbellied stove where we'd built no fire that morning, had been hanging in my mind, but I didn't realize it until the bloom-laden country air took its place.

That first hike was pretty easy. We went out at a slow pace, feeling nothing much for the first three or four miles. But at the end of five, when we took our second ten-minute break, we were glad we had only another hour to go. Our backs were aching from the load, which didn't surprise us. But it was a surprise that our feet were stinging. We thought we could hike with no trouble at all, but the weight we were carrying made all the difference. Even without a full field pack, our load was heavy.

When we got back to barracks, our feet were inspected by our platoon leader, Lieutenant Siebold. Marciano was with him. We took off shoes and socks and sat on the lower bunks, waiting for experienced eyes to look us over. The heels of our feet were red, and a few of us had blisters. As the lieutenant and the sergeant moved among us, they actually lifted our feet by the ankles so they could look close. When they finished, they talked quietly for a few minutes, and then the lieutenant nodded his head to the sergeant before turning toward us to speak.

"Men, your condition is normal. You've done well for the first time out. Keep up the good work. Your feet'll harden up in no time. Good job. Now get yourselves showered, then rest before chow."

Lieutenant Siebold was a less mature man than our sergeant, in years and temperament. A graduate of Bowdoin, he went through Officer Candidate School by the shortest possible route after he was drafted. He was about five feet ten, lean and hard. His eyes were sparkling blue, and his face and hair seemed almost the same light tan. He was intelligent, sensitive, cheerful, and kind, believing he could lead men by getting them to like and respect him, and in this he was right. When he gave us instructions to prepare us for a platoon field problem, he spoke with easy good humor and wit. If we were on a long, hot march, the lieutenant would never drink from his canteen. He'd save his water to divide it among the two or three men whose supply would run dry. We respected his endurance, as he meant us to. When we lined up for chow in the field, Siebold made sure he was the last in the platoon to be fed.

Once, during a lecture on handling various kinds of barbed-wire barriers, he surprised us by leaping up and throwing himself hard onto a chest-high tangle of barbs. They were staked across a narrow path that ran through heavy brush. Then he ordered Sergeant Marciano and the rest of us to use him as a human bridge for crossing.

"Come on, all of you, one at a time. You first, Sergeant. Just take two steps across my back."

Marciano led the way, stepping lightly, first on the rump and then between the shoulder blades. The lieutenant was wearing an overcoat, and he swore he wasn't even scratched. Though this show of his, and other demonstrations, had obviously been pre-arranged, he was a hero in our eyes, because despite his rank, he worked with us instead of commanding from above. He was hardly older than we were, probably no more than twenty-two. His way of leading us had a boyish side, which we liked. Twenty-seven-year-old Marciano, whose typical way of showing approval was friendly cooperation rather than praise, told a group of us at the PX one night, "Siebold is a prince of an officer, the best man I've ever met in the Army."

Marciano, our platoon sergeant, was quiet, matter-of-fact, hard-working, and he led us more by example than by command. Though only about five feet eight and 145 pounds, he was very strong. His hair was jet black and his face was ruddy-brown, with a beard so thick and wiry, he always seemed to need a shave. He wasn't a favorite of ours, like Lieutenant Siebold, but we unconsciously accepted him as our leader. We could see that he often helped Siebold, who was smart and generous enough to ask for the sergeant's advice and to act on it. Marciano was not a regular Army man, but he was drafted early, so he'd been around for several years when I got to know him. He could be tough on duty, but he was sure enough of his authority that he was often friendly with the men, after hours or during a march. Soon after we'd begin a long hike and the routine command, "Rout March," was given, the sergeant was likely to start a conversation with the man nearest him, speaking in a gentle voice that at first surprised me.

He liked to talk about life after the war, about his wife back in Brooklyn, and about baking. These last two subjects were in fact one and the same. His wife had used several of his mother's recipes, entirely to his satisfaction—Paloma, a kind of Italian egg bread; lemon cheesecake, made with ricotta and finely diced lemon rind; and stuffed zeppole, like donuts, though less sweet, and filled with anchovy or crisp bacon, or with jelly and then rolled in sugar. What pleased him most was that she had great success baking these confections, even though they were not part of her tradition, and even though she began to bake them after only one conversation with his mother, in which he swore little was said, and nothing written down. He was obviously proud of his wife. For him the end of the war meant returning to their home. I envied him for having a woman.

We were lucky in our company officer, Captain Porter, a reservist, and his executive, First-Lieutenant Endicott, a West Pointer. Like Siebold, they acted as if rank conferred responsibility rather than authority, though they used their authority effectively in their work. All three made us feel like participants in a common enterprise that was unpleasant but necessary, and we did our best for them. Starting with our first hike, we worked hard and we liked most of the officers and noncoms we'd met, but not all.

Stoddard was the corporal in charge of our hut. He was a pale-fleshed bird of a man. His small, beaky nose, which might have been lost in another face, was the dominant feature of his. Above it were gummy blue eyes, and below, a mouth and chin that dropped into the soft neck in a straight but indecisive line, except for his Adam's apple, the exact shape of his beaky nose. He was convinced that we "smart-asses" hated him and had no respect for him, and before long, what had not been true became so.

On the third night after our arrival, Stoddard walked into our hut. He'd been away on an assignment for several days, and he decided he'd better let us know who was boss. So he stood on the foot-high sandbox in which the potbellied stove was set, wrapped his right arm around the cooling stovepipe, and began a mad harangue.

"Ah'm in command o' this hutment. Younsis think ya so smart, goddammit, but ah'll show ya who's smart. Ya got scores higher than the officers'. I don't give a shit about ya brains. Ya don't look so smart. Don't get any ideas. Ya think ya gonna gimme the limbah dick, but ah'll show ya who's got the limbah dick. Ah'll bend y'all's backs and stick it in. Ah'll give the orders, and y'all are gonna snap shit or ah'll have y'all's asses."

He repeated these and similar comments at the top of his screeching voice for a full five minutes. I was too surprised to think about what the hell got him going, and I think the others were, too. Stoddard turned out to be a real bastard, dangerous because he would punish men to the limit of his discretion, which was considerable, whenever he felt his dignity had been wounded, a frequent experience for him. I suppose there was a limit beyond which he could not have gone without getting into trouble, but the Army did not interfere with the arbitrary exercise of discipline by any noncommissioned or commissioned officer. However irrational or unjust, rank had its way.

Stoddard assigned men to extra KP, had them run laps with a full field pack, made them dig foxholes and refill them, restricted them to barracks—all to punish them for his own discomfort. It was possible after a time to cope with him. As young as we were, it became clear that he was frightened because he was uneducated and unintelligent. There were times between his cruelties when we talked about Stoddard as pitiable, rather than hateful. But he'd soon remind us of his power to make us miserable whenever he chose.

Lieutenant Henderson, senior platoon leader, was a different sort of dangerous man. Smarter and a little better educated than Corporal Stoddard, he was in love with the power he could use at his discretion. Henderson, in his early thirties, was a big man—about six three, and 220 pounds, with some lard, but not a whole lot. He was red-skinned and red-headed, and when he wasn't scowling in a mean way, he was grinning in a mean way. Every time it was his turn to lecture the company, he would tell a dirty joke before he went on to his dirty lesson.

"One day a horny young feller was killed in a car wreck so fast he never knew what hit him. When he came to, he was on a big sandy space, walkin' towards a honky-tonk right in a grove of palm trees. When he got there, he saw a big barrel of beer settin' on the bar and a beautiful, big-assed blonde standin' in front of it. Before he went up to the bar, he asked the waiter, 'Where am I?'

"'Why, you're in Hell, Sonny,' was the answer.

"'Shit, this can't be Hell. Look at that beer! And look at that blonde!'

"The waiter looked at the young man, feelin' real sorry for him, and said, 'Sonny, the beer barrel has a hole in the bottom, and the blonde hasn't. If that ain't hell, I don't know what is.'"

After Henderson finished his opening joke, he would look at us to see who liked it and who didn't. A few laughed on cue, but most of us could not have laughed if we'd tried, and before going on with his lecture, he would chide us for being unmanly. He was crude. But if Prohaska or Nardelli, the Two Stooges from Camp Upton, had told Henderson's jokes, we'd have died laughing. They were comics, the lieutenant was a bully. When he lectured on the M-1 rifle, his advice was that we should keep our piece clean. He particularly stressed the importance of a clean rod and patch.

"Men, you wouldn't put a dirty thing in your best girl, would you? Then don't put a dirty thing in your rifle."

Henderson was hard not only on the men in his own platoon, but on the rest of us in the company, too. He was especially dangerous when he was Officer of the Day. I don't know whether he exceeded his authority then by looking in on the kitchen, as well as on the men mounting guard, but I know for a fact that he often ordered a man on KP to report for a second day in the kitchen, or for a second day of guard duty. I was not the only one on KP who had to do a second round, but I may have been the only one to tell him I hadn't had a chance to clean my rifle because I was on duty in the kitchen.

"Sir, I'm afraid that if I don't clean my rifle in the daylight, I won't pass inspection."

He looked down at me, scowling red. "Don't give me that shit. If your hair was short enough, you wouldn't have to worry about inspections. Get it shaved off as soon as you finish your second day in the kitchen, and report to me."

I couldn't believe him. I felt empty at the prospect of getting my head shaved. The idea was crippling. But I also felt anger. I hated Henderson's guts. I wanted to kill him. He had at least fifty pounds on me, but I knew I could knock him on his ass at least once before he got me—if he got me. But there was no way of opposing him without getting into bad trouble, so after I finished my extended tour, I went to the civilian barber on the post, depressed.

When I told him I needed my head shaved, he asked, "A punishment?"

I nodded yes. He said, "I'll take care of you."

He managed to give my already short hair a very close cut without leaving me entirely bald. I was still a spectacle. I hated Henderson—the son of a bitch. But nobody razzed me. Several had been punished unfairly by the lieutenant, and all were afraid of him. I reported to him right after the barber finished the job. He seemed surprised to see me. By the time I had gone for the haircut, I had been gigged for a dirty rifle, but no punishment followed. I don't know why. Maybe Henderson saw to the gigging and to the reprieve. But I never found out who inspected the rifle. Sergeant Marciano told me only that my rifle had failed inspection. But my record for discipline was first-rate, except for this one run-in with Henderson, and that may explain the reprieve.

So side by side with Moskovitch, O'Brien, Oliver, Marlowe, Peterson, Osterberg, Pollack, Melton, Norton, Pinkton, and the others, I went through basic infantry training, encouraged by a few good officers and noncoms, and threatened by some bad ones. We began training with young, healthy bodies, and the Army capitalized on that beginning. Our food was zesty, nourishing, and plentiful, we slept eight hours a night with few exceptions, we were gradually made to march longer and longer distances, we were made to do other exercises to improve our strength and agility, and we were trained in various skills—firing our rifles, the .30 caliber machine gun, the .30 caliber carbine, and the mortar; we learned how to use a bayonet, dig and camouflage foxholes, read a topographical map, follow a complicated compass course at night without showing a light, pitch a tent so as to stay dry, advance under intense small arms fire, with live ammunition passing just over our heads as we crawled forward, attack an enemy who was dug in. Though the work was hard and time-consuming, most of us adjusted to it well—even found some pleasure in our accomplishments. It wasn't only that we knew we were going back to college when training ended; it was also that we got into the spirit of things. It was a good war.

Nobody doubted that the Nazis and Fascists had to be stopped, so we gave our energy to the work. When we marched, we often sang vulgar infantry songs, with endless verses:

> I used to work in Chicago,
> In a department store.
> I used to work in Chicago,
> I did but I don't any more.
> A lady came in for a cake one day—
> "What kind?" I asked at the door.
> "Layer," she said. Lay her, I did,
> I did, but I don't any more!

Our generally good morale helped to make our training effective. Stoddard and Henderson were exceptions. Most of the cadre were indifferent to us until some duty brought us together, though of course the weight of their authority meant a constraint of freedom we'd never before experienced. It's not pleasant to realize that any noncom's whim might become an order you would have to obey. My essentially private, independent side felt the weight of this arbitrary power, which the Army exercised through the personal behavior of its officers and noncoms and through its various regulations and codes.

What the Army called "military courtesy" was a carefully worked out system of obeisances required of all personnel in their official and unofficial dealings with *any* superior in rank. Military courtesy prescribed that inferiors should walk half a pace behind and to the left of their superiors in rank, just as it prescribed when you should salute, when and how to wear your hat, and how often to say "Sir" when you spoke to an officer. These and countless other required gestures kept reminding us of who was on top, and on the bottom. Even the unintentionally ironic euphemism "military courtesy" implied that we had to accept the unacceptable. But as long as it seemed that we were all pulling together to win the war, we cooperated.

Whatever private worries I had, my body flourished in this dynamic environment. My weight increased from 160 to 180 pounds in two months, but I looked about the same—same waist, only a slightly larger chest, arms, and legs. I felt my strength increase, and I loved the feeling. I was divided, as I had been all my life—an introspective dark side, anxious and sensitive to death and beauty, and an outgoing animal side, full of confidence and vitality. Most people saw one side or the other, but those I was close to—especially Robert—could see both come to life. In the Army the two selves were more simple and more stark, separated by the kind of life I lived there—intense physical work and lonely brooding about the future.

Two men in the hut were drawn to me, and I to them: O'Brien and Oliver. Though different from each other, both were like the dominant parts of me. O'Brien was five ten and, like me, heavily built, narrow in the hips and full in the chest and shoulders, and he enjoyed his strong, healthy body. He had a good-looking face, too. He was usually cheerful, sympathetic to others, outgoing, and frank. He loved to eat, and he burned off as many calories as he took in by using himself tirelessly. Instead of moaning about a job, he plunged in and did it. He had a girl from his hometown in Kansas, a student at the University of Mississippi. He told me he needed to see her as soon as possible. I liked him, and he liked me. When he first saw me in my oversized fatigue shirt, he named me Chunky, and the name stuck. Even though "chunky" seemed wrong for me, I enjoyed being given an affectionate name by someone I liked.

Once, O'Brien was on KP just before an inspection. I remembered Henderson, the humiliation of my bald head, and the gigged rifle. O'Brien had been sympathetic.

"That son of a bitch," he said when he saw me back from the barber. "I knew a kid from my hometown who went to the Citadel, where they knob you the first day. He was in the dumps for weeks, even though all the other guys were bald, too. Chunky, if anything like that happens again, I mean if Henderson keeps you in the kitchen so you can't clean your rifle, I'll find a way to clean it for you."

"You know you can't handle another man's rifle. You'll get your ass in a sling," I told him.

"Maybe, but I'll do it anyhow."

I wanted to do O'Brien the same favor he'd promised me, so I looked at his rifle when he was on KP. I opened the chamber and looked down the barrel while the piece was still locked up. It needed cleaning. When the rack was opened, I cleaned O'Brien's rifle and returned it before cleaning my own. Nobody said anything, and he passed inspection in absentia.

On a field trip one cold, rainy night, we dug foxholes after a long hike. The weather was miserable, and we were soaked. I shoveled red clay like a demon, trying to get warm, but I couldn't shake the raw chill. As I was about finished, my back cramped nearly at right angles to my legs, and I couldn't straighten it.

"O'Brien!" I hollered, "Come here, will you?" He was only a few feet away.

"What's the matter? Hit a big rock?"

"No, it's my goddam back. It's frozen bent, and I can't straighten it."

O'Brien helped me out of the hole and rubbed my lower spine for several minutes, but it didn't do any good.

"I'll tell the lieutenant you want to report sick."

"Hell, no!"

I was dead set against sick call, but with the cramp, I could not finish the rest of the field work set for the night. O'Brien had another idea.

"Give me your mess kit," he said. "I'll be right back."

I figured he was going to get us our share of the midnight breakfast, then being served, so I waited, lying on my side, in one of the most comic postures imaginable, with the rain coming down and the mud getting deeper. When O'Brien got back, he quickly took both our portions of hot oatmeal, which he'd carried back covered, spooned them into a woolen sock, and reaching under my jacket, shirt, and undershirt, pressed the hot oatmeal bag on the unyielding muscles. They began to relax right away, and I was soon ready for work.

Oliver, my other friend, was physically and mentally tough, about as tall as O'Brien, wide-shouldered, and lean. But we didn't enjoy soldiering together. Our compatibility rested on our way of appraising the people and things around us. Oliver had dark brown, deep-set, intense eyes, a very high forehead, a tight drawn mouth, and a strong, square chin, which always showed the signs of his heavy beard. At eighteen, he looked thirty. The most dramatic feature of his unusual face was his long, slightly hooked, thin blade of a nose, coming out stark from flat cheekbones. He looked Spanish, but he wasn't. Few people could stomach him. He was too intense. I didn't like him in the easy human way I liked O'Brien, but I enjoyed being with him. His imaginative perception of the world around him never stopped. His mind kept reading and trying to interpret what he saw.

Occasionally he showed a comic side that gave a sardonic shape to things. Stoddard's crazy speech about giving us the "limbah dick," which bewildered us, left Oliver with a grim smile on his dark face. He would not, maybe could not, understand the world in terms made ready by others. Painful and exhausting though it was, he faced an eternally unfamiliar reality, which he wrestled with all his life. He saw afresh, moment by moment, as clearly as one can—neither sentimentally nor cynically. He was both unwilling and unable to change the way he saw things, and therefore, the way he lived his life. It turned out that he had seen me at Upton and had watched me when I was not caught up in activity. Then he watched me for two weeks in the hut, especially when I was alone, before deciding to speak. It was not like him to begin with small talk to warm things up. From his point of view, that would have been misleading. He was looking for a kindred spirit.

I understood the need very well. But mine was satisfied by friendships—like those I enjoyed with Robert, Helen King, my boyhood friends Kenneth Evans and Charlotte Walker, and others—and by my own thoughts as well. Of course there was a deep part of me that needed its complement. But I had accustomed myself to living alone in the midst of very satisfying company. And then there were my reveries. Oliver, who had no friends except for his brother, to whom he did not write openly, needed an understanding companion. So one day about two weeks after basic training began, he came up to me while we were on a ten-minute break and said, "You're an introspective person, aren't you?"

What a question. I couldn't have said no, and yes was unnecessary. So he got our friendship started, however awkwardly. We talked mostly about the people around us, checking out our perceptions, trying our best to characterize them accurately and to test our accuracy in extended exchanges. It was a new kind of activity, full of judgments about others, but not aimed at putting them down nearly so much as at giving us bearings in a strange sea. I had often played a version of the game by myself. But without someone else to talk things over with, I couldn't integrate what I saw into a general pattern—or if I did, I did so only slowly. So my deepest perceptions lived on in me side by side with my "normal" view of things.

For example, I had a poor opinion of Helen, which existed in my mind along with the image of the young woman I loved. There were two Helens, and I knew them both. The one I didn't like wrote vapid letters; told me in a stupid and cruel way that she was dating somebody else; put the past behind her more quickly than seemed possible. But my knowledge of this unlikable Helen didn't displace the Helen I loved. I held on to the good Helen with all the imagination of hope. If the bad Helen modified the lovable one in my mind, it did so only slowly.

There could have been only one Helen for Oliver. He was drawn to women sexually, but I don't think he could have fallen in love romantically. He recognized differences between one person and another more acutely than anyone I've ever known. But it was not like him to overvalue anyone, though he might value a person very highly. I doubt that he understood forgiveness, the crux in consciousness that willingly cancels the bad we know is real, for the sake of a future unencumbered by animosity. I could have forgiven the unlikable Helen if that would have given me the Helen I liked. But for Oliver, who saw things whole, such a possibility didn't exist. His friendship nourished the deepest part of me. But there was a great gulf between us nevertheless. He lived in an abyss and could not escape. I could see the place, but I often turned away from it.

Oliver and O'Brien never spoke to each other. They had little in common. But like me, O'Brien had a second close friend with whom he shared his interior life. His name was Marlowe, the son of a Wyoming sheep rancher, who from the age of fourteen took his lonely turn in the line shacks, like his father's hired hands. Marlowe was somber. He hardly ever spoke unless it was necessary. Small and wiry, he had an everlasting endurance on hikes, in all kinds of weather. But his energy gave him no pleasure. Though others tried to make friends with him, he seemed to trust only O'Brien, who understood his loneliness. At least O'Brien would tell me after one of their intense conversations, which they managed in such low voices that no one in the small hut could understand them, that Marlowe was suffering one of his depressions, in which he felt as much alone as he had in the line shack when he was a boy, far from anyone else for weeks at a time. His father was rich, and locally influential, but he thought his young son should experience all sides of sheep ranching firsthand.

My clearest sense of him during basic training, besides the image of his relentless marching, is the sight of his blond curly-haired head, brought down so low by his brooding as he sat on his footlocker, that it covered his knees. When he was in such a mood, only O'Brien could talk to him.

O'Brien enjoyed my company, as I did his. But he was drawn to Marlowe as to a kindred spirit. I guess I was drawn to Oliver in the same way. As I said, Oliver was indifferent to O'Brien, who felt the same way about him. But Marlowe was something else. Oliver, who watched, but never spoke to him, wondered about what went on in that lonely head. He told me Marlowe turned away from the company he needed, but it never occurred to Oliver that he did pretty much the same thing.

With the first weeks behind us, we found the routines of basic training more or less predictable. It's true that Henderson or Stoddard or some other man in authority would surprise us with irrational behavior from time to time, but we learned to put up with that side of Army life, without ever growing used to it. Time passed, and we got stronger and tougher. By the seventh week, we could march twenty-five miles in eight hours and still have the energy to dig in and camouflage foxholes before pitching our two-man tents and eating. We worked very hard five days a week, spent most Saturdays hearing lectures and doing close-order drill like wound-up toy soldiers, and on Sundays we rested—we got up late, ate a very full breakfast, including eggs cooked to order, wrote letters or waited on line for an hour or more to place long-distance calls home, and shot the bull.

Nights in our small hut before lights out were busy and noisy. We'd talk, shine our shoes, clean our rifles (leaving fine touches to daylight), eat food sent from home, and generally ease off from the discipline of Army life. The hut was close and badly lighted, and it was full of cigarette smoke, but we didn't mind. We enjoyed each other's company. Later on, in bed, there was time before I went to sleep to think about things, mostly my family and Helen and what would happen next.

About halfway through our training we were shocked by a rumor we heard from the noncoms. They said the ASTP would be closed down as soon as we finished basic. We had no way of knowing whether it was true, but just hearing it changed things. It was the first time we were hit with the reality that Army life was not an interlude between semesters. Somebody, somewhere, had decided we might see action at the front instead of going back to college. Like all the others, I was worried about myself. But there was Robert, too. He was almost seventeen, just a year away from the draft. If the ASTP was closed for me, it would be closed for him.

That night I worried about both of us. How would he take Army life? I tried to figure out ways for him to avoid the draft. If he enlisted in the Navy, he might have a better time of it. But he'd have to sign up for a four-year hitch. The Merchant Marine might be a better deal. We had written back and forth about the possibilities. I was surprised when I heard from my mother that he was about to apply to Virginia Military Institute, where he would study engineering. But even before he wrote to explain the decision, I'd figured out that he and my parents believed he would be exempted from military service at VMI until he got his degree. Then he would be commissioned and could serve as an officer. But I felt in my bones that such exemptions would be wiped out, just as mine had been, if the rumor was true.

Worrying about Robert was very much a part of worrying about myself, we'd been close so long. We didn't look alike exactly, but anyone could tell we were brothers. We were about the same height, and we both had brown wavy hair—his was a bit lighter than mine—and brown eyes. His body was set up like mine, but fifteen pounds lighter. We were both good athletes, with endless vitality. He was very fast. He boxed and did gymnastics at college. And he was handsome, with the best features of both parents cast in a classical mold. Women turned around when he walked by.

The night the bad rumor reached us, my mind took me back to our house in the woods. I remembered that when I was about eight and Robert six, my father cleared a small section of land behind the house for a vegetable garden, which Grandma Pagliaro took care of. We built a coop there too, where we kept a dozen or so chickens for a couple of years. We had to replace them often because some predator tore out their crops. Despite the losses, we kept hoping they'd start to lay eggs, but we never found one. Robert and I looked for months without luck.

One day, early on a Saturday morning, my father came into the kitchen with what my brother and I had been looking for, an egg.

"See what I found," he said.

"Who laid it?" Robert wanted to know.

"I think it was Babybird. I'm not sure. I'll cook it right now."

My father scrambled it in butter and divided it between us, tasting a bit himself. His strong mouth and chin were relaxed in a loving smile.

"That's what a really fresh egg tastes like," he said.

At the time we unthinkingly accepted our father's good luck in finding the egg we had so long looked for, but after a while we talked things over. It wasn't long before we decided that he had planted the egg and retrieved it just to please us. But we didn't feel hoodwinked, we felt loved.

If my sense of family hadn't been strong, I'd have had a really hard time making it through basic after the rumor about the end of the ASTP. I still missed Helen, even though I knew it was over between us. God, how I wanted a woman all my own. I'd drift off to sleep sometimes, imagining she'd written to say she wanted us to wait for each other. Sometimes I imagined an old friend like Charlotte Walker wrote to tell me she had dreamed about me and wanted to stay in touch until the War ended, when we'd get together forever. It was crazy, but the fantasies had a power all their own. They filled my lonely life before I went to sleep and during the long marches when my mind could wander as it would. Often a song would sing its way through me.

> Our love is a dream, but in my reverie,
> I can see that this love was meant to be.
> Only a poor fool, never schooled in the whirlpool
> Of romance could be so cruel, as you are to me.

Letters from home didn't fill the void exactly. But they told me I had a kind of emotional Headquarters for as long as I needed it. Once, even that security seemed threatened, when I first heard that my father's company was sending him to the ship-yard in Mobile, Alabama, to sharpen tanker production there. I had the feeling the family was breaking up, even though he'd worked on out-of-town jobs before, taking us with him when that was the reasonable thing to do—to Miami when he did the foundation for the Dade County Courthouse, and to Portsmouth for the dry dock.

But then I began to think, "Alabama is closer to Georgia than New York is. Maybe Dad will visit me. Maybe Mom will move to Alabama to be with Dad when Robert and Edward finish the school term, and she'll visit me too." Still, the family would be divided or at best relocated.

After the rumor about the end of the ASTP, other things showed us that Army life is unpredictable. First of all, Henderson was reclassified—reassigned to God knows where. By itself, that was a good thing. He was a first-class bastard who'd done a lot of harm. But after Henderson, Siebold was reclassified too! The best man in the outfit, reclassified. So what had at first seemed like the just treatment of a bad guy—Henderson scragged—looked like another irrational Army action when Siebold got the same treatment. Our battalion commander made both decisions.

He was the recently promoted Major Harris. According to rumor he was a longtime reservist on weekends away from his job as a shoe salesman. He was visibly proud of his rank. A sleek, baby-faced man of about thirty-six or seven, he paraded himself decisively—under a dimple-crowned, broad-brimmed hat. His boots were soft, each one clasped from ankle to upper calf by three little belts and buckles; and he carried a short quirt he used to whip the air from time to time. Otherwise it was tucked under his left arm. Before his promotion his uniform was like every other captain's. Apparently field officers—those with the rank of major or higher—were permitted certain deviations from standard military dress.

It was Major Harris who spoke intently with Captain Porter, the company commander, in the jeep, just before Henderson came to the end of the road. Even to my young eyes, Harris seemed so full of himself that it was hard to take him seriously, except, of course, as a source of danger. He was probably a better officer than he seemed. He himself set the pace for our first twenty-five-mile hike—not a simple thing to do when you're moving a whole battalion over an irregular stretch of ground, and doing the job in eight hours, not more or less. The rate of march helps to assure that the men won't be overtired when they reach their destination and it makes their time of arrival a matter others can count on.

Captain Porter did not like Henderson any more than we did. We had known this for a while, well before the captain broke the unwritten law that officers are not to be reprimanded by their superiors in front of the enlisted men. It was Henderson's insensitivity that got him into trouble. Though it took many forms, we connected one in particular with his downfall. We could all see when Porter thought Henderson was marching his lead platoon at too rapid a pace, forcing the rest of the company to keep up. The captain would look troubled, glance at his watch, and then gradually overtake Henderson, hoping to get him to realize his mistake without saying anything to him. But Henderson, who was likely to be telling somebody a dirty joke, never got the message. So Captain Porter would finally come up alongside him and whisper an order. Only then would Henderson slow down.

Porter played his part in this scene several times over. We wondered whether this quiet, gentlemanly southerner would ever lose his patience. One day he did. Henderson was as usual marching like a bat out of hell, while Porter and Harris rode alongside in a slow-moving jeep, engaged in an intense conversation. The jeep stopped, Porter dismounted, and called out to Henderson in a subdued but distinctly audible voice, as he began to overtake the lieutenant. Henderson didn't hear. Porter repeated the subdued call three times, to no avail.

Then, past self-control, he shouted, "Henderson!" at the top of his strong voice, his body shaking with anger. Henderson heard at last, but apparently too late. He disappeared. There was no explanation. Rumor had it that he was assigned to a frontline outfit.

Lieutenant Siebold's removal was another story. Our battalion did a night hike of fifteen miles to a place where we were to bivouac for several weeks. The pace of this relatively short march was more rapid than usual—it was a forced march—so that we were tired well before it ended, looking forward to the breakfast we knew would be served when we finished. When we were still five miles or so out from our destination, Harris told Porter to send an officer to the battalion kitchen (company kitchens were merged for the bivouac), to confirm our time of arrival. Porter sent Siebold, who got to there in a jeep, found everything in readiness, and accepted an early batch of pancakes from the sergeant on duty, who happened to be our company mess sergeant. Meanwhile, Harris, satisfied that the forced march was ending well, had himself driven to the kitchen to be doubly sure that everything was ready. There he found Siebold, eating before the men had been fed. He got rid of him on the spot.

Shortly before we reached the bivouac area, entirely ignorant of what had happened, we saw Siebold in a jeep, being driven slowly toward us as we marched to the encampment he'd just left. The driver stopped, and the lieutenant told us he'd be leaving us for another assignment. Then he wished us well, and before we had time to realize what was happening, he rode off forever.

The Army never explains itself. We never found out why Henderson was reclassified. In fact, we never found out that he had been reclassified. He just disappeared. The same is true of Siebold's reassignment. He said good-bye to us one day, and that was that. Henderson's unexplained reclassification was at first acceptable to us because we had experienced his unjust ways firsthand. But Siebold's left us stunned. We grew wary of Harris, and wary of the Army, which seemed perversely mysterious and unfair.

We were frightened by our new status as long-term infantrymen, but we got on with the job at hand, though with less trust than we'd had. We were still kids. The bad news forced us to grow up some, but it also made our immaturity obvious. One day I overheard one of the Italian prisoners of war filling potholes in the company street make a wisecrack I didn't like. "What soldiers! America is winning the war, but it's hard to see how. These guys look like babies."

Even Marciano reinforced my doubts. One day as he marched next to me, he asked in a tentative voice, untypical of him, what I thought about the men I'd been training with for almost three months. I said I liked them fine, and then I talked a little about O'Brien, Marlowe, Oliver, and Moskovitch. I knew he liked O'Brien, and in fact Marciano said so, before getting into the subject that was really on his mind.

"Yeah, O'Brien is a good man all the way round, but I don't see that in many of the others." Then he added, "These kids are supposed to be the smartest in the country. I don't see it. They have IQs higher than the officers', but I don't see the brains. Most of them don't know where they are or what they're doing."

He wasn't jealous or afraid, like Stoddard. Just perplexed. I started to say that many of us were immature, but we could learn languages quickly and handle abstract subjects that had practical applications in navigation and artillery. But I stopped myself, because the answer I meant to give him seemed an evasion of his recognition. Besides, he had made me aware of a sense I'd had for us ASTP brainchildren, without quite knowing it. So instead of countering or amplifying what the sergeant had said, I vaguely agreed with him. His view of us, and his crisp expression of it, had rumpled my complacency, even though it confirmed a half-formed sense of my own.

The weeks passed, and like all foot soldiers, we worried about the future, and at the same time, lived out the Army routine, day by day, with an eye on Stoddard and his likes. Home became more important than ever, and Helen began to fade. Life had changed not only for me. It had also changed for my family. My mother had asked for a picture of me, which I wasn't able to have made. I don't think she wanted a facsimile to cherish so much as she wanted to see what I looked like after nearly two months of Army life. She was not sentimental, but she was worried about how I might be getting along. Letters from Robert suggested they felt the strain of my new status as infantryman. That and my father's assignment to the shipyard in Mobile and Robert's last year before the draft brought the war close to all of us.

I didn't send a picture of myself home for weeks, and then it was Lieutenant Endicott's snapshot of me running a bayonet course. His photographing us was not just unusual, it was unique in my Army experience. Right after Lieutenant Siebold was reassigned, Endicott, the company executive officer, began staying close to our platoon, probably aware that we'd been hit hard by the sudden loss. Marciano might well have told him, or he himself may have guessed how we felt. I suppose he was trying to let us know that somebody in the Army liked us. Anyhow, he surprised the hell out of us by spending a whole afternoon taking pictures of us as we ran the bayonet course, and the next day he handed us the results, which included one of me. It shocked me when I saw it, because it showed me looking like a young version of my father at his toughest. Everyone said I looked like my mother. But the picture made it clear that my father's mouth and chin had become mine. It was one of the most startling disclosures of my life.

My father was tough and kind. So were my mother and Grandma Pagliaro. They were all loving and yet independent-minded. They never said so, but I knew from all three of them that it was important to get along with the people around you, without giving up your own view of things. This idea was brought home by a hundred examples while I was growing up. It helped me to resist my father's pressure on me to be an engineer. It was even included in the way we thought about religion. My parents made my brother and me take instruction for First Communion and Confirmation, but apart from that, we were allowed to attend Mass or not, as we chose. After I was confirmed, I sometimes went to church with Grandma Pagliaro. But when we moved to Virginia, I stopped hearing Mass altogether. I never believed God expected ritual behavior from me.

As things turned out, I saw my father in Columbus just days after he and the others had received the picture of me in New

York. He arrived in Mobile shortly before mid-February to begin his new job, and he came up to Columbus to see me on the following Saturday. Marciano got me a special pass from Captain Porter. It wasn't routine because we were on bivouac, but the captain said okay as soon as he heard what it was for.

It was a peculiar meeting for the first few minutes. Only two days before, my father had begun work on a demanding job, and he had traveled overnight to see me, uncertain whether the promised pass would come through. The Columbus bus depot, where we had agreed to meet, was crowded and noisy, like so many other public places during World War II, with hundreds of soldiers waiting for friends and relatives. My father and I were lucky; we found each other right away.

We embraced. He said, "I'm glad to see you. You look great. Your overcoat is dirty."

I knew right away he didn't mean I'd grown careless of my appearance. He was telling me he knew life had changed enough that I had to accept the dirty coat as inevitable. He was right. I had just come back from the field, where the coat had served as a coat in the day and a pillow at night.

My father had traveled by train and I had taken a bus. To shorten his return trip after the weekend, we agreed to go south to Montgomery, where we shared a suite at the Jefferson Davis. After dinner, we had a cot moved into the sitting room, where I slept. I showered before going to bed, and came out wrapped in a towel, ready to dress for bed in a T-shirt and shorts, regular Army night wear. When my father saw me, he came into the dressing room and said, "They're doing something right. You look terrific. How much do you weigh?"

"One-eighty," I said, smiling.

"I can't believe it. You look terrific," he repeated. "You pack so much in a small space."

He couldn't have pleased me more.

I ate a full breakfast the next morning, but the rest is vague. The visit had a sad undercurrent for both of us. Even so, the time went too quickly, and towards the end—when we said good-bye after an early lunch—we knew we would not be able to see each other often, if at all—with my father's job over two hundred miles from Columbus and the uncertainty of free time for me.

On the bus back to Columbus, I thought about home, where my mother and Robert were, and about my father in Mobile, and me, in the middle of nowhere. And for the first time in days I thought about Helen. I wasn't thinking about her very often, though when I did, I still felt a deep sense of loss. It was mostly Robert who was on my mind. During the last eight weeks of basic, he didn't write to me as often as I liked, and I used to nag my parents about it. I was expecting a lot of him. He had school to worry about, besides big changes in family life. I didn't want him to be drafted, and when he asked me about the Army, I tried to explain the regimentation. He knew how much I had thrown myself into the work of training, and he knew that I was in one sense flourishing in the Army—happy, not at all gloomy, he believed. So he had a hard time understanding what I meant. I wanted to help him, but there was no way I could. I used to be able to reach out to him. Now it was impossible.

As the bus rode along, I went back in time, to a winter's morning in 1933, after a night of heavy snow that continued to fall, gathering the world into a single white mass of rounded shapes. Robert and I walked out of the house through the cold, a quarter of a mile to the place where we caught the bus to P.S. 105. He had just begun school; he was not quite six. I was almost eight. The bitter air whipped the falling snow across our faces. I didn't know my mother could see from the kitchen window most of the distance we'd covered. We felt we were taking care of ourselves. When we finally realized the bus wouldn't be coming that day, Robert and I started for home. I carried his schoolbag, and then I got him to put his arm around my shoulder, as I held his waist to give him support. By the time we reached the house, my mother had hot chocolate and cookies ready. But I felt proud and satisfied that I had got us home.

Robert was my responsibility. Even his sins were mine. During the Depression, a man named Paul Hawks ran a small real estate business out of a one-room building located at the edge of a sandlot baseball field about a mile from our house. On Sundays, when a game was played and a large crowd gathered to watch, Hawks sold cigarettes, candy, and soda off a foldout counter, half of one wall of his little office. Robert and I were hired to pick up empty soda bottles for a penny apiece; we knew there was a two-cent deposit on each bottle, which Hawks had already collected from his customers.

One Sunday, we came back with a large haul of bottles, and Terrible Paul said he'd give us only half a cent for each. Robert, no more than seven, complained, citing the correct pay. Each of us was owed twenty cents, not ten. We got nowhere. Robert was angry, and so was I. But I was more involved in my brother's anger than in my own. Owing to the dispute, we were paid nothing. We hung around the candy counter for about ten minutes, hoping Hawks would change his mind. Then Robert, obviously frustrated, helped himself to four five-cent Hershey bars.

Hawks was out and after him in an instant. I stood by and heard him threaten us with jail unless we paid him twenty cents. The power was all on his side. Robert had to stay with the man as hostage, while I ran home to get my one quarter from the living room rug, where I had unthinkingly left it. I tried to look nonchalant as I collected the coin, but I could tell my mother and father knew I was doing something serious. They didn't interfere. I returned to Hawks. I hated him, but I paid him, and he let Robert go.

The bus rumbled on through the night. "Why is it that every time I think of Robert and the Hershey bars, it comes up from the depths of memory as if I were the one who lifted the candy?" I didn't know the answer. I dozed off.

By the time we reached Columbus, I was groggy. But I pulled myself together, got back to the Company Area and hitched a ride on a mess truck leaving our kitchen for the firing range where the outfit was still bivouacked. We had a few days more in the field before returning to barracks for the last weeks of training.

The platoon finished basic trailing clouds of glory. We completed the thirty-mile night hike with no dropouts, whereas the other units lost an average of 9 percent of their men. We were first in marksmanship in the battalion. And we tied for first in firing the mortar and the .30 caliber machine gun. Despite our loss of Siebold, we held together as a unit, in part because he had helped us to imagine ourselves that way, in part because we needed each other, and in part because the Army reminded us that we were a platoon by measuring us against other platoons.

We'd have come out first in use of the machine gun, except that when our platoon began to fire, which was late in the day, after most others had finished the exercise, the inspecting colonel stopped us from using spotters, who helped us to adjust our aim without taking our eyes off the target.

"What is this, Harris?" he shouted, red hot. "Regulations don't allow for spotters. Get those men out of there, goddammit."

We enjoyed hearing the colonel chew out the major right in front of us.

Our last long march—the thirty-mile night hike—ended on a downbeat, even though everybody in the platoon finished. When we began, the dark sky was brightened by stars and the air was dry and cool. Then it clouded over, and during our long break at the halfway mark, it started to drizzle and never let up. We were soon soaking wet. Clothes and equipment chafed our bodies. Our pack straps and rifle slings dug into our shoulders, but we kept going. The last break was quiet. We were too tired to talk. With almost four miles still ahead of us, we got up and slogged along through the fine rain, heads low. No one was very happy.

"Start a song up, Chunky," Marciano said. "Give us drag asses a boost."

I was in no mood for singing. But Marciano wasn't giving an order. He just wanted me to give a sign of the energy he knew we all had in reserve. So without thinking, I started to sing "It's the Last Long Mile," a World War I tune Ken Evans and I used to sing at his player piano. I heard myself singing mock-tremolo, God knows why.

> Oh, it's not the pack
> That you carry on your back,
> Nor the Springfield on your shoulder,
> Nor the two-inch crust,
> Of khaki colored dust,
> That makes you feel your legs are growing older.
> And it's not the hike
> On the hard-turned pike
> That wipes away your smile—
> Nor the sock of sister,
> That raised the bloomin' blister.
> It's the last long mile.

O'Brien shouted, "Sing it again," and I did. He and a few others hummed the tune with me. Then we were quiet again until we got near the Company Area. Having been ordered to march in parade step, we counted the cadence on command—one, two, three, four, one, two, three, four. Our rhythmic shouts filled the soggy night.

After we'd taken hot showers and eaten breakfast, we walked back to the hut for a morning's sleep. Oliver came to my bunk. He had a smile on his face, but I could tell he was mad.

"I couldn't believe it when I heard you singing that goddam song. I wanted to strangle you."

I understood him. My own fleeting resistance to Marciano's request shared something with Oliver's anger.

"I get you," I told him. "But we're different."

I don't think Oliver could have sung if his life depended on it. He even resented music's effect on him. But the differences between us didn't really divide us. They gave us something to talk about, and they kept the idea of variety alive, in a context of endless uniformity. Besides, he needed me to understand him—a proof that he wasn't crazy and alone—and I needed him.

My need for O'Brien during these last days of training was less complicated. We were alike in so many ways that we were never conscious of getting along well. We simply took each other's understanding and loyalty for granted. I would have been lucky to go to the front with him, if going to the front is ever lucky.

Our training ended on schedule, and we were graduated with appropriate ceremonies and praises. For the occasion, we cleaned our equipment, and we dressed ourselves in Class A uniforms. Then we fell in and marched to the parade ground—several thousand men. We stood at attention, waiting to hear some official word about the ASTP. The inspecting colonel presided. A short, peppery man, with graying hair and a raspy voice, he called abruptly on the major as he was about to begin his speech.

"Harris, lower that goddam microphone six inches."

The major jumped forward, saying, "Yes, Sir."

When the order had been carried out, the colonel came forward and spoke.

"At ease. Men, I'm proud of you. You have completed a period of arduous training, and your performance reflects well on the Army and on yourselves. You have measured up to the infantry's highest standards. Your bodies and minds have grown tough, and you have learned skills that will enable you to give a good account of yourselves in combat, should the fortunes of war bring you there."

The colonel paused a full thirty seconds while we all thought grimly about the fortunes of war. But the pause was not for rhetorical effect, it was to give him time to find some statistics on our accomplishments, which he read to us so we'd know the achievements of the various companies and platoons in the battalion. We listened with a certain interest, and we were glad to hear that our company and our platoon had done well. But what we really wanted was official word about the ASTP.

After he finished with the record of our performance, the colonel paused again, looking to his left and right several times, as if to be sure he had our attention.

"Men, it is my privilege to inform you that almost all of you will be assigned to one of two infantry divisions for further training—the 87th and the 104th. Both of these outfits have a proud history of service, in peace and in war. Most of their well-trained personnel have recently been called to service overseas, so there's a great chance for you to fill the ranks. I know from your great training record here that you will take up your new assignments with a firm sense of purpose and acquit yourselves well. Orders will be posted on company bulletin boards this afternoon. The best of luck to each and every one of you. Major Harris."

We were called to attention, marched back to the Company Area, and dismissed. While we waited for orders to be posted, we talked about the colonel's speech. We weren't surprised by the snow job he gave us. But we were surprised that he could talk for twenty minutes and never once mention the ASTP. How could he praise us and tell us what our infantry assignments would be, as if nobody had ever heard of the ASTP?

Chapter Three

Ouija Says

ALL BUT TWO OR THREE of the men in our training battalion were divided between the 87th and the 104th Infantry Divisions, just as the colonel said we'd be. Marlowe was one of the exceptions. His father had enough political influence to keep him at Benning, temporarily assigned to Battalion Headquarters, while he tried to get his son a place at West Point. It didn't work out. Somebody with clout got to the U.S. senators from Wyoming ahead of him. But when we left Fort Benning, Marlowe was still waiting to hear. He didn't exactly like what his father was trying to do; still, he would have been happy to get an appointment to the Academy. We all felt pretty much the same way. The Army had made it clear it would use us however it wanted to. We were all hoping for something better than our assignment to the infantry.

The new 87th Division we were assigned to in Fort Jackson, near Columbia, South Carolina, was made up of three groups— the old-timers (a cadre of noncoms and officers, along with a few enlisted men, who had escaped being sent overseas a month before our arrival, when the well-trained division was gutted for replacements); a number of ASTP men who'd been taken out of the colleges where the Army had sent them after they'd finished basic training; and those of us from Fort Benning. The men in all three groups had just experienced the power of the Army to control their destinies. Old members of the 87th felt it as they read the daily posted lists of their buddies about to be shipped overseas and sweated out the possibility that they'd be shipped out, too. And those of us in both ASTP groups had just felt the Army's power to change its mind without explanation. All of us in the 87th were afraid the outfit would be sent overseas soon. At the same time, we believed—we wanted to believe—the war was too far along for us to go to the front.

This paradox of fright and hope was a commonplace during the war. We never talked about our fear, though there were many signs that all of us were afraid—from the sounds of nightmares we shared to our endless wishing out loud for reassignment to a noninfantry unit. On the other hand, our hope that we'd never see combat was so unsubstantially grounded that it needed a lot of discussion to keep it alive. I heard many reasons why we'd never be sent to the front—the Luftwaffe had been so weakened during the Battle for Britain that Allied airpower would be able to destroy the enemy with the help of the ground troops already overseas; the 87th Division, made up mostly of green kids, could not be brought to combat readiness for many months, by which time the war would be over; the proportion of high IQs in the 87th was so great (a regular national treasure of brainpower) that the Army would never risk the bad publicity of sending such an outfit into combat; a secret weapon was being developed in the Yakima Valley, and it would soon end the war. Though there was at least some truth in all of these notions, we used them as camouflage. We knew in our gut the chances of our seeing action were high.

Oliver was the only man from the hut assigned to my new company in the 87th. In fact, he and I served in the same platoon. Other hut mates in the 87th went to units far enough from ours that I never saw them again, except for O'Brien. He was with the heavy weapons company in our battalion and was made a jeep driver. At first we tried to stay in touch, but we couldn't connect as often as we wanted to, and we began to drift apart. And even though Oliver and I were in the same platoon, we stopped being close at Jackson, at least for the first two months. Once the ASTP closed and we left Benning, we stopped making believe we could find a family in the Army.

Maybe if we'd had time to become part of the real life of 87th, things would've been different. But that didn't happen. When we reached Fort Jackson, in March 1944, we got the first taste of Division's unofficial way of handling new arrivals. The old-timers made it clear that they controlled the turf. The noncoms and privates, with few exceptions, had been in the Army for only a year or two. But it was their outfit we were joining, and they wanted us to prove we were good enough to belong, even though we outnumbered them four to one. But even after we showed them that we were well prepared, toughened infantrymen, they accepted us only slowly, because they kept believing brainy kids could not be hardened field soldiers, though we kept up with them day in and day out.

An exception was our platoon sergeant, a big man from Cleveland named Kredinski. If he had a sense of humor, he didn't show it. His broad face, with its steady eyes and jutting chin, was always serious. You couldn't take him lightly. He was very smart and conscionable, a noncom who did his job responsibly. Unlike the other old-timers, he took us as he found us. He knew we were kids, but he kept an open mind about what we'd be like as soldiers. Kredinski commanded the platoon in a no-nonsense way. He never got chummy with us, like Marciano, but he proved to be kind and fair, as well as tough. We were young enough to need a leader like him. We never got to know the officer who commanded the platoon, Lieutenant Robbin, who was often on duty in company Headquarters. Kredinski was in charge.

The other noncom we had to deal with every day was Sergeant Raymond, our squad leader. A tall, handsome guy, Raymond wanted us to know he was a ladies' man. We could see he was much less sure of himself than the platoon sergeant. But he didn't give us much trouble once we realized that all he wanted was for us to follow the orders he passed along from Kredinski and to like him. So we listened to his stories about the women he'd laid and encouraged him to tell us more.

Apart from the clear signals that we were the newcomers who'd be judged by the old-timers of the 87th—though never promoted—there were some official attempts to make us feel good about our new assignment. Soon after our arrival, the company clerk, Corporal Wanlus, a regular Army man, pinned up a notice saying we were all invited to a dance in the recreation hall. But in posting the notice, he only followed orders. When he saw us reading it, he got nasty.

"Don't waste your time. You twerps haven't got a chance. You're wet behind the ears. You wouldn't know where to stick it in."

Wanlus was right. The women, mostly WACS and civilians who worked in the PX, wanted to dance with the older men, and they sat around, talking among themselves, waiting to be asked by the right guy. The four or five years that separated us from the others was a lot.

A better official boost to morale was free time. As soon as Kredinski and Raymond decided we were qualified to be regulars, we were given a Class A pass. Whether or not we used the unusual privilege of the pass to leave the post during off-duty hours, we understood that after we were dismissed for the evening meal, our time was our own, unless, of course, we were scheduled for a night problem or some other special duty. And in addition to the pass, we were encouraged to look forward to a two-week furlough to begin within a month or two of our arrival at Jackson.

All these things helped our feelings, but they didn't make us anything like charter members of the outfit. Besides, the dance, the Class A pass, and the furlough made us wonder why the Army was being so nice. The reason wasn't hard to imagine. It increased the weight of uncertainty about the short-term future. We were infantry privates, not taken seriously by most of the old-timers—in fact, resented by some. And though we tried not to think about it, we were afraid of being sent overseas.

Our furloughs were delayed for well over a month. We were all champing at the bit, but there was nothing we could do except wait. I used my pass almost every night to go to nearby Columbia, South Carolina, which was always packed with soldiers. And every week or ten days, I telephoned home before going into town. Occasionally I called my father in Mobile, but most often, the house in New York. I was free after a night problem one afternoon in early April, just a few days before Easter, and I telephoned. Robert answered.

"Hello, Rob. How you doing?

"Okay. Everything's fine, but Mom's out shopping." He sounded like she should be taking the call. I was in the Army, he was home.

"Well, that's okay," I said. "I talked to her last week. How's school?"

"Pretty good. Unless something gets screwed up, I finish on June 30."

"Yeah, I know. You still think VMI is right?"

"It'll work out. I want engineering, and I really like the idea of going back to Virginia. Graduating from there will get me a commission for sure. Dad thinks I'll be deferred. I don't know, it seems like a good deal. How are you doing?"

"Okay, no complaints."

"Do you hear from anybody in Portsmouth?"

"No, not really. You?"

"Yeah, I got a letter from Bradley last week. Tewksbury is going to VMI, too. You remember Red. What do you hear from Helen?" Robert had given me a warning before he mentioned

Helen—Bradley was her brother. But Robert and I had talked about her before. Besides, he was right there from the beginning.

"Just about nothing. She hardly ever writes, and when she does, she doesn't say anything. But I don't think about her the way I used to."

"She should write," he said, as if there were no other way. "How are the girls in South Carolina?"

"The one dance I went to, the girls were women, and they didn't want me, so I don't know. But I hear there are good church dances in Columbia. I'm gonna try one."

"Church dances? What are they? I thought you were never going to church again?"

"It's just that they have these dances in the rec room of the church. I hear they're okay." I wanted to change the subject again. "What do you hear from Dad?" I asked. "Is he coming up for Easter?"

"Last we heard he was saving the trip for your furlough. Any word yet?"

"Lots of rumors. No real word. I hear they're waiting till they know we'll be shipped out, and then they'll give us our last two weeks home. I don't know."

"I wish you could be here. How is it there on a holiday?" He was really curious.

"It's not like anything. You just forget it, unless some asshole noncom makes a speech, like, 'Don't worry, men. Think of all the holidays you'll have after the war.' Anyhow," I said, changing the subject, "I hope VMI works out the way you and Dad think. Stay out of the Army if you can."

"Yeah, I guess so. But what about you?"

"It's okay, I'm doing fine. I weigh one-eighty stripped, and my waist is twenty-nine."

"Jesus! Is the food any good?"

"It's really great. Not like food at home, but it's tasty, something different all the time, and there's all you can eat, and that's a lot."

Robert laughed; but he wasn't laughing at what I'd said, it turned out. "Hey, you remember that crazy goat meat for Easter dinner! We used to hate it, the taste was so gamy."

How could I forget? My father insisted on goat for Easter—a custom from his boyhood in Italy. Maybe for Grandma Pagliaro's sake. He hired a special butcher to come to our house on the day before Easter. When the butcher came, he brought a kid—a capretta, a baby goat—whose feet, he swore, had never touched the ground. Then, in one of the tubs in the furnace room, the butcher—watched by Grandma—sacrificed the innocent capretta, and by custom, set aside certain parts for himself. On Good Friday, the day before the butcher came, my Grandmother and I attended the Passion of Christ's dying, a three-hour service. There was the promise of new life in the young kid's death, just as there was in Christ's. My mother always got us out of the house for the slaughter, so I never saw it. But I knew what was happening. At dinner the next day, Robert and I would taste the kid, but we never made a meal of it. We had baked ham or roast beef instead.

"Yeah, I remember. But it wasn't only the taste, the goat was tough as hell. Nobody liked it." But his recollection of Easter at home set my mind going. "Maybe we can have Easter dinner when I get my furlough," I said.

"Yeah, why not? Better late than never."

"You really think they'll defer you at VMI? When you get there, stay on your toes, and find out what you can. It's not the U.S. Military Academy. Anyhow, you've got a year. I better sign off. This is the longest call of my life. They'll have a fit."

"Okay, maybe we better. So long. See you soon, Harry."

"Write to me, Rob. You haven't written in weeks. So long, take care."

"I'll write. Take care."

Soon after I hung up, I took a bus to town, skipping dinner in the company kitchen. I needed something to do. First I had a hamburger and a beer, and then I began to look for a Presbyterian church where I'd heard they had a dance. When I got there the place was jumping. Everybody was young, my age or younger. It was like a high school dance, crowded and noisy, with music and loud talk. There were girls standing at the edge of the large room, waiting to be asked, and I danced with two of them. After that I stopped and looked around. Then I walked to one of the serving tables for something to drink and cookies. But I saw a very pretty girl, with a small upturned nose and big brown eyes, talking to the church matron in charge of the nonalcoholic punch. I wanted to dance with her right away, but I hesitated to interrupt the conversation. Then I decided, "What the hell, you can be polite."

"Excuse me, please. Would you like to dance?"

The matron smiled, and so did the young woman. "Sure, if you want to."

She made dancing easy. We moved together so well, I had no sense of leading. It just happened. "My name is Harry, what's yours?"

She waited more than a few seconds and then said, "I'm Abby Wofford." She wanted my full name.

"I'm Harry Pagliaro. My last name is tough to pronounce." I didn't like myself for apologizing.

"Pagliaro," she said without hesitation. "That's a nice name."

I looked at her kind face and we both smiled. When the music stopped, I asked, "Do you want to dance again?"

"I'd like to, if you want to." We danced three numbers, and then we stopped for some punch.

"Where do you go to school, Abby?"

"I don't. I finished high school just outside of Columbia a year ago next month, and I'm living with my aunt and uncle in town, trying to decide what to do."

"Oh, I see." In fact I was surprised by what she'd told me. Then I blurted out a question. "Will you spend the rest of the dance with me?"

She laughed with pleasure and said, "Yes, I'd love to."

We both understood before the night was over that we'd see each other again. In fact we met again at the church just two days later, and we acted as if we'd be together whenever it was possible. She introduced me to some of her friends. They were kind, because they knew Abby and I had something special going.

Her home was in a suburb of Columbia, about fifteen miles outside the city. Her father had died when she was ten, and her mother had remarried within three years. Things at home were not bad, but Abby preferred living in town with her aunt—her mother's sister—and her uncle. They had no children of their own. She had come to rely on them during the years after her father's death—when her home had been a place of mourning, and later, a place of courtship. Like me, Abby obviously needed a home away from home, and like me, she never quite found one.

Her uncle was a car dealer, who during the war was forced to buy and sell used cars because nothing new was coming off the production line. He did very well. One of the items he'd picked up at the auctions was an open touring car, a six-seater, custom built. It was a powerful eight-cylinder Buick—deep green and incredibly long—with spare wheels mounted on the running boards, and built into the rear of the front fenders. He and his wife loved to drive Abby and me around the streets of Columbia on Sunday afternoon, before we went out to a movie or a dance. We rode in the backseat and the aunt and uncle up front.

Like Abby and me, they took our friendship as a matter of course. They wanted her to enjoy it on her terms, which suited me fine. She and I became close during my stay at Jackson, comfortable in each other's company. Sometimes we just walked and talked, and sometimes we hugged and felt each other. But we never went all the way. Not that we struggled to decide for or against it. Maybe if I had been sure of what I wanted, she would have wanted the same thing.

But there was something strange about the friendship with Abby. In one part of my imagination, she lived in the past. My fear of what lay ahead—I wasn't sure I had a future—made me think of her as if our friendship had already ended. Abby really liked me, and I liked her. But I couldn't change things. Helen wasn't the reason, though I still thought about her sometimes. It was my bogged imagination that made my feelings for Abby seem finished, not dynamic. There was no Becoming about them. I lived out our brief relation as if it were a dream, which nothing could alter.

During those weeks, my mood was grim. I wanted no part of war. I believed the Axis had to be beaten, and I accepted the chance that I might have to go into combat. I'd go if I had to, but it wasn't wrong to hope for a safer assignment. I began life in the Army believing myself to be part of a great crusade of Good against Evil. The view was naive, but it was not unusual among young soldiers in World War II. Everyone saw that Hitler and Mussolini were madmen, leading destructive forces that had to be stopped. Without entirely wiping out my idealism, two things changed the way I looked at the war. First, most of the older men around me were not interested in our mission to save the world. All they wanted was to get through the hard times as comfortably as possible, and we could see them acting on this principle day after day. With promotion came privilege, and we saw officers and noncoms bucking at every turn, without dignity, for the next rank or grade. What affected me more, though, was my own growing sense that I was about to put my head on the line. Worse, my head was about to be put on the line by someone else, without my having a chance to say yes or no. The Army told me what to do, minute by minute. Loss of the power to choose brings dark premonitions. Dying would be the end of me. For some crazy reason I imagined fighting in Europe and fighting in the Pacific. If I died in Europe, it would be a little like going home. But I couldn't stand the idea that a strange, remote island might get my cold body.

Still, with thousands of others, I soldiered hard every day. The work at hand was preparation for a series of tests for the Expert Infantryman's Badge. To get it, you needed stamina, skill, and lots of luck. The tests included a thirty-mile hike, with full equipment, in eight hours, and a nine-mile cross-country forced march, same equipment, in an hour and forty minutes. That one was hard. It wiped out over a third of us. You needed both skill and luck to pass the nighttime compass problem. For that one you got a slip of paper with three compass readings—azimuths— and the three corresponding distances to be covered—several hundred yards for each. You also got three matches. You got under your poncho so no light showed. Then you'd strike one of the matches, read the first azimuth, check your compass for the direction, blow out the match, and—in the dark—pace out the prescribed distance in the prescribed direction. You might waste a match and lose out. More likely, you'd start walking a shade off course and increase the error with every step. On top of that, it was hard to calculate the exact distance you covered, in the dark, over rough ground. After you lit up and headed out three times, once for each compass reading, you had to be lucky to end up at the right place, where noncoms were waiting to say whether you came out close enough to pass. There were about fifteen tests altogether—shooting the M-1 from the hip, camouflaging a foxhole, creeping up on a position undetected, firing the 60 mm mortar, and on and on.

The Army always surprises you. Right after we began the tests, our furloughs came through. First they said we'd get furloughs right away. Then after a long delay without explanation, they told us we had three hours to get off the post. It was a rat race. Calling home was impossible. The lines for the telephone were too long. Oliver and I weren't talking the way we did at Benning. I almost always went to town alone. But we were still close, and we both lived in New York, so I grabbed him and said, "Let's clear out of here right away. We can telegram from town. Let's get to the railroad station right away."

"Okay," he said. "But I bet it's already packed. I bet half the division's on furlough."

When Oliver and I reached the Columbia train station, thousands of soldiers were standing on the platform, waiting to board the next train north. I couldn't believe arrangements hadn't been made for transporting so many men on leave. We waited, hoping to hear an announcement about a special train, but there was none. After a while, the once-a-day train that went to New York pulled in. I told Oliver to hold onto my belt, and I made a sure path through the crowd to the train door, swinging him in front of me at the last instant, and throwing him and his duffle bag up the steps just ahead of me.

As he landed on the outer deck of the car, he laughed out loud, for the first time, in my experience. Then he asked, "How the hell did you do that?" I didn't answer. I wanted to get home real bad.

The conductor closed the outer door right after we landed. The train was crowded, even before it reached Columbia. I thought of the poor bastards left on the station platform, but just then, a voice over the loudspeaker announced a special train headed north. Oliver and I found out after we got back to Jackson that all the men on furlough were taken care of within an hour of our departure. The announcement made my furious plunge through the crowd seem selfish and crazy, but even guilt couldn't dampen my sense of elation at being on the way home.

There were no seats for the first part of the trip, so we stood together in the aisle, talking every now and then. We didn't have much to say. After a while a woman of about thirty-five waved at us from her seat, saying, "Soldier, come on over."

She was seated next to an older woman, and they were sharing lunch. Oliver and I walked the few feet to their seats.

The younger woman said, "This is my mother. We just been to visit my brother—in the Marines. Please take some of this food. We have more than we can eat. Anyhow, we'll be getting off soon."

"Oh, no thanks," I said, "we'll wait to get some." But they both insisted. They really wanted us to have the rest of their food. The sandwiches looked delicious. I could see the roast beef and lettuce sticking out from the bread.

"Well, if you're sure it's okay. Thanks a lot."

The sandwiches were as good as they looked, the beef dressed with mayonnaise and pepper. They watched us eat, smiling. The mother said, "You both have such strong faces, and you look so healthy and full of life."

We couldn't handle that one. So we just nodded our heads and looked amiable. After that nobody said much. But they'd told the truth about getting off. In about an hour, they got up to leave, and we thanked them again, and they wished us luck, more than once, as they walked towards the door and waved. Oliver and I took the empty seats, closed our eyes, and rested.

The train was taking me home. With any luck my father would come up from Mobile, and the family would be together. Then after Robert graduated, my mother would move south. He had to start training at VMI early in the summer. Did he really want to go back to Virginia? Maybe that was true. We had good times there. But Lexington isn't Portsmouth. The train lulled me. During our first three months in Virginia, June through August, we lived in a farmhouse, on the Western Branch of the Elizabeth River. Robert and I fished for hours, or we just rowed, looking down into the clear water, where we could see bait fish schooling and crabs mating, motions in a silent picture. Or we crept out over a section of riverbank six feet or so above high water, through the brush, carefully, so as not to disturb the ducks, which seemed to be there, close to shore, feeding in all seasons. We had a .22 caliber rifle, but we weren't allowed to fire it on the river because of the danger of a ricochet. We wouldn't have wanted to kill the ducks anyway, unless we could retrieve them for a meal.

About a hundred yards behind our natural duck blind, there was a small stand of long-needle pine—a few hundred trees, each about three or four inches in diameter, close together and straight as arrows, their boles bare of branches for eight feet above the ground, after which they flourished into each other in a thick green canopy. Underneath was a deep bed of sweet-smelling brown needles, which yielded softly and quietly to our footsteps. We often carried the rifle silently through this peaceful copse, the shortest way to a natural embankment against which we mounted a target to fire at. We grew to love the whole adventure, repeating it dozens of times. The smells and sights as we walked the soft path through the shadows of the pines, the staccato of the rifle fire, and the slow walk back home took on a shape as indelible as a poem.

The furlough went quickly. I saw my family—mother, father, brothers, grandfather, and endless aunts, uncles, and cousins—but few incidents stand out in my mind besides the train ride from Columbia with Oliver and the postponed Easter dinner during the weekend my father came to New York from Mobile. Besides family, I saw friends I'd known from childhood, but I have no clear memory of this. Even a date with Charlotte Walker, a girl I grew up with, is vague in my mind. All I can remember is that we went to Ryan's, on City Island, for dinner one night, and hugged when we said good-bye.

The weekend of the Easter dinner was the repetition of many former Sundays and holidays at the table, a ritual of family permanence. I reached home on a Saturday, and we decided to celebrate Easter a week from the next day, which would be about halfway into my furlough. My father was prepared to take a long weekend, and he got home on Friday, in time to shop for the meal with my mother. She had saved enough ration stamps for a large roast. They went out the next morning, and came back with a load of food. Then we all gathered in the big kitchen, as we had so many times before, to start work for the meals ahead. But before we began, we ate a scratch lunch of ham, cheese, and roasted pepper sandwiches on Italian bread, and we had some of the great wine Grandma and my father had made in 1934. There were gallons of it, stored in demijohns sealed with olive oil before corking, and topped with wax poured on the neck after the cork was tapped in.

After lunch, Robert and I prepared vegetables, both for supper and the Easter dinner—string beans, escarole, turnips, white onions, artichokes, frying peppers, potatoes, romaine lettuce. My mother baked the holiday cheesecake, made with ricotta. She had already baked cookies and egg bread for Easter breakfast. From time to time she would stir and add to the soup she had simmering. My father soaked snails in milk, preparing them for a light pasta sauce for the evening meal. He also prepared baked chicken to follow the pasta, setting aside the giblets, which he sautéd with eggs for breakfast next morning. And finally he trimmed the leg of lamb—the Easter roast.

Everybody was busy, and we all talked, enjoying the orderly commotion. But nobody talked about me or Robert or the war, at least not directly.

"Dad," I said, "Some of your snails are crawling up the tile. Don't you want them back in the colander."

"Yeah, I know. I'll get them in a minute."

"Boys, please give me four of the outer leaves of the escarole for the soup," my mother said.

"Okay, Mom."

"Harry, your choice, linguine or spaghettini?"

"No contest, Dad. Linguine. And please don't make the sauce too hot. I can't take your heavy hand on the red pepper"

"Harry," my mother said to my father, "we're low on wine. Do you think the boys can open a demijohn? I have some cheese-cloth."

"Sure. Get yourselves a knife and a corkscrew, and be careful with the wax."

Robert and I went down to the storeroom, where we used to keep canned goods, hams, and cheeses before the war. We rolled a demijohn away from the wall and I carefully scraped the wax seal from the cork, removing the particles with a damp cloth. The cork was so big, it was easy to pull out whole. After I got it out, Robert twisted a piece of the cheesecloth and lowered it into the film of olive oil that floated on the wine in the neck of the bottle, another air seal. I watched his strong, deft hands as they lowered and readjusted the cloth until the surface of the wine was clear.

"Okay, Dad," we shouted together.

"I'm coming."

In a minute he came down with four sterile bottles and corks and a slim rubber hose.

"Good job, boys," he said, as he lowered one end into the demijohn and put the other in his mouth and drew to get the flow started, skillfully moving the running hose from one bottle to the next as he filled them. Then we recorked the demijohn, rolled it back against the wall, and proudly carried the four bottles upstairs.

During supper that night, and at breakfast and the afternoon dinner the next day, it was the same. Only questions about our schedules got even close to mention of the war.

"When are you due back, Harry," my father asked at supper.

"I have to make roll call at 5:45 A.M., a week from this coming Tuesday," I answered.

"So you'll have to leave Monday morning, I guess," my mother said.

"Yep, that's it, Mom. When do you leave, Dad?" I asked.

"This Monday."

"So soon?" I was surprised. "I thought you'd stay a few more days."

"No, I've got to get back. It's a big job, and things go wrong every day."

"You going to Mobile as soon as Robert leaves for VMI, Mom?

"I'm not sure yet. Dad and I have to talk it over." My parents knew that if I went to Europe, I'd be processed in Fort Meade, Maryland, less than four hours from New York. Both of them wanted her to be close enough to say good-bye.

That's how the talk went. Even when Robert and I were getting ready for bed that night, we didn't say what was on our minds, except that I repeated a version of what I'd told him over the phone. "Don't let the Army get you unless you have a commission. Maybe the Merchant Marine. You'd still be a civilian."

"Yeah, I guess so."

Then neither of us spoke. There was nothing to say. We just waited to fall asleep.

At Sunday dinner, my father carved the roast. It was a spring lamb that reminded me of the capretta and Grandma. My mother served the plates with meat and a spoonful or two of the juices. Robert and I waited them out before we all helped ourselves to vegetables. Then we ate, drank, and talked an endless time over fruit, nuts, and cookies. The wine, made almost ten years before, had aged very well. But the best thing was that the meal promised continuity and abundance. The family would always gather at the table, share food and wine, and linger endlessly.

On my last night home, I went out. Maybe it was the dinner date with Charlotte Walker. When I came home, late, I went to the bedroom and found Robert sound asleep. I almost woke him up, but then decided against it. I knew it would be a long time before we'd share a room again. But there was nothing to say, so I got into bed and waited to fall asleep. It was a long time before I made it, and then I slept lightly. Even so I was the first one up. I showered in the downstairs bathroom, just off the kitchen, and then made a pot of coffee and sipped it until Robert and my mother came down. Almost as soon as they joined me, I said I'd have to leave soon, and I went upstairs to get my bag, already packed.

"Take care of yourself, Harry," my mother said, kissing my cheek and hugging me. Her nose was red and her eyes were puffy.

"I've got a cold," she explained. I'd never seen her cry before. I'd heard her crying behind the closed door of her room when her mother died, but she never let any of us see her, not even my father.

"I hope you're well soon, Mom. Don't worry. I'll be okay."

"Take care of yourself," Robert said, putting out his hand. We shook. He looked grim. There was no way to acknowledge their sadness, not openly at least, and yet I found it hard to turn away. But I had to go. I walked to the bus stop that marked the first part of my journey back to the Army, feeling that I might never see my home or family again. As I started, I stumbled in a rut of the cinder path I was on.

The train ride back to Columbia was bleak—sad, scattered family at one end and Army life without much promise at the other. When I got to Jackson, we took up where we'd left off, taking tests for the Expert Infantryman's Badge. After three days, it seemed as though we'd never been away. All of us did our best, even though we didn't much trust the Army or the old-timers around us. We disliked our status as privates with no chance of promotion, and yet we were proud of our ability as foot soldiers. So we were glad that the same proportion of the ASTP guys as old-timers won the Expert's badge. I was proud to be among them—only 13 percent.

The old-timers stopped ragging us about our tender feet and weak backs. Instead, they got at us by telling us over and over about the Louisiana maneuvers they'd been through—the 87th against another division in mock combat—just before most of their buddies were sent overseas as replacements. They said no amount of advanced infantry training could give us any idea about the demands made on body and soul by maneuvers. We listened glumly. But some of the old-timers tried to get closer to us in individual friendships.

Sergeant Raymond, our squad leader—the ladies' man—was a heavily bearded man of twenty-five, from Brooklyn. He told me frankly that I wasn't like any New Yorker he'd known at home, and he wanted to find out more about me. We never grew close, but we often talked, and once, when we had a weekend pass at the same time, we took a thumb trip to Charleston and spent a day on the beach. Besides the Louisiana maneuvers—his chief topic of the moment—Raymond, an endless talker, told me about the women in his life. When he paused, it was usually to ask me what I thought about his successes. But sometimes he asked me various forms of a serious question—What do you think about love and women? The question puzzled me, because it seemed to contradict his view of himself as a stud and his view of me as a novice in all things. But bit by bit it became clear that he was interested in my answers because he sensed that I had different views from his and because his girlfriend, Jackie, had turned his idea of Woman upside down. The change had occurred in a dark hallway of the Brooklyn apartment building their families lived in, during his one and only furlough some months before.

When he returned home to Jackie, the Good Woman he was going to marry, he brought her flowers, took her out, and made plans to see her every day of his leave. But he also looked up old friends who were not Good Women, and he had a wonderful time with them in the sack. One day, after he and his brother Archie had visited twin sisters who liked getting it in the same bed at the same time, he went home to Jackie. Her mother was home, so they went to Raymond's apartment, which was empty, and necked for a couple of hours, doing all allowable things. When it was time for her to go home for dinner, he walked her down the two flights to her floor, gave her a hot soul kiss, and thrust his loins against hers. She moaned and reached for him, deliberately and efficiently opening his fly and clutching his hard penis.

He was horrified. "Jackie, don't," he said, "we musn't."

She rested against him as he explained how much he respected her, and how much he looked forward to the time when they would be husband and wife, after which there could be a life-time of love between them. Even before he mounted this uxorial discourse, his penis drooped. He solemnly assured me that it had become instantly flaccid in her hungry hand, a triumph of virtue over virility. At the time, he was sure he'd settled things with his logic of deferred pleasure. But ever since, he'd been haunted by doubt. His impression of Jackie's manual dexterity was indelible. It meant one of two things. Either she was a Bad Woman, a thought he could not bear, though the evidence supported the conclusion, he had to admit. Or he was so attractive that even a

Very Good Woman could not resist him—in fact, not only could not resist him, but could be so aroused that she became as efficient as a male in taking the lead in love. Neither alternative was satisfactory. For though he preferred the second, the idea of a Good Woman who took sexual initiatives, whatever the provocation, disturbed him.

If the encounter with Jackie had been less painful to him, it would have been only funny. But when he finally got the whole story out, I knew he was on red hot coals. His images of security, love, home, homecoming, fidelity, family—all the important nodes of his fantasy life, which he especially needed then—had been hit hard. Nothing I said (pompously, I'm sure) about the complexity of desire in women and men alike did a bit of good, because I threatened his idea of Good Woman, which he could not give up. It's funny that my confident insight into Raymond's sexuality gave me no clear sense of my own.

Raymond planned the trip to Charleston to get his mind off his worries about Jackie. He thought that if he could just leave Fort Jackson for a while, things would ease up for him. So we took the camp bus as far as it went, just beyond Columbia's city limits. Before trying our luck on the highway, we stopped at an inn for a beer. A pretty young woman served us, flirting playfully with Raymond as she took our order, and later as she served us. After that, she would pause to talk when she'd finished serving another table. There were several waitresses hard at work, but ours seemed really relaxed. Raymond was in heaven, half ready to give up the trip to Charleston, take a room at the inn, and try to bed the young woman. After a time, a middle-aged man came out of the kitchen and walked up to our table; he asked the waitress whether she'd take the place of a cook's helper, who'd just called in sick. Smiling, our new acquaintance placed her hand gently on the man's forearm as she agreed cheerfully to do the job. He went back to the kitchen. Then the pretty waitress said, "Daddy needs me. I gotta go. Have a good trip, y'all."

Raymond was surprised and disappointed. He was upset over her making up to him one minute and deserting him the next. But he was really shocked that she would flirt outrageously, as he saw it, right under her old man's nose, when she loved and respected him.

We hit the road, and within twenty minutes, we had a ride to Charleston—a real bit of luck, or so it seemed. The driver was a second lieutenant, with his wife beside him. Raymond and I were in the back seat. We had quite a way to travel, and whether to talk or not became an issue during the first five minutes, because the woman wanted conversation, and the man did not. I would have enjoyed talking, but as she chatted amiably, I saw in the mirror that his jaws and lips were tight, so I said little. Raymond was altogether silent. The woman continued the monologue, and pretty soon looked at her husband, maybe hoping he would give her some help, but his grim face moved her to silence instead. Things were awkward for about ten minutes as we rode along, with nobody able to speak when speech had become a necessity. Then, as if explaining everything, the lieutenant said in a strained voice, trying without success to sound pleasant, "My wife thought it wasn't fair for us to pass you by, with room in the backseat."

That was it. We finished the long trip in silence, with the uncomfortable couple occasionally mumbling to each other, in very low voices, which didn't sound too friendly. We were all tight and edgy, but there was no more conversation. I thanked them when we got to Charleston, and as Raymond and I walked towards our rooming house, he broke his long silence. "Jesus! What the hell was going on?"

While we were checking in, we decided to take the bus back to Columbia, to avoid the risk of another bad thumb trip. After washing up and leaving our few belongings in our room, we went down to the bar. All the tables were taken. But as we lingered, undecided what to do, three women called out and waved us over to sit with them. We dragged up chairs and joined them. One was Aunt Julie, a jolly woman of about fifty. The others, much younger, were her nieces, whose names I forget. All three had pleasant faces. They were in Charleston for the weekend, they said, from a small town in rural South Carolina. They told us they'd made room at their table because we needed a place to sit and because they wanted someone to talk to.

Raymond set out to charm them right away, obviously trying to decide between the two young women and hoping both would want him. But for the moment all the nieces seemed to want was conversation. Only Aunt Julie might have been thought to be flirting, and even she wanted to talk more than anything else. We ordered sandwiches and beer, and the conversation continued lively. I had no plan; I just wanted to see the scene develop. Raymond wanted the two young women. And if Aunt Julie was attracted to Raymond or me, I think neither she nor her nieces— if that's what they were—had any definite end in view. They probably wanted to relax and have a good time. Certainly they were enjoying the conversation.

Still, there was something odd about them. They were friendly, but they behaved as if they knew something we didn't, and our ignorance seemed to amuse them. I thought they might have taken the weekend off from a whorehouse. But the idea was stupid. After more than two hours of conversation that went nowhere, Raymond began to make it clear he was ready to leave. As we said good night, the women urged us to go to the beach with them the next day, after breakfast. Raymond was delighted with the arrangement, sure that it was the promise of a happy ending to our trip. As we waved cheerfully and left, the women laughed among themselves.

After showering the next morning, I slipped into my swimming trunks before putting on my uniform. Raymond watched, and as if stating an important conclusion, he said, "I'm not wearing my trunks, I'll just carry them."

I nodded and said nothing.

Then Raymond asked, his voice on edge, "What the hell were those dames laughing at?"

"How the hell do I know? Maybe they thought we were funny."

Later, at the beach, while Aunt Julie, in slacks and halter, reclined against the back of a rented half-chair, and Raymond stretched prone on the sand in his uniform, the nieces and I stripped down to our bathing suits and went for a swim. The sight of their trim bodies must have had the obvious effect on him. As soon as we got back from the water, Raymond said, "I think I'll get into my suit. Hey, come to the bathhouse with me, Harry." He handed his wallet and watch to Aunt Julie, and I pointed to mine, between the shirt and pants of my folded uniform, right next to her chair.

At the bathhouse, Raymond could hardly wait to get back to frolic in the water and play feelies with Aunt Julie's darling nieces. I thought he might be getting a little ahead of the game, but I wanted to get back to them, too. We didn't quite sprint, but we moved pretty damn quick. On our return, we found only the rented chair and my uniform on the sand, where minutes before the three women had been sitting, big as life. I searched futilely for my wallet and watch. They were gone, and so were Raymond's. We waited for thirty minutes, and then for thirty more, but the women did not return. Then, leaving me behind, Raymond went to the bathhouse to reclaim his uniform, hoping by the time he got back, they'd reappear. They didn't. We went back to the rooming house, but they weren't there either. No one could tell us anything about them, except that like us, they'd paid for their room in advance.

Shaken, and without a plan, we went back to the beach. For an hour or more, Raymond and I exchanged evidence we agreed should have warned us that the three were cold-blooded thieves. We had finished cursing ourselves as idiots and them as crooks for the tenth time, when they suddenly reappeared, apologizing merrily for their delay. They said they'd meant to be gone only a few minutes, but when they met old friends on the beach, they lost all sense of time. To this brief explanation, Aunt Julie added her summary view of us.

"You're a couple of damn fools to trust your watches and wallets to three strangers."

When Raymond and I boarded the bus back to Columbia, all the window seats were taken. He passed up the chance to sit next to a pretty young woman, and instead, chose a seat beside an old man. I sat across the aisle, but Raymond didn't want to talk. He and I never discussed Jackie again, nor did we ever talk about our visit to Charleston. Instead of diminishing the distance between us, the trip increased it, and our brief friendship ended with Aunt Julie's appraisal of us. I thought he would want to know that I was as baffled as he was by the merry trio, but when I tried to tell him so, he turned away skeptically, as if I shared a secret with them.

Not long after Raymond and I returned from Charleston, the Allies invaded Normandy. The whole outfit was glued to the radio, hoping for the best. All of us felt a reverent sorrow for the poor bastards in the first waves, knowing pretty well what they were going through. Our own vulnerability made us sympathetic to theirs. But after it was clear that our forces had established sound beachheads, we were relieved, knowing we wouldn't be called on to do that terrible job. It was behind us. We also began to hope the war would be over before we were shipped to the front, but we knew it was wishful thinking. The Army would want our bodies for action as never before.

Then in a day or two, we heard that a few men from the division would be sent to West Point and that we'd all be invited to apply for a place in Officer Candidate School. We laughed at both rumors, thinking some sadistic son of a bitch was enjoying a grim joke. Nothing ever came of the story about West Point, but the one about OCS proved true. Like all the other ASTP men, I applied, even though I knew I stood almost no chance. After filling out the form, I went to company Headquarters to drop it off. Corporal Wanlus, a crusty old bastard, who with the first sergeant was the only regular Army man in the outfit, reached out his hand to receive it.

I said, "Thank you, Corporal," and started to leave.

"Stick around," he growled. He looked over the application for a full three minutes, shaking his head more and more vigorously as he read.

Then he looked up at me and asked, "What the hell makes you think you could be an officer?"

I ducked the nasty question, saying, "I'd like the chance to prove myself in OCS."

With a biting grin on his face, he said, "You green little shit, you're wet behind the ears. Your application and all the applications from your smart-assed buddies will never get by me. You think just because you got high IQs you're officer material. I served in this man's Army for sixteen years, and I'm satisfied to be a corporal. How do you get it into your fuckin' head after a couple of months to be an officer? You shits. I'll fix you and your college buddies."

That was that. I never heard another word, and neither did anybody else in the outfit. The rumor circulated that none of the noncoms had a high enough IQ to become officer candidates, so they decided to stand in the way of those of us who did. But somebody higher up must have made the decision. Anyhow, the whole business came to nothing in our company. And we heard it came to nothing in the whole division.

I soon had other things to think about. Just days after I wrote home to say I had applied for OCS, I found my name on a list of men placed on alert. About thirty in the company—roughly one in six—were to be ready to leave for parts unknown on very short notice. Oliver was among them. It was Army policy—we heard for the first time—to single out men who turned nineteen to be solo replacements; younger men were sent into combat only if they were part of a regular outfit, surrounded by men they knew. At nineteen we were eligible to serve at the front among strangers.

A few days after we were placed on alert, Oliver was told to report to the supply room to turn in his old clothing and to receive a special issue. He was given light underwear and outer clothing—nothing at all that he would have needed for cold weather. So we assumed he was being sent to the Pacific. But in fact he waited for two weeks without hearing another word, and when the thirty of us who'd been placed on alert received a new clothing order, his name was listed with ours. Nobody explained anything to him. Like a good soldier, he simply turned in his light duds, and with the rest of us, received a new issue of all-weather clothing. Though the company supply room seemed to be giving us a strong sign that we were headed for Europe, we thought of Oliver's very recent experience and remembered that the Army would decide what to do with us as often as it chose, without explaining a thing.

During this time of waiting, I was easily reabsorbed into the Army routine during duty hours, and into the social life I'd made for myself in Columbia when I was free. Both were ways of escaping the anxiety I felt. I'd stopped thinking about a promotion or a change in assignment. I just did the work of the day as it came along. When I told Abby I was about to leave, it was as if I were repeating a message I'd given her before. Our sense for the inevitable was being fulfilled, and as far as I was concerned, we both accepted the outcome. But it was only in some dull sense that I understood my stay at Jackson to be ending. I felt no vitality of regret. My life was fixed in a dream. My letters home seemed to carry on as usual, though I think my anxiety broke through from time to time, especially when I talked about another furlough.

My mother came to Columbia a couple of weeks after I was put on alert. The company commander had agreed to keep me off duty so I could use my pass once she was in town. We spent most of her visit—from lunch, Saturday, through early afternoon, Sunday—in our own rooms or in one of the hotel dining rooms, because Columbia was far too crowded, especially on the weekend, to make walking attractive. After Sunday lunch, we went back to our suite, which included a pleasant living room. My mother took the easy chair, and I sat on the sofa bed. She quickly led the conversation to a game she said I might like to play—Ouija. I'd never heard of it, so she explained. Then she suggested we make a set of small cards—the letters of the alphabet and numbers from zero to nine. I had a piece of cardboard from a freshly laundered shirt, and with my mother's nail scissors, I quickly made the items we needed, and then distributed them in a circle on the smooth surface of an end table. My mother toweled a water glass until it was very dry and shiny, placed it rim down in the circle of letters and numbers, and we were ready to go.

We placed the first two fingers of both our hands lightly on the upturned bottom of the glass, and my mother began to ask Ouija questions.

"What day is it?"

The glass began to move, indecisively at first, and then with more assurance, spelling out S-U-N-D-A-Y, letter by letter.

I knew I wasn't pushing the glass, but I thought she was, so I laughed and said, "Okay, it's your show. What are you up to?"

She understood right away and answered, "I'm not pushing the glass any more than you are. Watch my hands. It's moving by itself."

I asked ironically, "Will it move by itself if we don't touch it?"

"No," she said. "We have to keep our fingertips on it, but only lightly."

I decided to go along with the game, a little surprised that my mother seemed to be serious about such hocus-pocus, and a little surprised that the glass had moved so smoothly under her light direction. I wanted to see how she had done the trick.

"What was Grandma Pagliaro's first name?" she asked.

"F-A-U-S-T-I-N-A," said Ouija.

I watched carefully. It didn't seem she could possibly be controlling the glass's movements. Obviously one or both of us were determining the action, but maybe in a less direct or conscious way than I had supposed. I settled into Ouija's world, grinning. But my mother's demeanor was uncharacteristically serious. Once she was sure I was enjoying myself, she suggested I ask a few questions, and I did. They were trivial, like, "What time is it?"

Then she asked some trivial questions herself, mostly about family. Ouija was eager and swift in providing answers.

After a pause, I heard the heavy question: "What will Harry's profession be when the war is over?"

Ouija moved somewhat more slowly, and yet decisively, as if recognizing that the information was important. "E-N-G."

Ouija went no further. My mother asked again, but by this time she was no longer tense. "E-N-G," Ouija said.

My mother tried again, palpably relaxed, laughing at Ouija's stubbornness. But the glass would move no further.

I tried with the same result, "E-N-G," except that the glass now began to grate on the table, making a terrible scraping sound.

My mother certainly thought the game was over. She began to chat in a brittle, easy way that was as uncharacteristic as her intensity had been a few minutes before.

She eased back from the table and said, "Isn't it nice that you're going to be an engineer after the war? You can go to Columbia and take up where you left off. Dad and I will be so happy when you get back."

I agreed without much spirit, wondering why Ouija refused to say "E-N-G-I-N-E-E-R," but when I asked her, she brushed off the question as unimportant. I could not understand her change of mood, from anxiety to relief, nor her willingness to turn away from Ouija's stubborn brevity.

That night in the barracks, before I fell asleep, it came to me that my mother hadn't really asked Ouija what my profession would be; she had asked, rather, whether I'd live to have a profession. Ouija had answered affirmatively, and she was satisfied. She wasn't superstitious exactly, but she must have been desperate for some assurance I'd survive the war, and as I knew, she half believed the future is lodged in our unconscious. As for Ouija's stubborn brevity, I was less certain. But E-N-G is as good a beginning for "ENGlish professor" as it is for "ENGineer."

About a week after my mother's visit, I left Fort Jackson with the other replacements, headed for Fort Meade, the replacement depot, just outside of Baltimore. When we got there, the Army processed us for the trip overseas. I don't know how they kept track of us all. We were not an outfit with noncoms and officers to keep tabs on us from day to day, just individual soldiers since the Army's decision to use us as replacements. But their administrative control was complete. At the same time, they tried to give us the sense that we were all united in a great undertaking by ordering us to attend daily news briefings on the war. We laughed grimly at the anomaly, all our former experience having demonstrated it was Army policy to keep us ignorant of our predicament. Our skepticism was confirmed by almost everything else the Army did. They kept us in the dark about when we'd be shipped out, and where we'd go, and most important, about what awaited us as solo replacements. We knew they needed some system for filling the gaps left by dead and wounded, even though it undercut the very basis of Army morale—esprit de corps. We could accept secrecy about when and where we'd go—it was a reasonable policy, though it was often foolishly implemented. But we couldn't understand why nobody said a word about what happens to replacements. Was it really their policy to send very young men to fight alone among strangers? Couldn't they at least send two or three friends up together?

After three weeks at Fort Meade, I was sent to a Port of Embarkation, near Hoboken, with thousands of other men, the last stage before the ocean voyage. My last letters home from the States were brief and trivial, except for a few sentences that say what's really on my mind: "Just a short note to let you know that I'll be moving tonight for parts as yet unknown. But it looks like it's going to be the short ride, not the long one." And buried in another paragraph is this one: "So far, Oliver is still with me, but time may change this."

I tried to sound cheerful despite the loneliness and the leaden worry that I'd never return.

Chapter Four

Journeys to England and France

THE *MAURETANIA* WAS A big ship, capable of enough speed to avoid submarine torpedoes, provided it followed an unpredictable zigzag course across the Atlantic. Because it could see to its own safety—at least within limits—it traveled alone, not in a convoy, which would only have slowed it down and increased its vulnerability. Spotters and gun crews were nevertheless prepared for attack, from the surface or beneath it, or from the air. The September seas were heavy most of the time. When you stood to the rear of midship on the main deck and looked forward, you could see the bow dip low and disappear from view for long seconds, while mountains of ocean loomed. Then the bow would reappear, blocking the forward view of the sea. The great ship and the immense ocean displaced each other in these deep, protracted rhythms for almost the whole voyage—giant, remorseless motions that deepened my isolation. Oliver was the only one I knew among the thousands on board.

But the needs of the moment kept me from brooding. We were far too many for comfortable quarters to be available. We were young, and we had been hardened to discomfort in the field, so we didn't mind the sleeping conditions, not at first, anyhow. Enlisted men like me were assigned to any space on the ship that was more or less protected from the weather and out of the way of the ship's business. With Oliver and about forty others, I was given a space in a mess room, under one of the fixed tables. I didn't mind the hard deck, but the lights in the nearby gangway and the intermittent traffic of our own restless men and the ship's night crews made for broken sleep.

During the whole trip, we were spoken to only twice by an American officer, a complete stranger to us—once as we began the voyage and once as we were about to disembark. For the rest of the time we were left to ourselves, without any sense of connection to the people around us. We were several days at sea before we found out that officers had been assigned to private or semiprivate cabins. Though we knew our officers in the States had better living quarters than we did, and a separate mess, the fact was never driven home as it was on the *Mauretania*, where the differences were right under our noses, and, as it turned out, far greater than they were in any American installation I knew about. Besides, in the States our officers most often ate with us, and they worked with us, day in and day out. On the *Mauretania*, we saw them opening and closing their cabin doors, behind which there was sanctuary from the mass of humanity on board. Even so, I think we would have accepted the differences as inevitable if one of them had been there to assure us we'd not been forgotten—thousands of replacements, left to a blind English authority. It was one of the British officers who spoke to us two or three times during the journey, asking us how we liked the food, which the United States paid England to provide.

He was a colonel, who strode into the mess on the third morning, right after we'd finished the first of our two daily meals. He was tall and lean, with a red mustache and red hair emphasizing the redness of his freckled skin. Like Major Harris, he carried a quirt under his left arm. A British sergeant-major who was with him shouted, "Ten-HUT."

We came to attention, wondering what the hell was going on. The tall colonel walked up to an American private, smiling and bending towards him, completely sure that his friendliness was appreciated.

"How do you like the coffee?" he asked, still smiling and bending.

"Sir, it's lousy."

The colonel got a truthful answer, but he'd asked the wrong question, at least from our point of view. We all wanted him to know the food was bad and the portions—without seconds—far too small. Our two meals a day were never varied—one slice of Bologna, two slices of bread, a boiled egg, half a dried apricot, and one cup of very watery coffee. But we didn't have the guts to complain, and he confined himself to the question about coffee.

"Well, we British used to be great coffee drinkers, but we long ago switched to tea. Awfully sorry we don't come up to your standard."

His upper-class accent and his sarcasm, intensified by facial expressions of jovial mock-patience, were maddening. The red-cheeked colonel obviously enjoyed playing the scene.

The dense numbers on board, topside and below, might well have bred more trouble than they did. To my knowledge, at least three fights broke out during the trip, but we were able to stop them ourselves. Once, Oliver, impatient with the uniformed mass pressing him on deck, plunged and elbowed his way through fifteen feet of the crowd around him, as if he could free himself. But I was the only one who paid attention to him. All in all, we behaved well despite the dense crowding and despite the sleeping quarters and bad food.

Oliver and I, along with two men who slept near us—ASTP-ers from the 87th, before then unknown to us—took daily turns standing in line to buy whatever candy, chips, or nuts the American PX would let us have that day, and then we shared our take. From our sleeping quarters, we could look into the galley and mess just across the gangway and see and smell the food being served to the English gun crews—bacon and eggs, bread and butter, rich meat stews, fried fish and chicken, fresh vegetables and fruit. But we agreed that these hardworking men, whose daily job was tough and dangerous, deserved good food. We shipboard transients, who were far too many to be fed well, could wait until we reached our next camp to be taken care of.

My feelings were probably like the feelings of the other replacements. I'd been cut off from the people I knew, except Oliver, and I was afraid of going to the front alone. And for the crossing, we had bad quarters and terrible food, and our officers had turned us over to the British. I tried to reconcile myself to the idea that nothing more could be expected under the circumstances, but I felt a muted resentment as well as fear.

Around the seventh night of the journey, I took a walk, my only night walk, just to take a walk. I strode down the gangway, right off our make-do sleeping quarters, to the place where American officers gathered for their meals. Directly opposite the entrance to their mess, I saw three pairs of huge mahogany doors—refrigerator doors, I thought—massively hinged and clasped with brass fixtures. I looked behind me and ahead, and seeing no one, I opened the nearest pair. Inside were heaps of cold cooked meat and other food—shell steaks, small broiled hens, fried chicken, rolls and butter, cakes and pies. Seeing the lavish remains of the officers' meals sent a hot pulse of anger through me.

"The dirty bastards," I hissed.

My willingness to accept crowding, poor sleep, scant food, and my own reduction to a numbered unit in an anonymous mass was destroyed when I saw the food. I was incredulous for less than a second before I felt the anger mount. We weren't starving or anything like it. But why the disparity between us and the officers? I closed the refrigerator, and then I pulled out the tucked-in length of my fatigue shirt to make a receptacle of it. Again I looked in both directions, and with the coast clear, I swiftly stashed steaks, hens, and rolls and butter—enough for half a dozen meals. Then I walked back to my quarters, woke up Oliver and the two men who'd taken turns with us in the long PX lines, and together we went up to the main deck to eat. We ate ferociously, great crunches of cold beef and chicken, congealed fat and all, and rolls and butter. What a feast after days of fasting.

Stealing the food left me feeling less helpless and alone than I had for months. It was an act of self-sufficiency. Poor Siebold. Eating that early batch of pancakes had always seemed an innocent act to me and my friends. But here on the *Mauretania* the infraction that got him reclassified was built right into the system. I didn't feel guilty, either for the theft itself or for the thousands of enlisted men who did not share the meal, though I would have if I'd eaten it all by myself.

The days passed, uneventful. I never returned to the giant refrigerators near the officers' mess. The first theft was the last. For the rest of the journey, I put up with our two bad meals a day, supplemented by nuts and candy from the PX, and so did Oliver and the others. Near the end of our trip, we sailed past the coast of Ireland. The green low mound of land rose bright and clear against a background of ocean and pale sky. We spotted a small silvery plane flying in to look us over. It barely contrasted with the clouds above. Our voyage was almost ended. Late that night, the *Mauretania* landed at a dock in Liverpool. The American officer who had assigned us sleeping quarters when the voyage began at last reappeared to instruct us about disembarking. We were among the first troops to get off. I had expected a blackout, but the area of the port near the ship was dimly lit, though the lights were canopied. We were greeted by cheerful looking women, both English and American, who offered us donuts and hot, strong coffee. We enjoyed the treat, even though we had to keep moving toward a railroad platform, where we boarded for the Midlands.

Our train was slow-moving, never speeding, and sometimes stopping on a sidetrack to let faster trains pass through. At about three o'clock in the morning we stopped. We were told to get our gear together and to assemble in ranks on the flat ground outside. We did so in a groggy state, and then we moved, at rout march, into the dark English countryside. Oliver was near me, but I had no sense of his presence during the march, which lasted until well after dawn. I enjoyed the stable land, a relief after the endlessly plunging and rising ship. During the first break in the march, I pulled out a cigarette and lit up, something I hadn't done since the beginning of the voyage. I had been a light smoker from the time I began college, only occasionally having more than three or four cigarettes a day, when I was tense about something. I would have enjoyed the relaxation of tobacco on the ocean, but my very first drag left me feeling queasy. I tried once again a day later, with the same reaction. I guess it was a form of seasickness. If I smoked, I was queasy, but if I didn't, I felt more or less okay. Here on steady ground, somewhere southeast of Liverpool, I dragged deep and got myself a little light in the head before we got up to march.

The dawn was slow in coming. There seemed to be glints in the east long before we saw the certain glow of the new day. A trick of the light—maybe it was my frame of mind—made objects I could barely make out seem many times their actual size from a distance of a hundred or two hundred feet. A stone that seemed as big as house as I approached it, turned out to be only a few feet high. And something the size of a mastodon became a small sheepdog, silently watching us pass, his head hung low. He seemed to see in us a familiar sight that made him gloomy. We marched on, into the brightening east. The sight of England's beautiful countryside stirred me as no landscape had before. I felt I was returning to these rich green fields and meadows, not seeing them for the first time. Their beauty was a combination of the natural world and the patient care of countless generations.

A few hours after dawn, several thousand of my former shipmates and I, including Oliver, reached an American camp, which was to be our home for a few weeks. It was good to sleep in a steady bunk again and to eat good Army food, which included fresh meat and a few vegetables. The eggs were powdered and the fruit preserved, but given the circumstances, we did very well. We were also issued new rifles, having traveled overseas without personal weapons. It would be no trick getting used to the new piece, a standard M-1, but I was glad when we got the chance to fire and get the feel of it.

Our officers were not as remote as they had been on the ship, but we had no sustained contact with them. In fact, I never had the feeling that I belonged to an outfit again, even after I was assigned to one at the front. My sense of isolation began to grow after I left Fort Benning. From then on I felt more and more that the Army used me as if I were a tool. They caught me and others like me in endless systems of processing, and moved us from where we'd been to where they wanted us, delivering us in good physical health. But the state of our psyches was something else. Each of us was being sent up alone, to fill a hole in the front lines.

There was little chance to see England and its people. Movies were shown on the post, and twice dances were sponsored by local clubs, but I couldn't get near them, they were so crowded. Those who did said the men outnumbered the women, and they could dance for only half a minute before being tapped. Except among ourselves, social life was limited. But once, I got a pass to leave the post, and I visited a village several miles away. A friendly Englishman directed me to a church dance, where I was surprised to find more women than men. I danced with several. They were friendly and open, quite unlike the reserved English people I expected them to be, but they made it clear, without saying so, that they wanted just one dance with me. I could tell their interest was an American soldier, about four or five years older than I, but no taller. His bright face beamed with pleasure as a dozen women kept cutting in on each other for the chance to dance with him. They were gentle and quiet as they rapidly tapped each other for a turn—in every instance, a brief one. But they were also energetic, persistent, and unembarrassed as they buzzed around their sugar cane, cutting in again and again. I suppose they were inviting him to single one of them out for the evening, but he didn't. I enjoyed the short man's success for obvious personal reasons, but for other reasons too. He looked happy and healthy—full of life. And so did the women.

As I walked back to camp, I thought about a high school dance in Portsmouth, which Helen couldn't make. I missed her, but it turned out I had a good time. Women then almost always waited to be asked to dance. Some of them, though, like the English women I'd just seen, were beginning to take the initiative. Chicken Gillespie, a friendly sexpot in our class, was one of these. I never heard her real first name. She had a reputation for direct-ness. I knew who she was, but I had only spoken to her across the counter at the ice cream parlor where she worked. The night of the school dance, she tapped my shoulder at the end of a song, as I was finishing a Lindy with Mary Louise Coggins.

"How about the next dance?" Chicken asked.

I turned to Mary Louise, who of course said, "Sure."

Chicken was unsmiling. She exuded body heat. As we moved together to the rhythm of a really serious fox-trot, I wondered what she might be expecting. I was glad she had asked me to dance, but I wasn't sure whether to relax and enjoy myself or to start talking. Since I was moving pretty well, but otherwise uncertain, I kept my mouth shut. I just danced.

After a bit, Chicken stepped back from me a little, smiled confidently, and said, "You're short, but it's okay."

I know I smiled to myself as I walked through the dark English countryside. "You're short." The Navy disqualified me because I was one-quarter of an inch short for the V-12. In the subway on the way back home, I wanted to yell to the whole Universe, "My height has nothing to do with my ability."

That night in bed, my mind's voice spoke. "I would have won the respect of the V-12 if they'd let me in. There was Aubrey Yost, the high school's only all-state player, a fullback weighing 175 pounds, challenging me, and I pinned him twice. I was the president of my senior class."

My self-indulgent fantasy began to slow down. "Well, maybe the Navy wasn't altogether irrational. Imagine admirals only three feet tall. Why not?" But then I thought of sexy Chicken, who had given me both the diagnosis and the cure. "You're short, but it's okay."

During our last days in England, we were given very few real duties. We just killed time as we waited our turn to be sent by rail to Southampton and then shipped to Normandy. Apart from testing our rifles, we were made to hike short distances, we were given lectures we'd heard before, and we stood in line for hours to receive an extra issue of socks or underwear—anything to chew up time. All of us knew we'd see action soon, and see it among strangers. Just under the surface of our minds lay the sickening dread that on the battlefield a bullet or a shell fragment might tear away a part of us or darken our eyes forever. I tried once to get Oliver to talk about it.

"I wonder how hot the action will be? Do you think we can take it?" I asked.

"I'll do what I have to, and that's it" was all he said.

"I don't know whether I can move ahead under fire. I don't think I'll panic, but I might freeze," I told him. I wanted him to say he was afraid and say we could both handle it. But he wouldn't help me.

"Why get excited?" he said as he grinned. "If you get it, you get it. That's it."

In those days of waiting for shipment to France, I wrote a series of brief letters to my family in Mobile and to Robert at VMI, using V-Mail—a single sheet, not very large, on one side of which you wrote your message before folding it so that it became its own envelope. These folded, unsealed letters were then sent to a censor, typically the platoon leader, a lieutenant, who read and approved, or read and deleted matter that was classified, after which the letters were photographically reduced, sealed, and mailed. V-Mail was supposed to reach home more quickly than Free Mail, which were letters written on whatever paper we could get and placed unsealed in a regular envelope before being passed on to the censor. Like V-Mail, Free Mail required no postage. It didn't take us long to find out that sometimes V-Mail and sometimes Free Mail was faster. There was a further uncertainty. If you used two sheets of V-Mail for a single letter, they would be sent separately, and sometimes page 2 would reach the addressee days before page 1.

During the last slow-moving days in England, Oliver and I and all the others waited for the move to France, feeling more and more remote from security. My letters home were written in a tone of lighthearted humor, which didn't really come off. They also answered questions about whether I needed money; what I'd done with an extra sweater my mother had knitted for me; whether the food was still good. My usually explicit answers gave me satisfaction. I guess tangibility of any sort is useful when your fantasy life is full of departure and perishing.

As if in sympathy with my condition, the giant weeping willow that my father had planted between the arbor and Grandma's vegetable garden came down in a violent autumn storm. He had used an ingenious method to erect it after a similar fall six years before, in 1938, when its upturned roots had lifted the arbor floor, a huge slab of reinforced concrete. He turned on the garden hose and directed its flow under the low end of the slab, undermining its earthen resting place, so that its high end was supported only by the tree roots, against which it pressed harder and harder as water washed away earth at the other end. At the same time, he began to pull the tree upright with a block and tackle, adjusting to keep the pressure on. Gradually, over several days, with my father redirecting the water flow every morning and several times during the day, the weighty slab returned to its level position, and the tree straightened up. Now it had fallen again, with no one there to work miracles. When my mother wrote to say what had happened, she told me they were having it removed. "Dad can't save it," I thought.

We crossed the Channel on a dark autumn day, having traveled by rail to Southampton, which seemed filled with shabby old buildings fronting narrow streets. Out on the dock, waiting for orders to embark, we breathed in the chill mist, looking silently at the three-hundred-foot ship on which several thousand of us replacements—all strangers to each other—would cross. It was an old tub. Its dirty gray paint and cramped spaces added to the bleakness of the mission. As we boarded, I looked out from the gray deck onto a gray, harbor-calm sea and a gray sky, drab extensions of my own spirit and those of the others around me. I have never seen so many sad men in one place. Unlike the new draftees on the train to Upton, the men on the ship did not tell jokes or shoot craps or play cards. Energy was damped by brooding.

We finished boarding just before dusk, still and quiet in the places we'd been assigned for the overnight crossing. Oliver and I were separated, but reunited for a few days after we reached the high ground above Normandy beach. I was self-absorbed enough not to miss him, but I was watchful nevertheless. All the faces around me were vacant and pale, expressions of lost life. The blank gloom of an older man—about thirty—was stark. He must have had a wife and children. His face looked like a death mask. We were all sad. Our inert melancholy was so heavy that even after we put out to sea, the violent waves of the October channel didn't stir it.

After lying torpid and yet awake for most of the crossing, I dozed off toward morning. But my sleep was shallow. I woke up as soon as the ship's engines slowed to drop anchor. Later, when we got to the open deck, we could see that the shore was about eight hundred yards away, Normandy beach, where so many had died, young men in the earth, rotting before their time. But we had business to attend to. Our ship drew too much water for us to get closer to the shore than we were. So we moved to a much smaller landing craft, with a flat bottom that could run right up the beach.

The transfer was not easy, with the sea running so high. It took expert handling and luck to get the landing craft alongside the larger ship without a collision. Even more difficult was the actual transfer of men from ship to landing craft. Of very different lengths, the hulls pitched at different rates in the high waves. We wondered how we'd get from one to the other.

Just then a sergeant climbed part way up the rail, and waving so we could all see him, shouted, "Here, men, watch me, watch me!"

We watched all right. We saw him climb over the railing of the ship, wait patiently until the landing craft was rising so that the two decks were close to level, and then jump. He made it look easy. Then he reversed the operation, jumping back to the ship from the landing craft.

The uneven motion of the hulls made the business risky. A false move would land you between two walls of shifting steel, real grinders. Violent noise added to the uncertainty—the sound of smashing water and the creaks and growls of ship's gear. But we began the dangerous transfer, and it was repeated a thousand times. I saw some close calls as I waited my turn, but everyone seemed to be making it. Willing hands on the landing craft grabbed those whose jump was unlucky. But then a man panicked, lurched, and fell between the bucking hulls. I saw him fall, but I didn't hear him make a sound. He must have been ground up. I put it out of my mind. It was my turn to jump.

Oliver and I were able to share a pup tent in the deep mud of Normandy. During the few days of our stay, the weather was raw, and it rained a lot. We didn't mind being half wet all the time, because we were in great condition, and our minds were on more basic things. We had nothing to do except to fall in twice a day so that the officer in charge of our bodies could be sure we were still around, ready to be assigned to an outfit. We whiled away the time talking and eating—Spam, D-Bars (a kind of dense, enriched chocolate that was hard to chew), and crackers. We had as much of this food as we wanted, but there was nothing else available. Though there was plenty of water to drink, there was none for bathing.

Occasionally we'd wander over to one of the fires that were allowed during the day. They burned in discarded 55-gallon oil drums with walls perforated to increase the fire's oxygen supply. There we'd warm up and look over our fellow soldiers. This was the Army at its least organized. Not that the officers lost track of us so that our transit to the front was delayed or confused. That didn't happen. But little pretense was made that we had to work during the day, a unique omission in my experience. There were one or two attempts at getting us to police the area—that is, to pick up the debris from the mud in which our tents were located—but the noncoms in charge of the operation seemed to forget to supervise us, so the job never got done.

Everyone knew we were marking time, each of us alone among many, waiting for the final assignment to a unit that would need us. I was lucky to have a friend there, though I knew

I'd lose him soon. During these last days together, Oliver and I played a new game. We pretended that war had improved our perceptions so that we could recognize the animals under every human facade. We decided I was a bear, benevolent unless pushed to the wall, and he was a horse, sometimes skittish, but generally strong and dignified. But we were less kind to others. We spent three or four days in the muddy fields, just above the beach, slogging to and from our tent for Spam, crackers, and water, observing the men around us, seeing through their disguise as humans to their true animal selves. We found almost no lions, tigers, bulls, or elephants, and only a few reptiles and rodents. For the most part we saw different kinds of birds, who were in a cautionary way alert and observant, but without real vision. They scratched and pecked, but their heads and claws darted meaninglessly, in abruptly ended motions. Their weather-raw necks were covered with chicken skin, anomalous above the olive-drab cloth and below the distinctly human ears. I laughed at each new discovery—keen adolescence, mocking life through fear. We verified our observations by comparing notes. Oliver never grinned so much.

At dusk each night, Bedcheck Charlie—a small, slow, low-flying German reconnaissance plane—visited us. Not knowing his mission the first time, I thought we were about to be bombed. Our heavy antiaircraft fire added to my anxiety, but Charlie soon headed east and things quieted down. Oliver was less disturbed than I by Bedcheck Charlie's unexpected visit. I thought it was the beginning of an air raid, and I was afraid. But I was relieved that I didn't panic.

On the fourth day after we reached Normandy, Oliver and I and dozens of other replacements were trucked out of the mud across miles of French farms and villages. All the towns in our path included buildings that had been hit by artillery. Several were reduced to rubble, probably by American bombers, which were preparing the way for our ground troops. After the break-through at Saint-Lô, toward the end of July 1944, the Allies moved quickly eastward. Paris was reoccupied by the end of August. In the south of France, the XV Corps, led by General Patch, began a new offensive in early August. Speeding north, up the Rhône Valley, they reached Dijon before the middle of the month. We replacements were trucked through territory recently taken by our troops. Though we didn't know where we'd end up, we were sure it would be far into France or in Luxembourg.

Despite the recent fighting, the farms were still being worked—just then being harvested, in fact. If the farmers had shut down because of the fighting, they'd have starved, and so would others who depended on them. I looked at the land for mile after mile. There seemed to be too much work and too few hands. Most of those in the fields were women and old men. There wasn't much livestock. The well-worked countryside, which despite danger had been brought to the fullness of autumn, seemed almost empty. It gave me a new feeling about the war. The quiet of the landscape seemed a strange aftermath of violence. It was like a cemetery. How far did the quiet after battle extend? To Poland, Russia, India, China? Across many, many thousands of miles of earth? The world's farmers labored against bad odds to support the demanding rhythms of plowing and planting, growth and harvest, even though their livestock and produce were bought or confiscated without their consent, and their sons conscripted for labor or military service.

The trucks that carried us across the French countryside dropped us at an old French military barracks near Toul, said to have housed French cavalry before the Franco-Prussian War. Though run down, the buildings were more than just utilitarian. They included elegant touches like molded plaster ceilings and paneled walls. The U.S. Army had installed hot-water showers in one of the large ground floor rooms, so we were able to get ourselves clean one last time before going to the front. There were no beds, but we could have clean straw, if we wanted it, to soften the wooden floors. Most of us chose to sleep on our overcoats, with our blankets pulled around us.

Our short stay in the old barracks returned me and the others to the sense of military purpose. If the Army had briefly loosened its grip on us in Normandy, they grabbed us firmly again in that old installation near Toul. We fell in after reveille and did a full day's work, including hiking and close-order drill. After dinner, which was good, our time was our own, except for special duty. Military discipline needed only three days to make us feel that we'd been living on the old post near Toul forever.

Among the men Oliver and I met there was Buck Sergeant Cruz, a thirty-five-year-old Mestizo from New Mexico. Before coming to France, he had served in the Aleutian Campaign, where he'd led an infantry squad in action. It was obvious that he was depressed about returning to combat. His face wore the gray look of dread I'd seen on the men around me when we crossed the Channel. We'd lost the look after the crossing, and I'm pretty sure it didn't come back to my face until I was about to go up to the front. But it stayed with Cruz for as long as I saw him. A corporal who'd served with him in the Aleutians told us a man in their squad had been killed in the fighting there, and that Cruz had taken it very hard. Shortly after we'd heard this, he confirmed the fact to a group of us who asked him about it.

"Yes, I lost a man in my squad," he said, as if he were personally responsible.

I hesitated to talk to him about the fighting. I didn't know how he'd take it. But I had to try anyhow. Oliver came with me. At first Cruz turned away from my question with sharp annoyance.

"I told you I lost a man!" he shouted angrily, his dark face contorted.

It would have been mean to say anything else, so I kept my mouth shut. But after a few minutes, Cruz relented. He looked at Oliver and me and told his story of combat reverently.

"We went on patrol every day, a squad. We left the company high ground in the morning, right after we ate, and walked down the slope. All snow, everywhere. We went across the valley, up the hill, one at a time, behind cover when we could. Near the top we crawled. Jap patrols worked the other side, behind cover. Our job was to see there was nothing else going on. If we saw a Jap, we fired. They did that, too. We worked the snow, quiet like that, lotsa times. Nothing happened. One day a kid from Beaumont got it right under the ear. Ortiz. We dragged him back. He was dead, like that. A little hole under his ear."

What held me was the depth of his feeling for the experience. He spoke as if the battle he'd fought were still going on, and would go on forever. The bare facts were simple. A few slow-moving soldiers, Japanese and American, stalking and crawling over snowy terrain as they maneuvered for single rifle shots at an occasionally visible human target. But his telling the story made it alive and terrible.

"I lost a man in my squad," Cruz concluded, as if he had not told us so twice before.

I was surprised that Oliver was as moved as I was. He talked later about Cruz as if he thought the sergeant knew something important, which we had yet to learn.

I know I pulled out before Oliver, but I can't remember saying good-bye. Others had left the barracks near Toul in groups of six or more, in trucks. As it turned out, I left alone, picked up by a jeep that had been sent by my new outfit to get me. Corporal Clewes was in charge. He picked up my papers and me at the replacement camp's Headquarters. Then we walked over to a waiting jeep, with a private first class behind the wheel. We drove off in a hurry.

The corporal was soft-spoken and friendly as he told me my military record was good. Then he asked me, "Where you from?"

"New York," I said, not sure I should mention Virginia.

"I'm from Kentucky," he told me. I liked him right away. He turned out to be a rarity among the men in my new outfit, friendly and open.

As we rode along, I asked him, "Where are we headed?"

"Raville. Troop A, 121st Cavalry Reconnaissance Squadron, 106th Cavalry Group," he said. "You been transferred from infantry to cavalry."

I guess I showed my surprise.

"The 121st asked Replacement for a private first class who could read a map, use a compass, a rifle, light machine gun, and mortar. Your name came up."

It was ironic that my Expert Infantryman's Badge had qualified me for a place in the cavalry. But it wasn't crazy. The cavalry's chief job is to track and probe the enemy, often in patrols of four or five expendable men, but sometimes in larger numbers. Whether they begin the patrol walking, or riding in jeeps or armored cars, they usually end up on foot. They may try to draw fire to gauge the enemy's power, take a prisoner for interrogation, or just nose around to see what they can see. Unlike the First World War, World War II had no continuous manned front lines, not for long at least. Typically, our "lines" were a series of positions, usually in towns or on high ground, joined by telephone or radio. So Cavalry could move between enemy strongholds, probing behind them. It was nerve-wracking work, where you'd want to have someone you could rely on.

The jeep headed east from Toul, through Luneville, which hadn't been badly hit, and then seven or eight miles southeast, into farm country. Like all the countryside I'd seen on the way to the old French barracks, this was autumnal, harvested or ready for harvest, with few visible hands doing the work and almost no livestock on the still-green pastures. The small village of Raville, our destination, was two or three miles west of Parroy Forest, Clewes told me.

"That's where the Krauts and us have faced off for a few weeks, like in the first War."

The .30 caliber machine gun, mounted above the dashboard, rattled loudly on the bumpy road. Clewes shouted to make himself heard.

Troop A of the 121st Cavalry Reconnaissance Squadron, the outfit I was about to join, was on break with the rest of the squadron, which had been relieved from its holding position in the forest by the 106th less than a week before. So I was to have a few days in Raville with my new outfit before going up to the lines. The 121st and 106th Squadrons, along with a Headquarters and service troop, made up the 106th Cavalry Reconnaissance Group, a small unit that worked at various times as probe, spearhead, and flanker for Patton's Third Army and Patch's Seventh.

When we got to Raville, Clewes and I reported to my new platoon leader, Lieutenant Lynch, a stern-faced man of about thirty-two or thirty-three. He was good looking, with small regular features, light blue eyes, and light brown hair and skin. He was about five feet ten, and maybe 150 pounds. He looked sinewy and strong.

"Find a place to sleep in the barn across the street," he snapped.

The lieutenant's billet and command post were in a room of the small house Squadron commandeered when it took the village a few weeks before. I thought he must have a lot on his mind, he was so brusque, almost angry. Or maybe he was having a hard time with the war. I wanted him to take me seriously as a soldier, right away, but things never worked out. I kept thinking he might be burdened by memories of combat, like Cruz. Maybe he was.

Before we left the building, Clewes showed me the troop's dayroom, which was furnished with some old easy chairs, a radio, and about twenty paperbacks, which he said I was free to borrow from. I chose *Mrs. Parkington*, by Louis Bromfield. Later, after I met a few of the men who already had places in the barn, I went back to the dayroom to bury my loneliness in the novel. Except for Clewes, who was very friendly, the men I met were pretty distant. They had their own troubles, some of them being recent replacements themselves. And the old-timers had lost so many of their friends they were in no condition to welcome strangers. The Army's replacement system was lousy. I was a lonely kid in a dream, with a good chance of dying before it was over.

Towards dusk, Clewes came into the dayroom. He told me I could have dinner with the French family whose barn we were sleeping in. Troop's kitchen had been giving the family food, which they combined with their own to produce evening meals for themselves and some of us. Other families in the village were doing the same. Even though I'd heard our cooks were putting out good chow, I thought I'd like to try the French table. Clewes also said he'd been ordered to take me out the next morning to see what I could do with a 60 mm mortar. He and I were to go to a field a few miles out of the village and fire at an empty oil drum from a distance of about a thousand yards. He smiled pleasantly as he explained the assignment, and I returned the smile. I had been reading when he came in. When he left, I turned on the radio, and for the first and last time during my fighting days, I heard some news, delivered by an Army broadcaster. After that, I wrote a letter home.

I knew I was close to real action, where I might be killed. I wanted to be somewhere else. I also wanted the terms of my being at the front changed, so I wasn't low man on the totem pole. But I never felt one shred of longing for home or for Robert or Helen or Abby or anyone else. I just wanted a way out of my predicament. I

October 25, 1944

Dear Mom, Dad & Ed,

You've probably seen by my return address that I've finally reached my outfit, and, as a matter of fact, my walking days in this army are over, because I'm in what is known, in army circles, as the mechanized cavalry. It's a little bit of a better deal than I might have gotten in the infantry and I'm familiar enough with my new job to do it well. This is the point at which I appreciate all the training that I thought

Letter home from the author, soon after arriving in his new cavalry troop think you have to be safe, however unsatisfied, to long for something. When you're really scared, all you want is reprieve. Hope is filled with possibility. The need for reprieve is empty and dead.

was additional and unnecessary back in the states.

I wrote yesterday and told you that no mail has reached me yet, but I have hopes of getting it before long now.

I'll sign off making this a quickie.

Love,
Harry

Letter home continued

Chapter Five

Raville, Parroy Forest, Raville

RIGHT AFTER BREAKFAST, Clewes and I headed out of the village in a jeep. We carried the mortar tube and base plate, six shells with propellant charges already fixed to them, and two pairs of calibrated binoculars—a pair for each of us. The jeep-mounted machine gun was loaded, and we carried our rifles. Clewes said it was unlikely that we'd meet Germans where we were headed, but that it was possible to run into an enemy patrol anywhere in the fields around Parroy Forest, so we kept our eyes peeled throughout the mission. But we saw no Germans, in fact no humans, only a pair of horses grazing at least fifteen hundred yards to the left of our firing position.

The place we went to for the mortar drill had obviously been used the same way before. I could see indentations in the ground, where other plates—the base of the mortar—had rested. And there was an empty oil drum—the target—in place when we got there. Clewes watched as I set up the mortar by the numbers. When I had made sure the base plate was as firm as I could make it before the first round helped to settle it further, I looked up. He asked me to judge the distance to the drum. I said, "875 yards."

All the rounds had a fixed propelling charge, so he said, "Set it for the distance, then, and fire."

I did so after fixing the elevation as I'd been trained to do. As soon as the shell was launched, I looked through my glasses and made out the landing spot to be accurate in distance, but five mils to the left of the target.

Clewes, who had also used his glasses, made it out to be ten mils left, but he said, "Let's go with five. It's your show." The second round blew up the oil drum. Clewes smiled with pleasure. But like me he realized I was lucky, even though I knew what I was doing. Vagaries of wind, propelling charge, base plate movement between rounds—all made for high odds against my second shot. Anyhow, our job was over, and we headed back to Raville. The ride was uneventful, except that I sighted a herd of large pigs running wild in a thinly wooded patch of land just off the road. I was surprised at this consequence of war, which for some reason seemed ominous.

As we drove into Raville, I took in the village for the first time. It was a small place, with no more than twenty houses, all made of stone—mostly farmhouses, with their stone barns attached. There was also a school building, a village hall, and a church with adjacent rectory. A few of the buildings had been pierced by artillery shells, but for the most part they were intact. The villagers I saw were all old men, women, and kids—no young or middle-aged men at all. The Germans had no doubt conscripted them to do forced labor. Beyond the village lay the farmlands that extended in all directions.

Clewes parked the jeep at the motor pool, saying I could go back to the barn or the dayroom while he reported to Lynch. I hung around the dayroom, hoping to hear from one of them, but nothing happened. Clewes must have told Lynch the kind of job I did. Not the lucky shot so much, but the way I handled the mortar. Lynch never mentioned it. I'd have felt more useful if he had.

The very last of the harvest had yet to be completed, but most of the season's field work had ended just before I got to Raville. The head of the family in whose barn I was to sleep, Emile La Croix, was still gathering crops from the land, but he spent most of his time storing potatoes in his root cellar, putting up green fodder for the few animals the Germans had left, and deciding which of those few to have slaughtered. Despite my deep running fear as the time approached for me to go to the front, I enjoyed fleeting pleasure when I read and when I ate at the La Croix's table. Their food reminded me of some of the Italian meals I'd known since childhood. The dinners were usually a vegetable soup, with little or no meat, lots of homemade bread, cheese or cured sausage, and pears and apples. As we ate, we drank small amounts of fermented cider. The diners included M. and Mme La Croix, their three daughters, all in their twenties, and four GIs—Clewes, Perot, and Trenard (Cajuns, whose first language was French), and me. No one spoke much. The Cajuns mediated what little conversation there was, switching back and forth between English and French, explaining now to the La Croix and now to us what was being said. But I remember the meals as quiet. La Croix may have been reticent by nature. He wasn't afraid of us. His wife and daughters would have reflected his fear if he had been. Still, the family can't have wanted us to be their guests forever. We knew they had sons to mourn and hope for.

Clewes was the only noncom or officer in A Troop who ever explained a mission to me. For instance, when we started out to the mortar range, he told me where we were going and what our chances were of meeting an enemy patrol. Three mornings before we left for the front, about an hour after breakfast, he told me the lieutenant had ordered him to lead a small patrol—me and two other privates—to the edge of the forest, to the northern flank of the 106th Squadron, the outfit we were soon to replace. He explained that Headquarters wanted to know whether the Germans were showing any signs of probing the space between the 106th's left and the infantry division dug in slightly to its north. There were no roads between the two units. He said there was no way to measure the chance of our meeting an enemy patrol. We'd just have to look and see.

The call to action surprised me. I was living in one of the last chapters of *Mrs. Parkington*, doing my best to avoid the war, and succeeding pretty well. But here it was. Clewes told me patrol work was routine. Our outfit was almost never near a large unit like a division of infantry or armor. We were typically isolated, so we had to keep checking the space around us, just to be sure we weren't surprised by the Germans. I was thankful that Clewes and not someone else was leading my first time out.

Every patrol in a combat zone is dangerous. I have never known a man who did not become grimly serious when he got such an assignment. The possibility of encountering the enemy— the expected event is always a surprise—was too great and unpredictable for anyone to take the job lightly. Besides, the countryside was loaded with antipersonnel mines, triggered so that the weight of a man was enough to set them off. If they didn't kill you, they would take a foot or leg, or worse, mutilate the genitals. It's part of the deadly game to look where you're stepping so you don't get your lower half blown off, and at the same time to take in everything between you and the horizon, far left and far right, so an enemy patrol doesn't surprise you.

I never got to know the two privates who worked with Clewes and me that day. As was standard, we spread out so all of us couldn't be hit by a single burst of fire or by a single artillery shell. We were all on the alert, but I think I did enough looking down and looking around for all four of us. We walked silently through a still landscape, three nervous miles out, across a series of empty farm fields, bordered by stone walls or hedges high enough to conceal any number of men. I kept waiting to be fired on by a large German patrol hidden from view. I was so intent on the enemy that I forgot about land mines, a much greater danger where we were. But it was danger in the form of living, hostile men that concerned me most—people ready to kill me. We didn't see any Germans. When we crossed the last of the open land, we entered the edge of a wooded gap between two low hills, on whose ridges the flanking American units were deployed. We didn't get close enough to either position to be challenged. Then we turned around and headed back towards Raville, looking behind us as well as forward and down. Halfway back, I spotted a horse two thousand yards off to our right, but that was the only living thing I saw, besides an occasional bird. Of course I pointed it out to Clewes, who nodded to let me know he'd seen it too. He later told me it was probably a grazing stray.

The Germans were by then using horses to pull some of their artillery, probably to save gasoline for their December drive into Belgium. But Clewes told me they never used them on patrol. Over the next weeks of action, I was to see horses, more than once, killed by our artillery, their rigid legs skewed, their eyes bulging, stomachs bloated, nostrils distended, tongues swollen beyond the open muzzle. Picasso's *Guernica* must have been inspired by such sights. All the dead men I saw concealed the fright of dying, but not the horses, with their bodies sometimes fixed in terror. We walked the rest of the way still worried about mines but relieved that our mission was over.

As the other men peeled off, Clewes smiled and said, "You were real cool on patrol."

Maybe I was, but I was also taut with fright, though we saw no Germans.

"Thanks," I answered, thinking he and I would go out together again, but we never did.

Then Clewes went to the lieutenant's command post to report. I knew in a way that the patrol was routine, nothing more, but I kept hoping Lynch would give me some clue that so far at least I was doing okay. Nothing. In fact, he never even looked at me when we passed on the streets of Raville. I'd salute and he'd walk by. We were to leave for the front early on Monday morning, and I needed some gesture from the lieutenant that would let me know I was part of the outfit. It never came. I began to realize the only way I'd ever have a real place in A Troop was to survive long enough to become an old-timer. A lucky shot with the mortar and a routine patrol meant nothing. Still, Lynch could have won over a kid like me with half a minute of his time. I'd have felt better, and I'd have served the outfit better.

On Friday morning, I heard that M. La Croix was about to have a sow slaughtered by the local hog butcher, right outside the barn where I slept. When I walked out and up the adjoining alley, which was cobbled with hard-worn boulders the size of a fist, the huge sow was already strung up by her hind legs. She knew she was about to be killed. Her alert blue eyes darted around, and occasionally she tried to kick against the rope that held her, as she panted for breath. But she seemed to realize things were hopeless. The butcher, a thorough professional, wasted neither time nor motion. With his very sharp knife, he cut the crucial vessels in her neck. Her long, soul-ragging squeal became a voiceless gasp, terrible to hear. It was an awful expiration.

"Pray for us sinners, now and at the hour of our death," I heard myself thinking.

This was not the best way to spend time just before going to the front. The sow was dying. Her blood flowed into a container that had been placed to receive it. I watched her transformation from fellow mortal to meat. After that, the butcher continued his work while the carcass was still tied up—a long skin-deep slit from throat to groin, and then a deeper cut and evisceration. Then he cut the body down and scraped off the bristles. They were part of his compensation for the job. Among the fascinated spectators were three children, no more than six years old, for whom the butcher blew up and knotted various sacs and handed them out as balloons. He and the rest of us were dead serious before the slaughter, but after the sow was dead, the butchering took on a festive quality.

The sow's slaughter carried me back to the Easters of my boyhood. In the cobblestone alley outside the barn, I remembered going to church with Grandma for the three hours of the Passion on Good Friday. Then, on Saturday, the slaughter of the kid whose feet never touched the ground. And on Sunday, roast kid for dinner. My past and present converged in Raville. The French sow, the Italian capretta, Jesus Christ our Lord, and me— all made one. A little crazy, but no crazier than war.

That afternoon we were ordered to fall in, mount, and drive halfway to Luneville to hear Colonel Nelson, the group commander, make his speech to us on the eve of battle. He's the officer Clewes said was no John Wayne, the one who wore hand grenades for show. The colonel praised and exhorted us, before he and Major Chalmers decorated four men with the Silver Star for gallantry in action. The war was getting close.

On Saturday I finished *Mrs. Parkington*, and on Sunday, I went to Mass, but not because I wanted to. I had spent almost a week in Raville, but I didn't get to know anyone except Clewes. The Cajuns I met at dinner had kept to themselves. Though we had shared four or five meals, we'd hardly spoken. But early that Sunday morning, Perot and Trenard awakened me. I thought they must be getting me up for some official reason. Short, fat, intense Trenard, who had shaken me with more fervor than was necessary, was the spokesman. Perot just looked and listened.

"Hey, kid, yaw name Pag-a-larrow, ain't it?" Trenard asked.

"Yeah," I agreed.

"Dhen you Eyetalian, and you Cat'lic, right?" he reasoned.

Instead of explaining, I agreed again, saying, "That's right."

"Dhen you comin' ta choich wid us," he concluded.

"I don't go to church," I said.

"Hey, tumara we go ta da front. You die, an yaw soul-in-sin be on us. Come or we carry ya!"

Perot and Trenard were of one mind, absolutely serious. It took me a little while to realize the fact, so they picked me up and began to haul me towards the ladder from the loft to the ground. I laughed with real pleasure, reading more friendliness in their concern than there was. They were dead set on saving their souls by saving mine.

"You comin'?"

"Okay," I said, and they put me down.

Together we walked the short distance between the barn and the church. On the way we met the parish priest.

"Bonjour, Monsieur le Curé."

"Bonjour, Messieurs."

The Mass did not draw me in, except for the choir of young women, whose voices were sweet and full. Though I seldom went to church, I had been moved by the Mass sometimes and by the Passion hours of Good Friday. But crucial as the moment was for me—the day before going to the front—I couldn't believe that a ritual observance would make any difference. The Mass wouldn't save me from death, and it wouldn't assure my resurrection. I didn't believe things worked that way, and I didn't want to believe they did. Cherishing life reverently is one thing. But looking for a refuge in the Church went against my instincts. Except for the music, which moved me, I was an outsider at the Mass. My deepest feeling was that the Army had thrust me out on my own. Alone, a feeling brain and thinking heart, I couldn't find anything to depend on.

That same afternoon, Lieutenant Lynch waved me off the street and into his command post.

"Pag-lee-arrow, this is Roper," he pointed. "He'll be your fox-hole buddy."

Roper was a huge man, lean and tall, about six feet six, a full-blooded Cherokee. He was old for a frontline soldier, maybe thirty-seven. At first I thought the lieutenant was pairing me off with an older man to help me out, but it was just the way it happened. Roper's foxhole buddy had stepped on a mine about two weeks before, and he was in the hospital with a bad wound. Roper, like me, needed a partner. The big man's eyes met mine and he nodded, obviously not very impressed with what he saw. As I faced him, I was tempted to reach down between his legs, behind his right thigh, heft him over my shoulders, and give him a spin. But I decided against the show of strength.

In a couple of seconds, he said, "I'll be glad to share a hole with you."

Was there something like a smile on his craggy face? In profile he was the Indian on a buffalo nickel, except for the hair. Roper's was short. His looks reminded me just a little of Grandma's—tough old bird. Roper had been with the outfit from before the time of its landing in Normandy, in early July. I'd heard about him from Clewes, who admired him. For one thing, Roper was shacked up with the local schoolteacher, an unmarried woman of his own age, a beauty who was crazy about him. But he was also a great soldier. Clewes said he could smell Germans. I was skeptical.

Roper and I were a strange pair, but a match nevertheless, each of us growing quickly confident of the other's alertness in tough situations. It's too bad the small patrols our outfit was called upon to mount almost every day kept us separated most of the time. I never went out with Roper. During my first week in action, though, he and I were always together, and that helped me a lot. He was quiet and sure in the face of danger, and he never took unnecessary risks. Lynch turned out to be something else. He loved to take a chance. I preferred Roper's quiet courage.

Monday morning saw a lot of grim men on the streets of Raville. I dreaded the experience I faced. The many others who were returning to it dreaded it even more. And I would soon come to know why. Their faces reminded me of Cruz and his squad in the Aleutians. It was time to go. Our vehicles were lined up and loaded, ready to start. Lieutenant Lynch had not yet mounted. He walked up and down alongside the waiting platoon. I was surprised to see that he wore a pair of open-holstered, pearl-handled, .38 caliber revolvers strapped to his thighs. He made them bounce as he strode. The lieutenant counted faces and checked equipment. Roper was missing. But before Lynch said anything, the door of the teacher's cottage opened, and out walked the big man, with his friend running behind him, weeping and wishing him well as he left her.

She'd lived out their brief affair openly, walking in public with him, leaving and returning to her house with him. One of the only things Trenard ever said to me is that the villagers believed this was her first love. She'd begun to teach in Raville about fifteen years before, when she was about twenty, and they'd never known her to have any but women friends. Everyone liked her, both French and Americans. I have no idea what Roper felt.

We pulled out of Raville. Though they stayed on the road, our vehicles covered much of the ground Clewes and I covered on my first patrol. We saw the same hedgerows, the same stone walls, the same fields. When we reached the western edge of the hill we were to occupy, we parked the armored cars and jeeps. My breath was shallow as we walked from our motor pool to the dug-in positions on top—I was about to face the enemy. We were told to stick to the narrow trail the engineers had cleared of land mines. I was careful, like everybody else. But here as on the first patrol, my deepest concern was that the climb eliminated the last barrier between me and the Germans. I was at the edge of war, where men were waiting to kill or be killed.

The Germans were holding ground stubbornly in Parroy Forest. In our sector, they occupied dug-in positions along the back and the forward slopes of a bald hill several hundred yards long. On the forward slope, facing us, they had observation posts running in a line parallel to the hill's crest, at intervals of ten or fifteen yards. Their back-slope positions were connected to the forward ones by trenches cut in a zigzag through the crest, so they could go safely from one to the other as their turns came to move forward to stand guard or to return for rest. We could see their movements during the day, though we hardly ever saw a whole German. Troop A of the 121st, my outfit, occupied a hill about the size of the enemy's, running parallel to it, about six hundred yards to the west. Our hill was bald too, and we were dug in, just like the Germans.

Locating the rest positions on the back slope was not just a matter of getting us a place to sleep away from the outposts closest to the enemy. It was also a way of minimizing casualties from artillery fire. Any rifled shell that cleared the crest was not likely to hit a dugout just beyond it. But mortars and howitzers could lob in their stuff in arcs so high that the descent was almost perpendicular to the ground. So these were a danger even to positions on the back slope. The valley between our hills, at its deepest about a hundred feet beneath us, was lightly wooded. This was the ground that a German probe or full-scale attack would have to cover before reaching us. In the daytime we could keep it well enough in view that no sizable patrol could surprise us. But the night was something else. Then we looked as hard as we could, of course, but it was our ears we had to rely on most.

The static warfare in Parroy Forest was unusual in World War II, where the front was most often not a line, but a series of strategically useful positions held briefly during fluid action. The Germans made a stand in Parroy. They had mined the pathways in the forest as they retreated into it, and our engineers had cleared narrow walkways for us at great cost. Even so, some men were wounded the day we came up, both in our outfit and in the 106th, which we were replacing. I heard the mines explode, but I wasn't near those who were blasted.

When we got near the top of the hill, we crawled until we got into the one of the trenches leading from a rear to a front position. Lynch paired Roper and me for guard duty, but we weren't assigned to the first shift in a front hole, so we stayed in the rear waiting our turn. I was surprised by our elaborate dugout on the back slope. The others on the hill were just as elaborate, we learned. They were deep enough to stand in—not counting Roper—and large enough to sleep four men easily. Along one wall of our hole, a natural earthen bench had been cut. And above, heavy timbers, jammed close against each other and covered with a foot of earth, provided a roof. It gave us some protection against the weather, and safety from flying shell fragments as well. Only a direct hit could get us. Unfortunately, the hole was wet, not just damp. But after two hours on guard in the front hole at night, where we strained eyes and ears for the signs of a German attack, and where we often took a mortar barrage and sometimes really heavy stuff, we were grateful for the relative protection and comfort of even a wet dugout. The entrenchments on our hill were old ones, from World War I, refurbished by Free French for use in our war.

The week at the front was nerve-racking. For the entire time, Roper and I took our two-hour turns together in the front hole, at four-hour intervals, while the other four men assigned to the same outpost got their four hours of rest on the back slope. Of the six of us, Corporal Peschak was the only noncom, and like Roper, an old-timer in the outfit. His new buddy, Willis, had joined Troop A in Raville as a replacement two days after I did. I never got to know the other two men who shared guard duty with us during that week. We six were located at the northern end of the hill our outfit occupied, so we had a flank to worry about as well as the ground ahead. The hill occupied by the Germans extended to the north, beyond our vision.

I kept dreading an attack by ground troops, and when I was on the front slope, my eyes and ears never stopped working. Meanwhile, I experienced that other terror, artillery fire, which I never got used to. It was always unnerving. The nights were long stretches of uncertainty, because even off duty in the timber-roofed dugout—where the sense of relief was palpable—you knew down deep that the Germans might make a move, especially after throwing in some heavy stuff. The barrages themselves were terrible, shaking the earth, making our hearts pound and our breath uneven. But when they ended, relief was destroyed by our anxious waiting for a ground attack.

By the end of the third day, all of us at our end of the hill knew that across the green valley, every afternoon, at 3:55 exactly, a German soldier stood up and adjusted his pack before walking a few yards parallel with the crest line. Then he'd turn and walk diagonally uphill. We could see him clearly, for almost a half minute, from helmet to waist. The German's punctuality—his predictability—seemed crazy.

The new replacement, Willis, who was from Kentucky, said to those of us he shared the dugout with, "I'd sure like a shot at that Kraut. I think I can hit him."

I couldn't imagine what he thought he was doing, but I kept my mouth shut. Corporal Peschak was silent too, though his face made it plain he thought his new buddy was not being very smart.

But Roper looked straight down at Willis and said in his soft, rich voice, "It's a dumb fuckin' shot."

I couldn't have said it better. The Germans were about 625 yards from us. Our standard M-1 rifles, with which Willis was armed, could easily cover the distance, but not accurately without some zeroing in, followed by some good luck. The chance of hitting a moving target with the first round at that distance was just about zero. Roper was right. It was a dumb fuckin' shot. But

Willis couldn't get it out of his head, so the next morning, when Lieutenant Lynch made the rounds, Willis joined Roper and me in the forward hole and told Lynch what he wanted to do. As he spoke, he wore a terrible grin, a sick longing for strength. It was the most unpleasant expression I've ever seen. I was surprised that he got an okay from Lynch.

"That's a great idea," the lieutenant said. "I'll be back to watch the Kraut get it."

It happened that Roper and I were on guard again when the time approached. Willis grinned the same awful grin and sighted his rifle dramatically for twenty minutes. He thought he was Alvin York.

Lynch showed up five minutes before the punctual enemy was to appear. At 3:55, the German stood up, adjusted his pack, and began his walk. Willis aimed very carefully and fired. We could all see that the bullet hit and bounced off a rock on the opposite hill, at least thirty-five yards short and wide. The precise German never broke stride. He may not have known he was fired at. Lynch left us abruptly, without saying a word.

Roper said softly, "Shit."

I felt contempt for the shot and revulsion for the motive. Still, Willis set me thinking about myself. I would have killed without hesitation to save my life, but I didn't know what it would take to get me to fire without immediate cause. Could I fire at a German from ambush, or would he have to attack before I'd shoot? I wasn't sure. My uncertainty raised other questions in my mind. If Oliver or O'Brien or Siebold or Marciano had been with me, I would have defended them with my life. I'd also have risked a lot for Roper and Clewes. But I wondered about others in the new outfit. What would I risk for them? I didn't know most of them at all, and the few I'd spoken to left me indifferent. But the main thing was that except for Clewes and Roper, where the ties were brand new, I was alone at the front, a stranger among strangers. They wouldn't die for me, and I wouldn't die for them.

During that week, the first shells to come in were from mortars, while Roper and I were in the forward hole. We could hear the late swish, just before the thud and bang. Mortar shells can have a very high trajectory, so I was sure one would come straight down into our hole. Many came close. Only three rounds came in that first time. We could tell from the sound of the explosions that one had landed on an outcropping of rock and two on the wet, soft earth. The earth absorbed the two shells before they went off, cupping the fragments so that most of them went upwards from the ground, covering a small radius. You'd have to be close to such an explosion to get hurt. But those that landed on rock, or later, on frozen ground, burst over a wide radius. They were much more dangerous.

Rifled artillery sounds altogether different from mortar, with its fast-twirling shells that break a textured path through the air with loud, sharp crackings and piercing whistles. When they come at you, they can sound as heavy and noisy as a freight train, but much faster. Their concussive power alone can kill you if they're big and land close enough. They set your brains vibrating hard against the skull. Like mortar rounds, their fragments disperse widely when they hit a hard surface.

At dusk of the day Willis took his crazy shot, the artillery started to come in, very heavy. Roper and I were in the forward hole.

"Jesus, it's close," I said, tense and shaking.

"It ain't so bad. Just stay low," Roper told me.

Nervous as I was, I could tell he was worried.

His face had a scowl that rejected things. His expression said, "Go away. I hate you."

And like me, he crouched lower in the hole than he had to. We both felt small and helpless. That's what artillery does. You know a single shell can transform you from a whole human into wet bits of flesh and bone, splattered by hot flying pieces of steel. After the first shell lands, you wait in tense expectation for the next and the next, hoping the fire pattern will move farther away.

I heard and felt and saw the artillery's tearing bursts, reverberating blasts, and evanescent fires—fierce and terrifying. There's nothing familiar about it. It leaves you not knowing who you are. Twice, I found myself biting clumps of the mud in the bottom of the hole, in desperate anxiety. I spit out the earth in impatient disgust. I thought my fright would kill me, but I kept it to myself.

After a long time, the barrage ended. Roper stood up and looked hard down the dark hill, and so did I. We listened hard, and we watched, expecting an attack, but nothing happened.

"That was a real one," Roper said, just as our relief came.

He knew I didn't need him to tell me that; he was relieving himself with the truth. The memory of the barrage was just under the surface of my mind, ready to come up and scare me all over again. I already knew the second real barrage would be worse than the first, and the third worse than the second. Artillery puts fear under your nose and in your mouth and lungs and guts. You know forever after that you can die at any moment.

When Peschak and Willis came to the forward hole, Roper and I walked back and got some food, more for something to do than from hunger.

We usually ate C rations or K rations at the front, though there were times when we got hot, freshly cooked meals. We didn't mind the tinned or boxed food, some of which could be heated if conditions permitted. The Cs included cans of precooked stews and hashes—mixtures like tomato sauce, bell pepper, and beef; beef, noodle, and gravy; beef and potato hash. I enjoyed opening a can and eating the food cold. The very thought of taking the time to warm it up was distasteful to me. It made me feel I would be doing something blasphemously incongruous with my predicament. The K rations came in a heavily waxed box that might include a piece of tinned American cheese about the size of a six-ounce can of tuna, a few strips of bacon packed in fat and ready to be fried, some instant coffee, biscuits, and three cigarettes, packed in their own little waxed box. At the front, I always had more food than I needed, and much more than I wanted. I was constipated most of the time, in part because I ate less than usual, and in part because that's the way anxiety affects me. Many of the men around me reacted the same way. I never experienced a loosening of the bowels from fright.

One morning late in the week, while Roper and I were in the forward hole, a young lieutenant-colonel appeared in the trench leading down from the back slope. He couldn't have been thirty. He paused in a crouch about twenty feet from us, looking around to try to decide, I later realized, whether he might be exposed to German small arms fire. Not knowing the situation, he asked us, "How should I approach your position?"

He was looking for advice that would assure both his dignity and his safety. If he crawled unnecessarily, he would look foolish. If he walked upright and got shot, he might be dead.

But it was Roper who answered the Colonel.

"What, Sir?"

Embarrassed, the colonel smiled amiably, but he didn't repeat himself.

I said, "Sir, just stoop a little and come down quickly."

Roper whispered, "Is that what he wanted?"

The colonel joined us, still wearing the stupid smile. "Any action?" he asked.

"Mortar or heavier stuff, mostly in short barrages every night, Sir," Roper told him, "but no German probes right here. They've been moving and firing up and down the line at night, though."

The colonel listened and nodded his head. He looked around for a full ten minutes, but said nothing more. Then he bent low and walked quickly up the trench to the rear.

"Good luck," he said.

It was a strange visit. We had no idea who he was or why he was there. We thought he might be a new officer with group Headquarters who felt the need to see things for himself. But that would have been very odd. We also thought he might have been a Special Services man who came up to provide himself with a basis for claiming that he'd seen action. We never found out. But the memory of his appearing and then extracting himself from the place of danger, as if it were a simple matter for him to decide, left us feeling gloomy. Why couldn't we leave too?

That afternoon the Germans dropped some propaganda leaflets. As if to capitalize on the colonel's reinforcement of our sense that those assigned to frontline duty had been singled out unfairly, the leaflets told us how cruel it was that we at the front numbered only 4 percent of the Americans in uniform. They said we should rebel against this arbitrary selection for combat.

"Where are the rest of your countrymen?" the leaflets asked.

But the German propaganda had just the opposite effect from the one intended. If only 4 percent of American soldiers were at the front, wasn't the same true for German soldiers? We all knew we were unlucky to be among the small number serving on the lines. We also knew that most men in uniform—including ourselves—had tried for better assignments and that more than a few avoided combat duty through political influence. But when you finally got down to it, there was no just way of avoiding the injustice of our being where we were. That didn't mean we were gung ho, only that we finally accepted our places at the front, grimly and sadly, hoping against hope for quick deliverance.

It turned cold that day. I didn't like the idea of wearing gloves—and I never did so at the front—because I thought it would slow me down if I had to fire. Some men cut the index finger—the trigger finger, right or left—off their gloves and felt confident that they could use their rifles thus prepared. But I wanted both my hands entirely free. So I'd put them in my pockets from time to time, with my rifle carefully propped near me or slung over my shoulder as the occasion prompted, and I'd briskly twist my upper body from side to side. The movement shifted my heavy ammunition belt and the damp clothes beneath it back and forth across my abdomen and hips, stirring the circulation and warming me. This hands-in-pocket motion became a habit with me, keeping my hands and the rest of me warm in very cold weather.

When Roper and I took our first turn in the outpost that night, it was freezing. We were barely in our position when a dozen mortar shells—three at a time—fell on the hard ground and dispersed, lighting up the black night. We ducked low, and everything passed over our heads. My breath was shallow. I waited for more shells, but none came. So we stood up, looking and listening, expecting a German attack. Five minutes. Ten minutes. Nothing. Then we were jarred by the rapid burst of a burp gun—an automatic handgun—maybe five hundred yards to the north, from the light woods in the valley on our left. It was followed by loud screams that seemed to voice unspeakable human anguish in the night.

"Someone's being ripped up," I whispered to Roper.

"Take it easy, take it easy," he said.

Obviously there was a patrol, probably not ours, between us and the German lines. I braced for an attack, ready to shoot any enemy who might come towards us. We worried about the flank. They'd have to come uphill. We could shoot down. Dark as it was I could still see Roper stiffen several times, as if he thought he'd heard or seen something he had to check out with special care, but each time he relaxed after a minute or two, sending me the message that everything was okay. I thought I could probably see and hear as well as he, but I relied on him nevertheless. Part of the reason is that he was older than I, a combat veteran, completely unpretentious and full of common sense. But besides his obvious maturity as a man and a soldier, there was something else. He had a warrior's assurance, some well-founded confidence I took seriously and wanted to share in. His intention was always to stay alive, if possible, but he was cool when the going got bad.

There was more gunfire, this time closer, only two hundred yards away, followed by more of the terrible screaming. But this time the screams became piercing squeals. Terror pulsed and thumped through my heart; it flashed hot up my neck and skull. Even scared half to death, I searched the darkness for German attackers.

Then Roper brought me to my senses by saying, "Some Kraut shot a hog or two."

That was it. I remembered the cry of the slaughtered sow in La Croix's alley, and I remembered the pigs I'd seen running wild in the woods when I returned from mortar practice with Clewes a week before. A German patrol, intending to probe our flank, fired nervously at some stray pigs it had disturbed on its sweep to our left. They must have thought the animals were a patrol of GIs. Those first pig cries, sounding all too human, must have frazzled them some. At least the Germans never came close to our position. Or was I the only one frazzled that night? The enemy turned back because they knew they'd lost any chance of surprising us.

That night, after the attack scare ended, I remembered Clewes had told me Roper could smell Germans. Though I was still skeptical, the image of Roper stiffening while we waited for the attack stuck in my mind. It was as if his body, and not he, were deciding what to do. I know the distinction between him and his body is dumb, but there are times when an action is deliberate and times when it is taken unself-consciously. What was strange about Roper's stiffening on the forward slope is that he seemed unself-conscious—willing to let his body decide—for long minutes together. Maybe he could smell Germans.

Two days before the end of that long week in Parroy Forest, Clewes gave me several ersatz cigars. He got them from one of the cooks who had delivered the week's one hot meal of beef stew, bread, and coffee the day before. By that time, I was smoking pretty heavily whenever I was in the back hole, and during the day in the forward hole as well. Smoking on guard at night would have been suicidal, of course, because of the light. At first the tobacco calmed me some, but the cigarettes were beginning to lose their kick. So I tried one of the cigars, reputed to have been left behind by retreating Germans. They were not so much tasty as powerful, and I began inhaling them to get that subsidence of jumpy nerves I wanted. Thereafter, I smoked several a day when I could get them, which was just about all the time. The cigars also gave me a renewed pleasure in my cigarettes, because I no longer expected them to do more for me than they were capable of.

On the fifth day, we heard the rumor that we'd be relieved soon, on Monday. It came with the first batch of mail to reach us at the front. I got about a dozen letters from family and friends. What a surprise. One was from Helen. But what she said was unreal. She wrote bread and butter sentences, not a letter for somebody at the front. I was more interested to hear that Robert was complaining about military discipline at VMI, but otherwise doing very well. He had good reports in all his subjects. Maybe he'd be deferred until he graduated, complaining and doing good work the whole four years.

Given the uncertain world of war, we didn't allow ourselves to believe the rumor about a break until the lieutenant told us, when Monday came, to get our gear together right away. There were smiles of relief all around. The 106th Squadron was coming up again. They arrived punctually, and with them came a few rounds of German mortar fire. Everyone scrambled for cover. At first we thought the enemy had found out about the relief and were trying to catch us out of our holes. But the firing ended too soon for that to have been the case. We waited awhile after the last shell exploded, and then we went all the way down the back slope.

Though a little jumpy, all of us were feeling good—too relieved to believe we might really step on a mine—and yet we were more careful during our return than we had been when we first entered the forest and climbed the hill. I walked behind Roper, doing exactly what he told me he was doing—walking in the footsteps of the man ahead, so as to avoid any chance of the deadly step. I heard myself laughing like an idiot demon, as if I were doing the cleverest thing in the world.

I was in a relaxed stupor during the short ride back to Raville. As we came in, we could smell the hot meal the cooks had ready for us. The whole village came out to greet us, including the schoolteacher, beaming and crying with pleasure, and the La Croix, mother, father, and the three daughters. Everyone looked happy, and we dismounted, feeling a great relief. My chest, which had felt tight and hollow while I was on the line, relaxed and became a full and free-breathing chamber of life again. During the first few days of rest, I forgot to smoke.

Our first morning in Raville was free and easy. Even though the front was only a few miles east, it seemed a world away. Of course I wrote home right away to report that I was safe. Towards noon, one of the sergeants told us trucks were available for the drive to Luneville, where we could take a hot shower. Most of us went. Others heated water in various make-do containers, and gave themselves sponge baths in one or another of the village barns. Roper and I enjoyed the ride over dirt roads and into the small city, less than ten miles south. The Army had rigged up showers in part of the ground floor of one of the buildings it had taken over in Luneville. The water was hot and the pressure strong. It was a luxury, after being wet, cold, and dirty for more than a week.

Seeing giant Roper nude after we'd spent a week at the front was a strange experience. It was as if there should have been nothing more to find out about him after we'd watched and listened for so many hours on the hill together, but here I was, witness to a new disclosure. His body was big, lean, and hard, and he looked even taller out of his clothes. He had a man-sized dong. But I wasn't the only one looking. So was he. And his impassive face took on the expression of wonder.

"Why if you ain't built like a fancy brick shit house. You mean that's what's been walkin' around under them dumpy clothes o' yours?"

Before leaving Raville, we had reclaimed our extra clothes from Supply, where they'd been checked while we were in Parroy. So we got out of our filthy underclothes, socks, and shirts, knowing we wouldn't have to put them on again until we could wash them. We didn't have a change of pants or field jackets, but except for these, we were clean through and through. My boots were still damp, but my woolen socks were clean and dry for the moment.

After Roper and I had showered and dressed, we went to a nearby bakery and each of us bought a couple of loaves of bread made out of wheat and potato. The baker told us about the mixture. I knew just enough French to understand him. Soon after that, Roper went back to the motor pool to get the first possible ride into Raville. He'd promised his friend he'd return to her as soon as possible. I went to a Red Cross shelter and just hung around for a couple of hours, drinking coffee and eating donuts.

While I was there, I ran into Corporal Peschak, who had shared the back hole with Roper and Willis and me in Parroy. We'd hardly spoken during our week on the lines because we spelled each other off, so that one of us was almost always sleeping while the other was in the forward position. And when we were in the rear at the same time, we were likely to be sleeping too.

Peschak was a tall, good-looking man, about twenty-five, with a friendly, open face. His hair and eyes were dark brown, but his skin was fair and his cheekbones covered with a light flush of strawberry. I saw him before he saw me, and I wondered whether to say anything. As it turned out, he yelled hello as soon as he spotted me, and we talked over a cup of coffee. He was easy to be with. He told me he came from Buffalo and he was engaged to be married, right after the war. His father and mother were Polish immigrants, devout Roman Catholics, and he had two brothers and two sisters. He was the oldest. Before he was drafted, he'd worked on construction jobs as a laborer, but he wanted to do something better when the war was over. He thought he would go to college to study engineering. He stopped talking. Then he looked at me and waited. I told him a little about myself. He listened with real interest. "So you have no girl."

"No, not really."

"That must be tough. Maybe that's why the front lines are so hard on you."

He meant to be kind, but he shocked the hell out of me. "Yeah, maybe. But what about Roper and Willis? Aren't they afraid, too? Besides, I don't know anybody here."

"You know Willis doesn't count. And Roper is only afraid in a tough spot. You're afraid for tomorrow. But, yeah, it must be tough to come up to the lines without a friend." Then he said again, "So you have no girl."

"I've never even slept with a woman," I heard myself say, hardly believing I could be so frank about my private life.

"Yeah, that's it. You have no girl, and you never slept with a woman. There's no future in your bones. And it's worse being alone up here."

Peschak smiled in a kind, reassuring way. The distance in our ages seemed much greater than the few years that separated us.

He said, "You know the look I see on your face. Sometimes I feel like that. Roper says you're cool in a clutch. That's the way he is. Cheer up. You'll make friends. You'll get laid."

That was our one and only conversation. As near to each other as the war had brought us, our paths never crossed again over the next month. We never went on patrol together, and the outfit didn't have another break from the fighting between Parroy and Erckartswiller, the end of the line for me.

Like Roper, I too returned to Raville early. At least some of the faces there were familiar. I walked into the dayroom to look around. Right behind me came Lieutenant Lynch. He'd just driven into town, and he looked a little drunk. Grinning from ear to ear, he told us about a beautiful young French widow who had succumbed to his masculine charms. He finished his story by repeating the courtly bow he'd executed when he said good-bye to her. It was good to see him relaxed enough to brag and frisk a little.

A soldier I didn't know asked Lynch, "Where did you get them guns, Lieutenant?"

Lynch stopped smiling. He lectured us. "These revolvers belonged to my great-grandfather. He used them in the Civil War. I come from an old Virginia family, and I take pride in being an American gentleman. Wearing Great-Granddaddy's guns is a way of keeping the tradition alive."

I liked his strong sense of family, but he was arrogant when he talked about it. He was better bragging about his love life.

I went to the La Croix's for dinner, where I was expected. Their place was the closest thing I had to a home, and I wanted to enjoy it while I could. A new batch of sausage was hanging from the kitchen rafters, meat from the slaughtered sow. I looked around and was glad to see that the dinner was soup, bread, cheese, and fruit—no sausage. The Cajuns were more talkative than usual, telling M. La Croix how we'd spent the week. At first the women listened, but then they got up, offering more soup and bringing the bread and cheese to the table. I had seen the La Croix daughters out of their work clothes and in their Sunday best, singing in the choir the day before I left for Parroy. All three were tall, big-boned women, with somewhat heavy features, but their faces were kind and strong, and they all had beautiful blue eyes. Nicely decked out and singing, they were wonderfully bright and alive. I didn't know their names. The middle one, around twenty-two, used to sit opposite me at the dinner table. I was not conscious of looking at her, but I imagine that without meaning to, I gave out plaintive signals, implying not love, but fear at the thought of returning to the war. She must have had a pretty good idea what I was feeling.

Next day we were issued boot packs, supple leather leggings fused to high-top rubber shoes. Each boot had room enough for two wool-felt pads, shaped to fit the bottom of the shoe. We were told that every day we should replace the upper one—next to the foot, where it got damp from perspiration—with the lower one. I followed the instructions for rotating the pads, and my feet were more or less dry from then on. It's odd that I felt the pleasure of possession in the boots. It wasn't just that they promised to keep my feet dry and warm. I enjoyed knowing they were mine.

In my new boots, I walked around Raville, looking for something to do to keep my mind off the front. I decided to buy some calvados, a crude brandy distilled from fermented apples or pears. Water was everywhere that autumn, in streams, puddles, canals, and of course in containers in our jeeps and armored cars. I wanted to carry a quart of the brandy, just in case I needed it. When I got to the house where they sold it, the big, red-faced man in charge filled my canteen and insisted on giving it to me for nothing. I thanked him, and we shook hands. Then I went back to the barn and tried to get into a book to avoid thinking, but it didn't work the second time. There was only one *Mrs. Parkington*.

The morning came when we had to return to the front. It was a bright, crisp autumn day, but our spirits were gray, and all our faces grim, as the vehicles lined up and we took our places. We would not be returning to our static positions in Parroy. The Germans were retreating, fighting stubborn delaying actions as they yielded ground. And we knew we would not be returning to Raville. In fact our departure was the beginning of our nonstop pursuit of the enemy through Alsace and to the Rhine, while the Germans sometimes held ground and sometimes counter-attacked fiercely.

The whole troop was in place and ready, except for Roper, who had yet to appear from the teacher's house. Lynch walked along the line of platoon vehicles, checking things. I was already seated in the jeep I'd been assigned to. Suddenly the middle La Croix sister came up to the vehicle, and reaching past the man sitting next to me, solemnly extended her hand. I jumped out right away and shook hands with her, smiling, pleased that she would take the trouble to be kind. Her strong face had a pleasant and serious look, with no trace of self-consciousness in it. I had the impression of falling into her large blue eyes, where there was comfort.

"Adieu, Monsieur. Bonne chance," she said, without a smile, only the pleasant, serious expression.

"Thank you very much. Good luck to you, too," I said, still shaking her hand.

Lieutenant Lynch scowled and said, "Hurry up the goddam foolishness."

I said good-bye to the young woman and got back in the jeep, thinking that Lynch was a son of a bitch. But I still made allowances for his having a tough job. He was bound to have a lot on his mind.

Roper's farewell to the schoolteacher once again had its public side, but the two brought it off with dignity for all of that. What we saw was brief, giving Lynch no time to interfere. Maybe he wouldn't have in any case. It's hard to know.

We left Raville and never returned. The La Croix, the three daughters, Roper's friend and lover, the hog butcher, the children with the sac-balloons, Monsieur le Curé, the choir of women, the man who gave me calvados, the lieutenant's widow—all were behind us. We headed east, bypassing Parroy on the south, rushing to catch up with the German retreat. Not that anyone in charge told us what was happening. In this case we didn't have to be told to understand that a new phase of the war had begun.

Chapter Six

Fighting in the Vosges

THE LONG, COLD MONTH of November 1944 is for me a blur of pursuit and attack over the roads of the Vosges Mountains. Every day had its dangers and anxieties. As soon as we left Raville, we began a pattern of advance that with few exceptions was to last for weeks. We'd ride for several hours and then move into a village as the Germans were leaving it. They'd retreat because they knew that a few miles behind us, in the form of infantry or armor, there was more power than they could match. We'd take a village in a dash, and they almost always found a way to make it tough. Their last vehicle to leave the place would fire at the first of ours to enter. And they routinely left a sniper, high in a tall building—the church steeple, for instance. He'd fire from above, often getting one of us before he was himself shot down. Another trick was to booby-trap a building they thought we'd occupy, which made the already risky job of clearing a house, room by room, doubly so. But the nearly invariable thing the Germans did after we took a village was to fire artillery at us, trying to hit the cobblestone streets before we could take cover. Exploding on the hard surface, the shells would spread their deadly fragments over a wide area. We used to duck down between huge dung-heaps—then common outside the front of rural houses—and the street-side wall of the nearest building, trying to avoid windows that might splinter and cut us up. The first barrages usually didn't last long. They were meant to get us before we had time to find cover, while we still had things to take care of in the open, like moving from house to house to be sure they held no Germans or getting a sniper out of a steeple. We had to find ways of doing both, more or less at the same time—finding cover from the artillery as well as we could and securing the town we'd just taken. That was always a dangerous time. But even after we'd searched the town and cleaned out any Germans left behind, we'd wait on edge for a counterattack.

They liked coming in at dusk, with plenty of armor. Even without word from one of our patrols we had time to decide whether to hold our ground or withdraw because we could hear the warning noises of their advance, powerful metallic grindings from heavy vehicles, sounding closer and closer. We sometimes fled to avoid being chewed up. Then we'd regroup, and if we could, return the next morning with enough power to get them to retreat again. It was a seesaw game in which with few exceptions both sides attacked or retreated, depending on their strength. But sometimes we held ground against the odds, buying time with our lives so that the giant action of which we were only a part might have a better chance to succeed. And sometimes I think we bought time with our lives to fulfill some officer's longing for glory.

On that first day out of Raville, after many hours of driving eastward, we stopped for the night on a gently sloping field. As we started to dig in, we were told to forget the digging and pitch our tents.

"What the hell's going on?" I asked Roper.

"I dunno, but it can't be bad. If we don't need holes, there's nothing to hurt us," he reasoned.

The weather was raw, but not quite freezing, and a fine rain fell all night. For the moment, at least, the world was quiet. We were surrounded by miles and miles of peace and quiet, I wanted to believe, even though I knew different.

Roper was much too long for a pup tent. But he managed to fold his legs and make do with the short space. We talked some, but neither of us made much conversation at the front. We used only the words we needed, and our social exchanges, which I guess we needed sometimes too, were always brief. So we settled ourselves for sleep. I was just going under when I heard the first rounds of very heavy stuff pass over from our rear toward positions far into enemy territory. I hadn't heard such big shells before, even during that bad night in Parroy. Within a few minutes the density of our artillery fire had increased so that the noise worked right through us. Our bodies vibrated with the trembling earth. Over where the big guns were firing, the sky fulminated, jags of brightness breaking the dark night fleetingly, in giant shifting patterns, and the air was filled with harsh whistling chugs for hours. The event was immense in time and space.

The morning after the great barrage ended, we started the chase. The towns we took during the month included Remencourt, Avricourt, Rechicourt, Sarrebourg, Rauwiller, Eschwiller, Weyer, Eywiller, Asswiller, Durstel, Ottwiller, and Ingwiller, roughly in that order. The first attack I was in took place about two days after the giant American artillery barrage that prepared the way for our movement toward the Rhine. We'd been riding, stop-and-go, most of the day. As usual, nothing was said about where we were going or what we might expect. We had no choice but to accept this uncertainty, and it grated on us. Even though we privates knew roughly where we were—in the Vosges, chasing the Germans—and knew the terms of our being there, we were surprised when our vehicles stopped and we were told to dismount and then ordered to the attack.

It was early November, but the air had become very cold, below freezing. The midafternoon sky was a hazy pale blue, fast becoming dismal gray. As soon as we were on foot, the platoon was ordered to spread out and cross a slightly rising field that was covered with a dusting of snow. The other platoons would follow. Through the light snow we could see the stubble of the past season's sheared crop. At the far end of the field was a small village, the size of Raville, about six hundred yards away. We moved forward, not knowing what to expect.

Why hadn't we driven our vehicles right into the village? There must be Germans waiting for us. Couldn't Lynch have said something? The lieutenant was by conventional hero standards the bravest among us, but he didn't lead out on this one. Maybe he'd been ordered to stay behind. Or maybe he was on patrol. We spread out, advancing in an irregular pair of lines, feeling at each step the crunch of snow and stubble underfoot and then the rigid surface of the frozen earth. Maybe the Germans didn't have time to lay mines. I was in the first rank, moving forward, towards the village, hoping things would stay quiet. But the prelude to the show was ominous.

Two light tanks, hardly ever assigned to us, cut out of the parked column behind us and lumbered ahead, blasting their guns at the stone buildings on the far side of the frozen field—our objective. That cinched it. The Germans must be dug in and waiting, or Group would never have given us tank support. We moved no more than fifteen yards before German artillery began to explode very near us. At first I thought it was coming from the village, but we could soon tell that the heavy rounds were passing over the stone buildings—big stuff from the rear. Every few seconds, clusters of German shells landed on the hardened earth. After they burst, we could hear the twirling fragments of hot steel racing close to the ground all around us. We were flat on our stomachs, but we weren't as low as we wanted to be with all that deadly stuff cutting through. Like the other twenty-five or so of us in the platoon, I had hit the ground fast and hard when I heard the first of the heavy shells tearing the air. The shells I'd listened to in the pup tent a couple of nights before had been on the same deadly mission. This time the direction was different. Fierce explosions reverberated, the ground shook, the air cried, torn by speeding metal.

It was much worse than the bad night on the hill in Parroy. Field and sky were shattered over and over until I was light in the head. Where the hell was I? What the hell was I doing here? I gasped for breath. I think I wanted to whimper, but I couldn't. I had to get through the bald space we were trying to cross. I got up and ran forward after a cluster of shells burst near me, trying to get clear of the fire pattern. I did that again and again. But I gave no thought at all to advancing toward the village, even though that's just what I was doing. All I wanted to do was get away from those hot, shattering barrages. I'd run thirty or thirty-five yards, and then I'd drop again, trying to stay low enough to escape the dense shell fragments that kept whirring overhead. I was so scared I chewed crisp snow and stubble every time I went down. I had a big wad of it in my mouth. I wanted to be part of the earth, but I didn't have time. Maybe I spit it out, or maybe I swallowed it. I don't know.

> Sound blasted purple on the frosted earth,
> Steel splinters sped and twisted low across
> The hardened field. Our faces, wiped by fear,
> Saw Death beneath, without a human mask.

Then a trick of the mind got me out of the tough spot I was in. In the middle of that violent confusion, I suddenly saw myself and the others from a distance. We were in a picture, and there was no danger. I just looked at us. Twenty-five men, a few wounded and bleeding, one with his red gut spread out around him, on a beautiful white field, sloping very slightly upwards towards a pretty village of stone buildings. And overhead a placid gray sky curved down to the horizon line beyond it.

But after a few seconds, I began to see things right again. Unless we wanted to be caught in the middle of the field until the shells got us, we'd have to move forward and take our chances, which in fact is what we'd been doing all along. By the time I was halfway across the open space, my sense that I had to cope with the danger dominated my fear. I was thinking again. I wouldn't wait for a piece of the low-flying stuff to get me, which it might do even when I was flat on my stomach. I ran the last hundred yards or so without stopping, being by then well ahead of the German shells, which continued to fall closer to the middle of the open land. By the time I'd crossed the field, I realized that most of the others had done the same. Surprisingly few men were wounded.

But there were other things to think about—the village and its defenses. German shells were still flying, but they passed over us, landing in the field we'd just crossed. I was glad the tanks were with us. They kept blasting away. What I could see ahead was rubble and partially destroyed buildings. But no humans, military or civilian, were in sight. And there was no small arms fire. The tanks moved through the main street and fired at a German car escaping from the far end of town, but they missed it. The men in the car had been left behind to report on our numbers and weapons. But they were the only Germans we saw. Those of us on foot moved quickly through the village, spreading out to minimize the number of casualties a single shell burst might cause. We searched the houses, a room at a time, just to be sure no other Germans were around. Nothing. Within a few minutes, the overhead bombardment stopped. The aural void left me imagining noises for several minutes. It was a distraught silence.

That was my first attack. Though the artillery had been bad, things could have been a lot worse. We might have hit resistance in the village itself. We were lucky that day. I'm not sure just when it occurred to me that after this hot baptism of fire, I would face danger with less fear. But I know when I found out I was wrong. It was during the very next attack against a German-held village. I was scared to death all over again. It's true that I never lost control as I almost did crossing the snow-covered field, though I came close a couple of times. But the same combination of helpless, gasping fright and vital self-control marked my weeks at the front. I was at the same time unnerved and cool, unwilling and efficient, shallow-breathed with the fear that I'd die and utterly confident that I'd make it. These are flat contradictions, but that's the way it was.

Within ten minutes after we'd taken the rubble-strewn village, we heard the sound of incoming artillery again. This time the Germans had zeroed in on the main street, which they covered pretty well with a close pattern of a dozen or so rounds. I got into the narrow space between a pile of broken stone and the wall of a building more or less intact. Nothing came really close to me, but I was still concerned about the return of the troops who must have retreated from the village only a short time before. The Germans made a habit of counterattacking. So when their artillery stopped, we faced outward towards the field beyond the village, waiting for them, but they never came. One by one, we got up and looked around, waiting to be directed by a sergeant or the lieutenant, who had by then joined us. The previous thirty minutes had been intense, to say the least. We began to let down a bit.

Our platoon was assigned to hold the ground at the far end of the village, where the German car had made its late exit. We took over the cellar of a house that had lost its roof and upper story and most of the ground floor. Just outside the broken entrance lay a dead German and two dead horses. The man's eyes and mouth were frozen open, his legs were stretched out, and one of his feet was missing. His fingers and arms were extended in grotesque resistance to the terrible unknown. He was the only dead human I saw in combat who had not come to rest. The horses were almost on their backs, with their bellies not quite straight up, their rigid legs and tongues pointing in different directions. Their huge carcasses held my attention until I was at the entrance to the cellar.

I happened to be the first one to go down the steps, and though it was beginning to get dark, I saw a trip wire attached to an exposed charge, running across the last step—a booby trap begging to be dismantled. After I called out the danger, I stepped over the wire, and so did the men behind me. Though we reported the rigged up explosive, no engineer came to dismantle it for the two days we were there. We never touched a booby trap because it might be a decoy concealing another trap. The job needed a specialist. So we improvised a left turn at the bottom step to avoid the wire as we entered and left our bunker. Though it's in some ways unlike me, I had complete faith that no one would forget to make the turn. I knew that the dead soldier and horses near the entrance would be our grim reminder of the danger at the bottom of the stairs, whether we were coming or going.

We dug a set of four holes, about seventy-five feet apart, in a semicircle that centered on our cellar and curved outward from the village. From any one of the holes we had at least a partial view of the terrain flanking the road that joined us to the enemy. We stood guard in pairs, two hours on and four off, as usual, returning for rest after guard duty in the holes. I didn't know the men in the cellar. Lynch was elsewhere, at Troop's command post, and Clewes and Roper were away, too. In fact Roper was not with me when we crossed the frozen field under fire, and he wasn't with me on guard in that village, which was Vaucourt or some nearby place. I shared the outpost hole with a much smaller man, and twice stood part of my two-hour turn alone.

It was during one of these times by myself that I took a willing German prisoner—a strange experience. As usual, I was straining to see and hear, turning my eyes continuously back and forth through the arc of vision that curved toward the enemy's position. Though it was the middle of the night, there was light enough to see things at quite a distance, a hundred feet or more. But I heard before I saw—the sound of someone crawling. I was sure of it. The hair on my neck stiffened, and I checked my breath as I threw up my rifle, pointing it in the direction of the sound, ready to fire as soon as I could see a man.

But before I saw him, I heard him say, "Friend, friend."

Then he stood up, about seventy-five feet away, his hands over his bare head. It was understood that those who surrendered voluntarily would not wear their helmets. As he walked slowly towards me, I kept an eye on him and an eye on the terrain around him—to his left and right and especially his rear. I didn't want him to distract me from the possibility of an attack by his comrades. But by the time he got to the very edge of my hole, there had been no enemy movement.

I said, "Stop," though I knew how to pronounce the German word "halt."

He stood still. Then I motioned him with my head and rifle to turn around and back off a little, and then I motioned him to lie down prone, with his arms extended. He understood me right away. In this position, he was easy for me to keep an eye on, and he didn't obstruct my view of the ground between me and the enemy. Two men from the cellar relieved me about a half hour later. During this time of waiting, I didn't speak a word, and neither did the prisoner. I was as alert as I've ever been, worried about him, and also worried that if there were an attack before I could deliver him to the cellar, he might change his mind about surrendering, in which case I'd have to kill him. But all went well.

As my relief approached, I called out that I had a prisoner, and asked one of the two men to go back and tell the others I'd be bringing him in, so they wouldn't be surprised into doing something foolish. After waiting a minute or two, I walked the German back to our bunker, curious to get a good look at him.

As he got near the bottom step, I stopped him, pointed to the trip wire, which he could see after I'd shown it to him, and directed his steps to the left. It wasn't until I reached the floor of the fully lighted cellar that I was able to see his face. He was no more than seventeen, Robert's age, maybe younger. His light brown eyes and light brown wavy hair reminded me of Robert, too. He looked frightened, and I felt sorry for him. He had been at the receiving end of the many thousands of artillery rounds Corps had just sent over. Maybe that's what made him surrender.

I pulled a can of C rations from my pack and opened it for him.

"Danke schön," he mumbled. He was subdued.

He tried to smile when he said thanks, but he couldn't. He ate slowly, gloomy and afraid.

Then some of the fellows in the platoon started to rag him. They said he was a coward for surrendering, and they told him Germany would be destroyed. He probably did not understand English, but I'm sure he got the message anyhow.

He remained silent through the continuing abuse until someone said, "Danzig ist kaputt."

To this he said, "Nein," afraid and yet emphatic.

He was right, Danzig had not fallen. For some reason this last taunt and his response triggered my angry intervention. I didn't know these bastards.

"Leave him alone! He's my prisoner! When Lynch gets back, I'll turn him over for questioning at Headquarters. Until then, stay away!"

At that moment, I felt closer to the German boy than I did to my fellow soldiers. Anyhow, they left me and the prisoner alone. Much later that night, very close to dawn, Lynch came into the cellar, and I turned over the prisoner.

We left that devastated village and its three exposed corpses after a second night. I didn't go on patrol during our short stay, but I know others did, and my guess is that Headquarters learned enough to conclude the Germans were retreating once more. Anyhow, we mounted and took off after them, as we were to do every day or two until we were stopped at Erckartswiller.

During those weeks of fast action, I had some close calls, sometimes during an attack, sometimes during a German counterattack, when we had to fall back, and sometimes on one of the many patrols I was called upon to join. The German retreat was complicated, and our apparently headlong pursuit had to be planned so we reduced the chances of leaving a strong German unit behind us. A reconnaissance outfit like ours was often way out in front, ahead of the enemy's north-to-south line of defense, but it wouldn't be a good idea to bypass a city that might be loaded with Germans ready to cut you off and wipe you out.

I figure that was the reason for a patrol led by the lieutenant in the early days of our push. It was larger than most. About a dozen of us, mounted in three jeeps and an armored car, which held our radios, set out in the early afternoon from a village we'd taken the day before. Neither Roper nor Clewes was in the patrol. As usual, we were told simply to get our gear together fifteen minutes before we were to pull out.

My best guess is that we set out from Rauwiller for Saarbrucken. Our destination certainly turned out to be a substantial city, with buildings larger than any in Luneville, and without the provincial-rural characteristics of the smaller cities of Alsace. To get where we were headed, we traveled fast through open country, but we stopped often in concealment, giving the lieutenant time to leave his jeep, walk to the armored car, and get T-5 Lane, the communications man, to put him in touch with Headquarters. I suppose he was letting those who ordered the patrol know where we were and what we'd seen. As usual, I kept waiting for a clue about what we were up to, but as usual I waited in vain.

Rauwiller is maybe thirty miles from Saarbrucken as the crow flies, but given our stop-and-go progress and our circuitous route, it took several hours to get there. We entered the city in the last light of the day, approaching downhill, slowly, on a paved street. As far as I can judge, we were sent there to see what we could see, in the expectation that what we reported might help those in charge to decide on the deployment of larger units than ours. During this period of the war, elements of the 106th Cavalry Reconnaissance Group often fought like mechanized infantry, as we had done only the day before, when we took Rauwiller. But units of our Group also did patrol work for the Third Army, which was to the north of us, and for the Seventh, which was to the south. At the same time, we were often deployed to protect both armies on their flanks. We privates slowly pieced out the nature of our complex obligations, which might result in a changed mission at a moment's notice. As for the patrol to Saarbrucken, we had only the most general idea what we were doing in that large city—miles away from the nearest American unit of any size—where we had no friends, and where the Germans might be waiting for us.

As the armored car that led our four-vehicle caravan moved deliberately down the city street, we all looked ahead, of course, but we also looked left and right and up. From time to time, we looked to the rear as well, not sure whether we'd been let pass, only to be boxed by tanks waiting in the side streets. But that didn't happen. For some reason the Germans had decided not to defend the place. Our own Headquarters may have had reason to believe they'd withdrawn and had sent us in to find out for sure. Air reconnaissance might have seen what looked like a German evacuation, but that would need a check on the spot. When we'd moved half a mile along the city street, a valley between stone and glass walls, we heard the grinding sound of a tank beginning its slow acceleration. Though at first we couldn't be sure, we thought it was moving away from us. The lieutenant ordered the jeep I was in to move ahead to check the tank's direction. We sped to the next side street and saw the lumbering withdrawal. As soon as we'd motioned our discovery, the lieutenant waved us back. We all knew by then that the tank had been left behind to look us over, not to engage us. So far, so good. But the night was ahead of us, and we didn't know what it might bring.

We parked our vehicles in an alley, just off the street we'd traveled, and dismounted. Then Lynch led us back to the street, walked up the stairs to the front door of a three-story town house he seemed to choose at random, and knocked. I admired his cool behavior. He obviously meant to get us a comfortable place to sleep if he could.

A full minute after the lieutenant's loud knock, a woman of about thirty-five opened the door. She was a handsome blond, dressed in drab tweeds. Her face was war weary, and she was afraid. The lieutenant spoke confidently in English, wishing her good day and saying that we'd like to spend the night. Though she spoke German and French, but no English, she understood what he wanted. She waved us in, trying pathetically to smile her fright away. We followed the lieutenant. She told us over and over that there were no men in the house, but we searched every room and closet anyway, from cellar to attic. Except for an old woman in the second-floor sitting room—the young woman's mother-in-law, she told us—there was no one else in the building. By this time it was dark, but the house was well lighted, protected from observation by anyone outside by heavy, close-drawn curtains. We had to stand guard in pairs until morning, but there were enough of us that I pulled only one turn.

Soon after the lieutenant gave us the schedule for guard duty, I wandered alone into a room with a small bookshelf and browsed the titles, trying to get my mind off the fact that we were miles from nowhere, with the chances of our being cut off for keeps very high, if the Germans were so inclined. Why would they let us get back to report Saarbrucken was empty? Or was it empty? We really didn't know anything about the city except for the bit of it we'd traveled through. Well, if they didn't explain the mission to me and wouldn't listen to my opinion if I gave it, what was the use of thinking about it—except, of course, to give my anxiety a tangible shape I could cope with. But I gave up speculation for the moment. I looked quickly at book spines on the shelves, with titles I recognized from a college course, by Kant, Schelling, and Goethe. I left them where they were. Even if I could have read tough German, looking into one of the books on the shelf was not what I wanted to do just then. I stood around waiting, as I pretty much had to, until the next thing happened to me.

While Lynch was giving us our orders for the night, I had seen the frightened women beginning to prepare a meal for us, using their own food and some of the C rations we had brought with us. I figured we'd be eating soon. But before the call to chow, I was approached by five of my fellow privates. I knew only one of them, and him slightly. They came up to me in a group, looking very serious, and waited for their chosen spokesman, the one I knew, to tell me what was on their minds. They looked like a committee with a report to deliver. What I heard shocked the hell out of me. Three of them had been through the old woman's bedroom during the house search, and they returned to it afterwards, looking for whatever they could find. Among her scarves and gloves, they discovered a jewelry box filled with earrings, rings, and pins, most of them gold. Somehow, they were sure that Lynch and the noncoms knew nothing of their discovery, but they weren't sure about me. So to cover themselves, they offered me a share of the jewelry to guarantee my silence. I couldn't believe what I heard.

Here were five average American boys. Though I didn't know them, I would have thought them decent. But they were not only ready to loot, but eager to explain the justice of doing so. They argued the case passionately. They said we'd drawn the lousiest assignment in the Army, for which we received the lousiest pay, less than the infantry. It followed that we had a right to take care of ourselves by robbing the old woman, who was the enemy. There was more. Anyone with the same chance would certainly do likewise, so why should we leave what we'd discovered, only to have someone else grab it. Finally, they said my ridiculous unwillingness to join in made it impossible to take the loot without running the risk, whatever I said, that I'd report them. In short, it was unfair of me to stand between them and what was rightfully theirs. But I just couldn't take a share of the old woman's gold.

I have no idea what they did, finally. I tried to read their faces at the dinner table, but it was impossible to tell. At the time, I thought they were dead wrong, and I still think so. But they may have needed to steal the gold for reasons as personal and as irrational as mine when I stole the officers' cold food on the *Mauretania*. Maybe these young men had to be compensated emotionally for spending the night in a German city, far closer to the enemy than to our own troops. Closer? We were right in the midst of the enemy. It was a crazy patrol we were on. No amount of explaining it could make it anything but crazy.

I made another error that night, much more serious than the first. Lynch and I would probably never have hit it off anyhow. And he may have been looking for something to confirm his sense that I wasn't his kind of man. As things turned out, I know he wasn't mine. All of us were at the dining room table eating, except the two on guard outside. Both women had been at work for over an hour, getting the meal together, setting the table, and bringing the food. They were trying to find ways to keep us friendly. The younger woman, clearly worried, said some things intended to be flattering. Her face was worn by care, and her attempts at polite manipulation, pathetic.

"Im Feld und Strasse.... Whether you're in the field or in a town, you American soldiers have fresh baked bread served to you." Then she marveled at America's egalitarian Army. "Wonderful! Officers and men eating at the same table."

Lynch wanted to know what she was saying, and I told him. He grunted. Then we began to help ourselves to the food. The women hovered nervously, asking whether everything was all right. Probably Lynch didn't understand them. Or maybe he wasn't interested in what they were saying just then. In fact, no one seemed to be paying them any attention, except me. I understood their need to please us and to be reassured that they had done so. They were completely at our mercy and afraid. So I thanked them and told them the food was good. They seemed a bit relieved, though I think they'd rather have heard the reassurance from the lieutenant.

Then the younger woman said in German too simple to be misunderstood, "I'll serve the coffee after dinner, yes?"

I looked at Lynch, waiting for his answer. But he hadn't understood her. "What'd she say? What'd she say?"

"She wants to serve coffee after dinner. Is that okay?"

The lieutenant turned red with anger, which he directed at me. He hit the table top twice, very hard, with the heel of his right palm. There were two loud cracking sounds. Then he yelled at the top of his voice, "I want my coffee NOW! By God, I'm an AMERICAN! What are YOU?"

The women ran to the kitchen to brew the coffee. I said nothing, of course. I was as shocked by his anger as I was by the proposal to steal the old woman's jewels, though in a different way. What the hell was he driving at? I wasn't an American? What did he think I was doing in the Army? What about my father and his service in the American Navy in World War I? And the dry dock in Portsmouth and the tankers in Mobile? And the Navy E he got from Admiral Moreell? Yet instead of being angry with the lieutenant—that came later—I tried to reassure myself that the woman's expectation and mine had been reasonable. I thought to myself, naively, "Most of the Virginians I know drink their coffee after dinner."

Besides, I thought, both she and I had given Lynch the last word. He had the choice to make. But from his point of view, there was no choice. Every American knows it's un-American to drink coffee after dinner.

We had no trouble that night in Saarbrucken. Next morning we drove out the way we'd come in, and in a few hours rejoined the outfit just in time to move out to the next village. There's no doubt I was heartsick with fear all during my time at the front, and in some ways I felt like a child without any power at all. But it's also true that after I took part in the first attack under heavy fire, and after the German boy had surrendered to me, and after I'd been on a few patrols, I felt a new self-sufficiency. God knows what it means that I experienced both these feelings at the same time—fear and confidence. I knew deep down I might not survive the chances of war, and that if I were ever to get back home, I'd have to find ways of reducing my vulnerability. Patrolling and attacking are dangerous ways to spend time, but that's what our outfit was called upon to do, day in and day out. And we did the work using the fewest men possible, to minimize losses in case the job ended badly. Most important, I was a private, who took orders from anyone with rank, unable to decide things for myself.

From the time we left Vaucourt—the place we attacked by crossing the frozen field under heavy fire—until we got to Erckartswiller, our pattern of action was the same. We'd follow the retreating Germans, attack a town whenever we caught up with them, and then wait for a counterattack and try to hold on. Whenever the Germans withdrew, we'd take up the pursuit again.

As if this work weren't exciting enough, we'd go on patrol every time we were in a place for more than an hour or two, just to see what we could see. After Vaucourt, we moved through Sarrebourg and then headed into the Vosges Mountains, riding quickly into landscapes whose beauty I could see but hardly appreciate. The green, forested hills and valleys seemed endless, but I had no heart for them then. The roads were not great, but they were passable. As hard as we drove, we were at first unable to overtake the Germans. But however fast they moved, they found time to slow down long enough to pour in the artillery whenever we took a village.

Shortly after the patrol to Saarbrucken, the troop rode down the main street of Eywiller, meeting almost no resistance. I heard the machine gun on the lead jeep chattering away. Then a wounded German was carried to the captain's command post for preliminary questioning before his transport to Group Headquarters. There was a little more firing, but nothing to speak of. We were told to dismount and spread out, ready to return enemy fire, should there be any more of it. I had already begun to look for a safe position in case of artillery fire, but the only cover I could see was a dung-heap next to a wall that included several low windows. Flying glass can kill you as dead as any shell fragment. I was just walking past the windowed wall, looking for better cover, when the shells began to come in. Caught in the open near the glass, I ran a short distance before I dropped, but there was no real safety because the fragments twirled low over the unyielding cobblestones. The pattern of fire was near me and it was dense. I thought I'd had it. There was nowhere to go and no earth to eat. I was gasping. Then I heard a voice and felt a hand on me at the same time. A young woman was trying to pull me towards an open door in the wall I'd passed just moments before.

"Komm' mit!" she said.

I couldn't believe she was there. But I got up right away and pushed her between me and the wall, covering her back as we moved quickly toward the doorway and into a ground-floor storage room. She was my age. Her skin was white, her hair blond. But she had brown eyebrows. Her eyes were blue. She kept looking at me. When I stopped breathing hard, I was mute. I wanted to thank her, but at first I couldn't speak.

"God, she's beautiful," I thought to myself. "It's a miracle she wasn't killed."

She kept looking at me.

"Thank you. You saved my life. Thank you." I put my hand on her shoulder. She smiled.

The artillery stopped falling. She sat me on a low stack of milled timbers, and then she took off my helmet, gently but firmly, and offered me a piece of dried sausage and an apple, speaking simple German words in a kind voice.

"Iß etwas. Sie müssen keine Angst haben."

I wanted to unwind, to change my gloomy face, but I couldn't. She herself was unafraid. She must have come out to get me after seeing me through one of the windows I'd passed, looking for cover.

I didn't stay with her in the storage room for long, less than ten minutes. I was not eager to leave her, but I knew I had to get back or I'd be missed. Though I had no appetite for the food she'd given me, she insisted I keep it. Her good looks registered on my numb senses, but what I felt most was the deep comfort of having been saved by her.

I smiled, saying "Thanks," and we waved good-bye.

I stuffed the sausage and the apple into a pocket of my field jacket, and I walked away.

When I got back to the street, it was a different place. Not only had the German artillery stopped, but part of a U.S. armored division had moved in, and at least six heavy tanks were spaced along the main road. Many unfamiliar GIs were walking around as if there weren't a war going on. We learned from them that most of their armored division had passed along our flank and were pressing the Germans who had just withdrawn. It was one of the rare times when the odds were we'd be safe for a while, though artillery fire was still a threat. In fact, those of us in the 121st Cavalry Reconnaissance were so used to being far ahead of any big American unit and so used to being outnumbered by the Germans, that we felt we were on a holiday that afternoon, surrounded by one of our own armored divisions. They had great firepower. But most of all they had men. Their sheer numbers were a relief to us.

One of our sergeants pointed out the lieutenant's command post, and told us we didn't have to report there until 4:00 P.M. In the holiday spirit of that unique day in combat, when we felt strangely safe, Clewes, Roper, and I walked the main street for a while. Then we dropped into a small shop, just reopened for business. We went there more to look around than to buy. We got into a halting conversation with the proprietor, a man of sixty or more. After a while, he said something to his assistant and then invited us to his home, directly above the shop, for a glass of beer. We accepted.

When we got upstairs, he introduced us to his wife and father, who was about eighty-five. As he promised, we were served beer, which was light in color and full-bodied, very good, though I was not used to drinking warm beer. The woman went into another room, and the five of us sat at a round dining table, with the white-haired old man next to me. He dominated the conversation, telling us in French that he'd witnessed war from the time he was ten. He'd been a boy when the Germans took Alsace from the French in 1871. He recalled when the French reclaimed it after the Treaty of Versailles. And he'd seen the

Germans return to occupy the ground again in 1940. Now the Germans were being driven out once more.

We couldn't understand all his words, but his subject and his sentiments were clear. He didn't like Hitler, who had to be defeated. But he didn't like war either. He spoke the word "baïonnette" over and over, gesturing thrust and withdrawal with his arms and hands, and grimacing disgust with each repetition. He obviously thought war was a bad way of settling differences. I must have been looking at him with utterly open eyes, fascinated by his passionate delivery.

He stopped, looked at me and smiled, and then patted my cheek, saying, "Bébé, Bébé."

The others looked at me, but I didn't mind what the old man said. I must have seemed like a real kid to someone like him. Anyhow, we soon finished our beer and offered our thanks and good-byes. When we reported to Lynch's command post, we were told we'd be pulling out right away. We were sorry to leave the heavy armor and the many men behind us. But the holiday was over. The Germans were on the move, and we followed them to the next village.

On the morning of Thanksgiving Day, I came off guard in a village we'd just taken and were about to be driven from. As the official history of the 106th Group says, "Thanksgiving night. It was rough. An entire fresh Panzer division, bold with new tanks and tactics, attacked at night, each tank surrounded by tough, experienced doughfeet. We gave ground, but we didn't give up. We lost first Eywiller, then Eschwiller and then Rauwiller. But with the help of fresh infantry, we stopped them there" (*The 106th Cavalry Group in Europe, 1944–45*, ed. Major Thomas J. Howard; Augsburg: J. P. Himmer, 1945, p. 73). I remember we got the shit beat out of us, but I don't remember the fresh infantry.

Anyhow, when I came off guard that morning, it was still pitch dark. We weren't yet sure the Germans were going to counterattack, but we could all tell from the sounds of their tanks in motion and from their heavy artillery fire that they had massed a lot of big stuff not far from us. Heavy trucks were moving, too. I walked back to the command post and heard that many in the platoon had already been fed Thanksgiving dinner, about which there'd been a lot of fanfare. With the others, I walked the half mile rearwards to a back slope, where the cooks had set up their kitchen. I hadn't looked forward to the promised meal at all—too much like a Last Supper—and I remember eating just one mouthful of meat and stuffing and cranberry jelly, and then drinking a cup of very hot coffee. I threw away the rest of the huge mound of food, which I'd tried to keep the cooks from serving me in the first place. But they wanted to get rid of it fast so they could clear out.

I walked back to the platoon, nervously waiting till my next turn in a forward hole. The Germans kept moving big stuff around. The metallic churning and grinding of heavy trucks and armor kept us on edge. We were sure they'd attack, especially after a barrage, which they'd send in every half hour or so, but nothing happened. It got to be afternoon, and there was still no attack. What the hell was going on? I guess Headquarters was asking the same question and decided to find out. About 4:00 P.M. a noncom came up to me and said, "I'm Sergeant Conroy, Pag-lee-arrow; you and Corporal Shinn and Edwards are going on patrol with me after dark. Be ready. I'll pick you up."

That was it. He gave me no exact time, and said nothing about where we'd go or what the mission was. I knew better than to ask. Headquarters had to learn what the Germans were up to, of course, but I didn't like the assignment. I didn't know a single one of the men I'd be going with. Besides, with the Germans moving a lot of machinery around, there was a good chance they'd chew us up. Knowing Conroy's orders would have helped me some. But there was nothing I could do but put up with my anxiety and wait.

Clewes saw me and asked, "What's wrong?"

"Uh, I'm feeling pretty tight about the patrol with Conroy," I told him.

"Tell Lynch. It's been done before. They take it like you ain't volunteering. They don't say you won't take an order."

"I don't know. I think I'll see what happens." Bad as I felt, I couldn't bring myself to beg off. So I waited out Conroy until about 10:00 P.M., when word came down that the patrol had been called off. Like the sergeant's original order, the change of plan was unexplained, but it seemed obvious that Headquarters knew we were about to be attacked.

Before the good news about the canceled patrol, while I was still waiting for Conroy, Roper and I had stood watch together. It was pitch dark. We were between two houses, looking in the direction of the Germans. Though we couldn't see much, we knew the ground sloped gently downwards away from us. Given the darkness and the noise, we were uneasy. We wouldn't be able to see or hear Germans on patrol until they were very close. Roper was never so tense. He was rigid with anticipation, holding his submachine gun in a position for quick use. I waited for his usual letdown and relaxation—the signal that things were okay. But he just stood there, tight and ready. Then I heard him grunt loud and fire a short burst, then another, then another.

A cursing voice in pain cried out from the darkness. There was shouting in German, and in a momentary silence, we heard men running away.

"Jesus, Roper, I couldn't see them."

"I smelled 'em," he said.

I kept my mouth shut. A short time later, my patrol was called off, and in less than thirty minutes after that, we sped out of town as German tanks began firing at our positions, lumbering toward us at the same time. I couldn't wait to get out of there, even though I'd wanted to check the ground where Roper hit the German next morning. I could still hear the sound of the wounded man's curse.

Our withdrawals were always complicated by our responsibility as a reconnaissance outfit to stay in touch with the enemy as he redeployed, so as to inform ourselves and, more especially, our comrades in the infantry and armored units of Corps. I was sent on more than a few patrols during the last two weeks of November. In fact, just about any movement we made in units no bigger than our troop—which was always light in numbers while I was there, and never totaled more than a hundred—might be regarded as a patrol. We probed ahead of the infantry, and we were small enough to be overrun easily, unless we had some support from Group's light armor and artillery, which was very seldom the case. Most often I went on really small patrols of four or five expendable men. These actions are wearing because you're made to stretch your luck to the breaking point. Before we ever set out on a small patrol, our outfit would already be isolated from a really large unit, like an infantry division, and we all felt vulnerable. To go on a patrol from there was to move even farther from help. The tension grew partly as a function of size and distance and time. How many of you were going? How far from a big outfit was your unit? How far from your unit would you travel? How long would you stay? Transportation was a concern, too. It was good to have vehicles along—an armored car for protection or a jeep for fast escape. But in fact I almost never went on a mounted patrol without having to get out and walk, to see what I could see. Finally a sense for the enemy—his position and strength—contributed to how we felt about a patrol. And yet, whatever sense we might have was the result of what we privates ourselves could hear or see or somehow deduce.

It was just like the Army not to forget that I'd been relieved of a tough assignment—the canceled night patrol with Conroy, Shinn, and Edwards. A few mornings after our hasty retreat from the German tanks, Lieutenant Lynch came up and said, "Pag-lee-arrow, you're going on patrol with Sergeant Conroy. Be ready in ten minutes."

Conroy showed up at the appointed time, with Shinn and Edwards in tow. We set out right away, without a word. It was the middle of a very cold morning. The weather was freezing. I suppose Conroy had been given more or less explicit orders. He may have shared them with Shinn, but he didn't tell me anything, and I don't suppose he told Edwards anything either. We spread out in a file, about thirty feet apart, sticking to the shoulder of a very straight dirt road that passed through a wide open valley. We could feel the hardness of the frozen ground underfoot. As we moved we took in the ground's natural contours, the trees, walls, hedgerows, and buildings, places that might hide the enemy. Nothing. After the first mile, the country was flat and barren, with no concealment. The feeble sun, which we saw dimly through a gray-clouded sky, was on our left oblique—we were moving roughly south. It was a bleak hike.

We walked about three miles along the straight road, seeing no signs of life. I don't think I even saw a bird. The world was cold, silent, and empty. Hardly a tree was in sight. We'd walked about as far as we ever did on a foot patrol. Much farther and we'd have had a lot of ground to cover if we got into trouble. Why hadn't we taken a jeep? A little over three miles out and the road we were on took a sharp turn away from a natural shallow declivity—probably a creek bed through which water had once run. We turned with the road, and soon saw a flat, dark gray village in the distance—maybe half a mile away. It was unlike any hamlet I'd seen in the Vosges. Conroy said nothing, and neither did we. We just kept walking. It seemed the village ahead of us was our objective.

The thought of exploring it a house at a time, almost four miles away from Squadron, with no vehicle for quick escape, left me feeling grim. This might be one of those patrols that provide Headquarters with the information it wants by not returning. Maybe that's why we had no jeep. We'd only lose it.

But we hadn't yet found out the worst of our predicament. It wasn't until we got within two hundred yards of the dark village that we saw a canal running perpendicular to the road we were traveling, and it ran between us and the village. As we got closer, I could see that it was not very wide, maybe forty feet, but it looked very dark and very cold, probably near the freezing point. When we got to the bank, there were the early signs of a freeze on the surface of the water. Beyond it stretched the dark, flat, quiet village. I thought this was as far as we'd have to go. We'd probably hang around the bank awhile, to see what we could see, and then head back. But I was wrong.

Sergeant Conroy said, "Pagalarrow, you and Edwards cross the canal and reconnoiter the village. The corporal and I'll cover you from here."

I couldn't believe he'd given the order. There was no time to think, but I knew I'd be crazy to obey. If I didn't get killed crossing or searching the town, I'd be soaked to the skin, and I'd freeze to death. I wasn't afraid. I wasn't angry. I wasn't in the least uncertain. I didn't hate the goddam sergeant. I wasn't worried about the future. I just knew in a hard rock way that I wasn't going to cross that freezing canal miles from nowhere.

Not more than a second after Conroy gave his order, I heard myself say, "Sergeant, I'm a better shot than you. Edwards and I'll cover you and the corporal. You cross."

He couldn't believe what he'd heard. I could hardly believe it myself, but I was past all doubt and questioning. I looked straight at Conroy. I'm sure my face wore nothing like an expression. But I could see his fear and incredulity plain as day. He exploded.

"You goddam chicken shit bastard!" he said in a trembling scream.

Then he walked through the pitiful consequences of his own command. Weighed down by his helmet and his loaded ammunition belt, holding his heavy M-1 rifle high over his head, he waded into the freezing canal of unknown depth until the water came up to his boot tops.

Then he whirled back abruptly, and walking madly towards us, said in a loud, hysterical voice, "There ain't no Germans in the town." The grin on his face was ghastly.

I have no idea what he reported on our return to Troop, but I doubt he told the truth. He probably covered me to cover himself. What could he have said to Lynch or the captain that would not have meant as much trouble for him as for me. Was there a conspiracy between officers and noncoms to treat privates as expendable? I don't think so, except in the sense that they gave us the dirtiest jobs to do. But as for excusing themselves from the obligation to behave courageously, no. I'm sure Lynch was brave, and I have no reason to believe Conroy wasn't. He could never have admitted to Lynch or the captain that he hadn't crossed the canal after I'd refused to do so, assuming he'd been told explicitly to get someone across to reconnoiter the village. And even if he hadn't been so ordered, he wouldn't have admitted to them that I'd refused his order, when he hadn't himself followed through by crossing.

Still, I couldn't be sure. I had taken a terrible risk in disobeying a direct order. Conroy was certainly pissed off with me, and he may well have found some way of doing me harm without giving himself away. But I've never regretted my decision. Crossing would have meant almost certain death. It would have meant drowning or freezing or being shot or taken prisoner while freezing. Wearing water-drenched clothing on a bitter day like that one, with no chance to dry off and get warm, is death. Sergeant

Conroy's slow imagination must have told him that when he began to execute his own order.

"There ain't no Germans in the town."

The following day we took a village without opposition, and for the next twenty-four hours we neither heard nor saw any signs of the Germans, an unusual state of affairs. With three other men, I had searched the farmhouse and barn at the far end of town from our unresisted point of entry. It was the house in which the Germans were most likely to have left a man or two to size us up before attempting to rejoin their outfit with the information. We started with the barn, part of which was the basement level of the house, and then went through the two upper floors of the house itself, room by room. It was nerve-racking. I happened to search the kitchen, directly above the lowest portion of the barn, where I was relieved to find an old woman at the sink, calmly peeling potatoes. Though her relaxed demeanor implied there were no Germans in the house, we continued our careful search, just to be sure. Having completed our job, we waved to the old woman and went down to the low section of the barn under the kitchen.

It was very cold, as it had been for some days. My bulky clothing had many irregular sharp edges of frozen mud, especially at the knees and pants bottoms, sleeves and cuffs. My bare hands were stiff and chapped. I wanted something hot to drink and to hold. This was the only time during my weeks on the lines that I wanted to make a cup of hot coffee, so I asked one of the men whether I could use his sterno heater. I never carried one. He nodded. I stood partway up from a crouch to reach the heater at the same time that he got up to hand it to me. We jostled each other slightly, and my rifle, propped butt-down between my knees, went off. It made a tremendous noise in the enclosed space. I had carelessly left off the safety after the house search, and as near as I can figure out, one of the hard edges of my clothing had penetrated the trigger guard when the other man and I collided.

"My God! The old woman upstairs! Maybe I hit her!"

I doubt it took four seconds after the shot to reach the kitchen, where I found her transfixed—her back to the sink, her palms at shoulder height, facing outwards, and her mouth and eyes wide open.

I said, "Mama" (she was at least thirty years older than my mother), and I hugged her. "Thank God I didn't hit you."

Her body relaxed in my arms, and she began to cry and laugh. The three men came up to see what had happened but left when they saw she was okay. I stayed with the woman for about fifteen minutes, waiting for her to calm down. During that time I tried to get her to understand that the shot was an accident. If she didn't understand my explanation, which was more in sign language than in French, at least she understood I was sorry for what happened. I went downstairs feeling like a damn fool but deeply relieved that she was all right.

Apart from that bizarre violence, things remained quiet in the village. Those of us on the line would have been happy to leave things as they were, knowing the enemy would quickly enough stir things up again, but Headquarters must have thought we needed to relocate the Germans. So next morning our troop moved out again. After hours of riding, we rumbled into a small village in the late afternoon. Located halfway up a low ridge, it comprised only one row of houses, all built on the same side of its single street. They were on our left as we entered. The street was no more than a hundred yards long. Falling away from the back of the houses, which faced the street, was an expanse of meadowland, a gently sloping valley leading to the next ridge over a thousand yards away. As the jeep I rode in came to the middle of the village, we drew fire from two burp guns. It came from a German vehicle that had been concealed behind some bushes growing between two houses. None of us was hit, though we could hear the bullets whistling. By the time we saw the enemy's car, it was flying across the meadow, headed for the far ridge. Our jeep swerved left to give the machine gunner—who was Roper—a last chance to hit the fleeing Germans. But it was too late. He missed, and we made no attempt to follow.

There had been a lot of noise for a few minutes. It must have sounded even louder indoors. An hysterical woman came out of one of the two houses between which the firing had occurred. It soon became clear that she was not frightened for herself, but for her husband, who had been caught outside, at the back of the house. Maybe he'd been working there, or maybe he was back there to help the Germans somehow, willingly or not. Or maybe he was a hostage, held to keep his wife or some other villager from warning us of the German car. Whatever the case, she was sure he'd been hit, and she cried his name in misery, over and over—"Robert! Robert! Robert! Robert!"

She wailed the name in German, without sounding the final "t." Weeping and groaning, she called for him. The tears fell down her cheeks and into her twisted mouth. Her anxiety ended a few minutes later, when Robert appeared, looking very frightened. She shrieked her deep relief, clasped him to her, and then began chanting his name over and over. It was not a pleasant scene. He must have had a close call in the exchange of fire. God knows what it sounded like to her, just a few feet away inside the house. Robert disengaged himself from his wife and looked at Roper and me. He must have been afraid we'd accuse him of helping the Germans, but we had nothing to go on, not even a strong suspicion. Robert spoke briefly to his wife, and then they went inside.

The lieutenant posted Roper and me near their house and told us what hours to stand guard during the night. Robert, who must have seen us there, came out to invite us in for supper. He still looked very frightened, probably concerned for his wife and family in case we had it in our heads that he shouldn't have been out there with the Germans when we took the village. He was one of the very few men under fifty years of age I'd seen since I got to France. I suppose he was a farmer who was most useful to the Germans in the fields. Or maybe he was ill. Or maybe he was working for the enemy. Anyhow we accepted his invitation. Suspicious of his fright, I sat down with my helmet on and my rifle between my legs. (I made sure the safety was locked.)

Roper gently reprimanded me, saying, "He ain't dangerous, just scared to death. Probably never been shot at before. And he's got his wife."

So I took off my helmet and leaned my rifle against a nearby wall. Robert and his wife smiled a stiff smile, but they were still very nervous.

The meal was an ordeal for them. They wanted to assure us that Robert had not cooperated with the Germans, and they weren't sure how well they were doing. Robert was so red and taut with anxiety that his face looked skinned. And his wife, Helga, a frenzy of motion, moved back and forth between the kitchen and the dining room table, complying with her husband's shouted orders. She brought us a large platter that held a thick bottom layer of home fried potatoes, covered with a layer of cooked-to-brown fresh sausage, topped by a layer of hot, crisp sauerkraut. I didn't relax—Roper did—but for the first time in weeks, I ate a full meal. The food on the platter was good, and so were the cider and bread. I was pulled between Roper's ease and the couple's distraction. But their fright was dominant. It never lessened as they made tense efforts to please us. Eating little himself, Robert encouraged his wife to run back and forth, and she hurried anxiously to do so.

"Helga, bringe das Brot!"

She reached into the oven and brought us hot bread. Their raw fear was awful to see. I got out of the house as soon as I could.

Headquarters must have gotten information about where the Germans were gathered. At least the day after we took the village Helga and Robert lived in, the troop was ordered to mount, and we headed roughly northeast. We traveled quickly through several places recently vacated by the Germans. They almost always left a single soldier with a bicycle, or two or three in a car, who stayed long enough to make a count and then tried to get away. In some of these villages, the civilians were not as friendly as they had been. They never tried to resist us, but they were not at all welcoming, and in one town some of the young women walked ostentatiously up and down the main street after we rode in, pretending to be enjoying each other's conversation as if we weren't there. Meanwhile a voice in German gave instructions to the townspeople through a loudspeaker. Even though I could pick up only an occasional word, it was obvious that the message was Authority's Directive to the Populace.

For some reason it was there, in the early afternoon, that I thought about a Christmas card to mail home. Clewes had one to spare, but I didn't write on it then because I got orders to join a group of two jeeps and an armored car to go on patrol. Lynch was leading, but Roper and Clewes weren't included. I tucked the blank card in my pack.

We left the German town almost immediately, heading northeast. Our little unit moved over a good road for about two hours, covering maybe thirty miles, and then we passed swiftly through a dead-quiet village, hoping against hope that it was empty. It was. At least we saw nothing and we drew no fire as we zipped along. It's hard on the imagination to drive toward the enemy, looking, when you can't see what might be concealed behind a stone wall or in the woods or beyond a rise in the ground. And it's hard to listen for sounds that might clue you when your own vehicles are grinding right in your ears. But we covered miles of road, doing our best. We saw nothing. The world seemed very quiet except for the noise of our own little convoy.

It was late in the afternoon when we came to the open gates of a private park and manor house. After pausing for a couple of minutes at the entrance to the property, Lynch ordered us to move up to the house, where we stopped and got out. It was a large residence—four times the size of our house in New York—and its architecture was spare. The outside walls were sand-colored, made of flat, unpolished granite. You could tell the walls were thick because the window openings were filled with unusually deep-set steel casements. The main door, also set deep, was a simple but massive combination of glass and steel. The whole structure was modern looking.

Four of us were ordered to search the house, which we did with as much care as possible. It was empty. There were neither soldiers nor civilians in it. After we were sure it was safe, we looked around to satisfy our curiosity. Fresh scrapes in the wooden floors suggested that furniture had been recently removed in haste. How had they managed that in the middle of a war? We decided the people who lived in the house were important Germans we'd been sent to capture. Obviously we arrived too late.

We were fascinated by the place. Despite its size, the house didn't have many rooms. They were all large, with high ceilings and big windows. I was surprised by the simple richness of everything I saw—glass, wood, brushed steel. Apart from this strong general impression, I was struck by the huge bathroom on the upper floor. It was finished in tan and pink marble, simply mounted, without ornament. The sink and tub seemed immense, and so did the shower stall, which had a heavy glass and stainless steel door. The fixtures—spigots, taps, radiators, towel and clothes racks—were plain and massive, and lots of cylindrical lighting fixtures were sunk in the ceiling. The quiet opulence of the place, unexpected as it was, made for a dazing contrast to the cold squalor of our recent lives. It was also a dream-like ending to the long anxious ride through the enemy countryside. My sense of reality was out of balance. But it was to be really blown away during the next stage of the patrol.

Lynch ended our moment of relaxation with the order to mount up. We didn't know it at the time, but our trio of vehicles was about to be divided. We rode together slowly for a few miles, continuing to increase the distance between us and Squadron. I didn't like what we were doing at all. And of course the lieutenant said nothing about our mission. Body and mind, we were his to do with as he decided. I hated being kept in the dark. The weather was clear, and though the sun hadn't set, it was hanging low in the autumn sky. We'd start to lose light pretty soon. I wanted to be somewhere safe before night fell.

While the sun was still above the horizon, our vehicles stopped at an intersection of roads. I was ordered to leave the jeep and find room in the armored car, which already held three men. I recognized T-5 Lane, who was put in charge even though his stripes gave him no official authority—they were only the technical rating of a radioman. I didn't really know him, except by sight. But he was the only one I knew even that well. While I was still lowering myself into the car through the turret, I saw the jeeps go off in one direction, while we went in another. I wanted more than ever to know what was happening, but Lane was a clam, like all the other noncoms except Clewes. Even when I was inside the car, I could tell it continued to move in the direction we'd followed earlier, northeast. I'd already seen the jeeps take the road that headed west, maybe to continue the patrol, maybe to begin the southwest swing back to Squadron.

The armored car kept moving slowly in a more or less northeasterly direction, stopping every mile or so to radio Headquarters, give our position, and receive orders. It wasn't long before dusk began to close in. We were told by radio to go to a hill not very far ahead of us and to report on whatever we heard and saw. For the first of only two times while I was in action, I actually heard instructions from Headquarters. But what I learned hardly gave me the big picture. They weren't about to let us know that. In fact, the unexplained instructions, given almost moment by moment, increased my sense that I was being used impersonally, even indifferently, without being given the ghost of a chance to feel myself part of the mission. They would have improved morale by telling us more than they did, without giving away secret information

By the time we reached our destination—a low, bald hill, maybe forty feet above the surrounding land, with a flat crest about half the size of a football field—it was almost dark. Lane told me to get out and stand guard. That was all he said. He didn't say how long we'd be on the hill. Maybe he didn't know himself. I wondered why I'd been sent outside. Probably to see what I could see, free of the car, while those inside were busy with the equipment—radios, 37 mm gun, and turret-mounted machine gun. I stopped thinking about it. I thought we'd be leaving in a few minutes, so like a damn fool, I didn't dig in. I just stood a little to the left and ahead of the vehicle, which was near the southwest edge of the flat crest of the low hill, and I faced in the direction we'd been headed when we stopped.

The early part of the night was quiet. I strained to see and hear, but there was nothing. At first I felt only temporarily separated from the armored car, which afforded fairly good protection against most kinds of firepower. I thought I'd be getting back in soon. From time to time I heard Lane talking to Headquarters, but not distinctly enough to understand what he said. After a while I began to wonder when we'd be pulling back. Up there on the hill, we couldn't see or hear anything worth reporting, and moving ahead in the dark was hardly safe. But time passed and nothing happened except for the intermittent conversations between Lane and Headquarters, which I couldn't make out.

When I'd spent about an hour outside the armored car, a man climbed out and stood with me for ten minutes.

"See anything?" he asked, looking as far as he could into the night.

"Nothing," I answered.

"You sure?" he asked, nervous and annoyed, as if I might be holding out on him.

"Yeah, I'm sure. See for yourself," I told him, irritated. He could climb into the armored car whenever he was ready.

He heard nothing and saw nothing. Then he went back into the car. As soon as he left, I began to feel really alone and exposed for the first time. I didn't care anything about his company. It was just that I began to realize we might be on the hill for a while yet. The man from the car must have wanted to pull back as much as I did. He was just hoping I'd be able to report something Lane could give Headquarters so they'd be satisfied and give us the order to withdraw. But that's not the way it happened. I waited hours in the dark, straining to see and hear. During that time, it should have occurred to me to dig in. It was not like me to forget such a basic thing. But for some reason I didn't do what I should have done—what I had always done.

Toward midnight things began to change. I thought I heard the sound of vehicles far away, so I walked the two or three steps to the armored car to let them know, telling them I wasn't positive. By the time I turned around, the sounds were distinct. I listened for a full minute. What I heard suggested a long convoy, including armor, passing within a thousand yards of us at the closest. I returned to our car to report, but by that time Lane and the others had heard, too.

"Yeah, we hear it. We're calling Headquarters. But we're ready to fire canister from the 37 and use the machine gun."

Our weapons would be effective only against personnel, not armor. It would be damn foolish to fire on the convoy with what we had.

"God, I hope Headquarters knows what it needs to know, so we can pull out," I prayed.

Just then a burp gun fired at us from maybe five hundred yards. I hit the ground right away and tried to sight something I could shoot at, but there was no target. It wasn't twenty seconds before our 37 fired in the direction of the burp gun's burst. A German patrol flanking the convoy had moved between us and their vehicles, probing to test our strength and warning us off at the same time. At this point I moved for better cover from the side of the car to its rear, where I could still look forward.

Within a minute of the small arms fire, my breath was taken away by the screaming whirl and concussion of about six heavy artillery shells landing no more than two hundred feet ahead of me, just beyond the forward ridge. I couldn't tell where they were coming from, but my first assumption was that the Germans had withdrawn their personnel and were directing a pattern of fire up the hill. When another clutch of big shells landed as close as the first, my guess seemed to be confirmed. The Germans must have overestimated our strength or else they just weren't taking any chances.

In the silence that followed the artillery fire, I heard T-5 Lane at the radio, in a strangely loud exchange with Headquarters. The voices at both ends were excited. Back and forth they went, with Lane asking questions and somebody shouting answers that Lane seemed unable to accept.

All I could make out was Lane saying, "It's landing two hundred feet from us, Sir, two hundred feet!"

Then the voice from Headquarters would say something I couldn't understand, except the tail end. "Stick it out. Stick it out."

When the radio conversation ended, I heard Lane gabbing with the others in the armored car. Why were they making so much noise? What the hell was going on?

Finally a voice from our armored car, sounding a little crazy, shouted down to me, "Colonel Nelson himself called to tell us not to worry about the artillery because it's ours."

The message was a grim joke. A hair's breadth of deviation, and our artillery might wipe away the crest of the hill and us with it, armored car and all. They must have been lobbing the stuff very high, or we'd have been able to tell where it was coming from. More shells came in, this time much closer to the convoy than to us. Then the pattern changed again, and shells landed much too near us, on the far side of the hill's crest. Was our artillery trying to hit the convoy or to save us from patrolling Germans or both? It was obvious by this time that we were not going to be pulled back. Headquarters wanted us out there to keep tabs on what the convoy did, crude as our information would have to be. Would it keep moving? Would it deploy? Meanwhile our shells kept pounding in increasingly dense clusters. Group didn't have that much firepower. Corps had added some of its guns to ours. They were dead serious about getting the German vehicles. Lane was on the radio again, but nothing changed.

Between our barrages, the Germans sporadically fired burp guns and rifles. I lay prone, behind the armored car, perhaps foolishly expecting they would miss me. Our machine gun and canister answered. But neither the Germans' small arms nor our answers seemed like much. It was the artillery that got to me. It kept telling me that we'd been ordered to take up a madly isolated position, barely tenable, and then so only if our big guns kept threatening any Germans who might come close enough to try to take the hill, which is to say, kept firing as close to us as to them. I wondered when the enemy would direct artillery at us, but they never did. Their aim must have been to relocate their armor as quickly as possible, so they had to keep it moving to minimize its exposure to our heavy fire. Meanwhile, our guns kept pouring it in, the shells sometimes bursting a thousand yards away, but just as often dangerously near. I couldn't believe we were being shaved so close. I was tense with fear as shell fragments ricocheted off our car. I ducked low and stayed low. The dense firing lasted for hours, and it wore me down. Over time, artillery batters the commonplace assurance that sustains us. With the shattered air and ground, the soul is shattered, too.

Time wore on, torn by shell bursts, and when dawn was still two hours away, I was at the edge of the world, feeling unconnected from anything I knew. I had shut down the capacity to feel. Any shot from a German rifle would have killed me as dead as a shell could have done. But I paid no attention to small arms. And toward first light, our heavy barrages became only the repetition of what I'd already survived. I was numb by then. But somewhere along the way I began to believe that each repetition was preordained to include my survival. My mind was blank and my spirit wrung. I lay on the ground behind an armored car on a low hill somewhere in northeastern Alsace, where I had no business.

Then somehow I was back in the armored car. Somebody must have told me to return. We had completed our withdrawal from the hill before I began thinking straight. We left very early in the morning, before the light was full. The ride back to the outfit is a blank. The troop reassembled that same day. All patrols were in. Lynch said something about the next part of the campaign with a mad grin I couldn't read. I thought about the modern German house with its huge rooms and great marble bath, the crossroads where we'd stopped our little caravan so we could divide the jeeps from the armored car, the crashing nightmare on the bald hill. I was still a little dizzy.

On the following day, we were to attack Erckartswiller for the first time. Before we pulled out to start the job, I wrote a lackluster holiday message home, using the Christmas card I got from Clewes and packed away some days before. The simple design on the otherwise blank card is made up of a green wreath decorated with red berries in the upper left-hand corner. A wide ribbon, represented by two parallel wavy red lines, passes through the wreath and runs down the left side and across the top. The illustration is completed by two large bells, outlined in red, which hang from the wreath. The reverse says, "Merry Christmas and A Happy New Year, 121st Cavalry."

November 29, 1944

Dear Folks,

I hope this reaches you in time, but if not it won't miss by very many days.

I wrote a letter several days ago, but so far I have not been able to mail it. Probably you'll get both together.

Have a Merry Christmas and also have a drink on me.

Love,
Harry

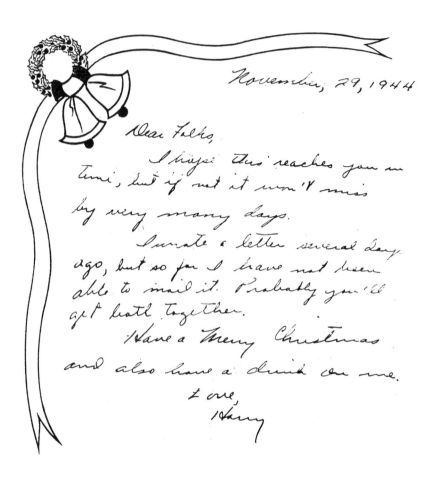

November, 29, 1944

Dear Folks,

I hope this reaches you in time, but if not it won't miss by very many days.

I wrote a letter several days ago, but so far I have not been able to mail it. Probably you'll get both together.

Have a Merry Christmas and also have a drink on me.

Love,
Harry

Christmas card sent home by author in 1944

Erckartswiller, a Tough Road Home

AS WE MOUNTED FOR the move to Erckartswiller on November 30, Lynch said more about what we faced than he'd ever said before.

"We're going for bear!"

I didn't know what to make of his statement, which he spoke with a funny strained grin. It was the same grin he'd worn the day before, just after my return to Troop from the mad night on the hill. He must have known something then. Maybe our officers had been told we'd be going after an entrenched enemy. That German convoy's movement I'd heard all night outside the armored car could have had something to do with it. Maybe the Germans were defending access to the convoy's route and we were being sent to break through. But why not send for Armor or Infantry instead of calling on eighty-five reconnaissance men to make the attack? I wanted more answers than I had.

On the morning of November 30, we approached Erckartswiller in a small motorized convoy, very slowly descending a forested mountain road. I was again assigned to the armored car, which was the second vehicle, right behind the lead jeep. T-5 Lane's face and fingers worked tensely, as he kept us in radio contact with Headquarters during our descent. He had been on the patrol to Saarbrucken, where the mother and daughter-in-law had served us dinner and coffee with the meal, and on the patrol to the bald hill where we were almost killed by friendly fire. "Friendly fire!" He was visibly nervous. As radioman, he probably found out more than the rest of us about "going after bear." I listened as he spoke to Headquarters in a breathless voice, trying to understand what we were up to. But his end of the conversation was little more than a series of confirmations.

"Yes, Sir, that's right, Sir. Maybe one thousand yards. No, Sir, I can't tell. Yes, Sir, we will, Sir."

Then we'd descend another two hundred feet, and Lane would engage in another dense conversation that told the rest of us nothing. Still, it was clear that Headquarters wanted him to report often. They'd want to know if one of our vehicles hit a mine and blocked the road, which was too narrow for passing. The lead jeep and even our armored car might pass over, or pass by, a mine without detonating it. It would depend on how the Germans had set it. Our heaviest vehicles, two light tanks and two assault guns from Group, were most likely to explode one. Headquarters would also want to know if we met resistance from German armor, or if we were fired at by antitank guns. So the armored car paused often, coming down the mountain in stages. And the jeep ahead stopped and started when we did. All of us were tense, like Lane, who spoke in taut, breathless undertones. Between calls, he'd look around at us, and then he'd fidget with his equipment until the car stopped again for a conversation with Headquarters.

Once, between calls, when we were pretty far down the mountain, he looked straight at me and said with some annoyance, "You'd like to know what's going on."

I didn't know what to say. He hadn't asked a question. The tone of his voice told me he'd made an accusation. But there was no need to answer. Lane finished the conversation himself.

"You haven't been in combat long enough to be nervous."

It was a nasty thing to say. He had a right to be nervous, but I didn't. In a way he was right. He'd been in it since Saint-Lô, and I'm sure he'd seen a lot. But if you begin your days in combat with the clear sense that you're not immortal, it doesn't take long to realize that war can kill you. Besides, had he forgotten I was the one who spent the night outside the armored car? Lane didn't say anything else, and I kept my mouth shut. He just didn't like to have the rest of us seeing him as tense as he was, prickly as a trapped cat. The night on the hill had frazzled him too. Anyhow, it was time for another call to Headquarters. We were very near the bottom of the mountain.

While Lane did his job, we listened for the sounds of German armor. All of us shared the heavy sense that we faced a formidable enemy. But we knew nothing else. I don't think Lane knew much either. There were so many questions. Would we attack in our vehicles? And just what would we be attacking? A village? A perimeter of dug-in men supported by heavy armor? A wooded mountain slope? We could only wait to find out by doing the job.

After what seemed an interminable conversation, which turned out to be the last, the car started to move again, and though we moved slowly, we soon came to the bottom of the mountain. We turned right, heading north, through a man-made clearing in the forested lowland, following a straight dirt road that was rutted, maybe by tree-cutting equipment. We could see felled trees that had not yet been trucked away, and the landscape was dotted with fresh stumps only a foot or two high. As we drove, we kept the mountain we had come from to our right and then to our right rear, moving just about parallel to its crest line. After traveling about half a mile, the convoy stopped. We parked the jeeps and armored cars near some trees for partial conceal-ment, and the troop commander left two men in charge of them. The rest of us, on foot, followed the two tanks moving in the same direction as the rutted dirt road, but we fanned out over the cleared land to our left. Our two assault guns came behind us.

We walked about two-thirds of a mile farther north. Though we didn't know it at the time, we were approaching Erkkartswiller, a small village we never saw, hidden as it was behind two or three hundred yards of dense forest. And we didn't learn the name of the place until the next day. As soon as we stopped, we dug our holes in a circle with a diameter of about fifty yards. The rear of the perimeter was not quite closed. The assault guns were located inside the perimeter, and the tanks flanked the forward holes, those closest to the village. To our right rear we could still see some of the mountain we had descended.

The woods between us and the village were dense enough that we could not expect to have tank support when we attacked. In fact, the woods ahead of us were contiguous with the woods to our left and right. It was only to the rear of the clearing we occupied that the trees were thin. Within our perimeter there were many fresh tree stumps and recently felled trees.

I felt lucky to be with Roper again. We dug in together near the tank on the perimeter's left. Our hole was at its forward edge. Shortly after we'd prepared these modest defenses, the Germans sent in some shells, not many, maybe eight. We dived into our holes and waited out the barrage. Then we began to move around again. By this time it was early afternoon. The day was bright and clear, as were all three of our days outside Erckartswiller, and it wasn't very cold, for a change. Though anxiety made pleasure in the good weather impossible, the mild brightness helped to make things better than they would otherwise have been. I wasn't exactly looking on the bright side of things. And I hadn't suddenly become resigned to my predicament. It's just that for a fleeting instant my fear let up, and I saw the clear sky. It seemed too peaceful for a battlefield. But right then and there my attention was taken elsewhere. Lynch stood on a stump near his hole. We could all see him. Our whole platoon was on the forward side of the perimeter. What the hell was he doing, standing up like that? Officers in the field make a habit of being inconspicuous so they're not picked off by a sniper.

"Men, get ready to attack. Five minutes. We have the honor, we'll lead the way. Keep an eye on me. Let's get 'em."

In five minutes, our platoon began to move toward Erkkartswiller, somewhere in the woods, the place we couldn't see. As Lynch signaled, we spread out, covering a span of about a hundred feet, and then we walked forward over the remaining fifty yards or so of the clearing and into the woods, the way to the unknown village. We moved ahead with the reluctance of men stalking a deadly unknown. The forest was dense with trees and low growth. There were no paths I could see. Trees and underbrush made direct forward motion hard, but we managed to keep roughly abreast of each other. We penetrated about one hundred fifty feet into the woods, and then we paused. Lynch had slowed down to take stock of things, and the rest of us followed suit. It was very quiet. No birdsong. Only the dark silent forest. There was nothing to take stock of. Was there really a village ahead of us? We moved forward again.

Then all hell broke loose. Rounds from rifles, machine guns, mortars, and 88s came flying at us in the most dense fire we'd experienced since I joined the outfit. It turned out to be the most dense fire the troop had ever experienced. We couldn't see the enemy or any origin of enemy fire, but we could tell it was coming from ahead of us over so wide a band that our strung-out line was catching it from the left and right oblique as well as from the center. All we could do was hit the ground and stay low. Some of the 88s were coming at us in direct fire rather than in a lofted trajectory, but the outcome could be devastating either way. The woods were so thick that most of the shells—mortar shells included—were bursting against the trees before they could hit the ground, their fragments twisting in all directions, often coming down at us from quite a height. It was obvious that we couldn't make headway except at great cost—deadly cost—so we were relieved to get the order to crawl back. We turned around and slithered low, moving fast as hell until we got to the clearing. The German fire stopped. Miraculously, no one was wounded in the first attack. The lieutenant had got us out of the woods fast.

Like all the others, Roper and I went back to our hole, expecting the enemy to follow up its advantage with a counterattack. To judge from their firepower, they could have overrun our defense perimeter with little trouble. We waited tense with expectation for a long time. Nothing happened. Gradually we let down some, thinking they might wait until dusk to move against us. That would be in less than two hours. I needed something to do, so I opened up some K rations. I ate the cheese and then left the hole to get a drink of water. When I got back, I opened the packet of three cigarettes that came with the meal. I barely noticed that the olive drab color of the box was unusually dark, and the wax unusually heavy. But I became conscious of the odd packaging when I opened the little cigarette container, which was also unusually dark and heavy. Inside were the most delicious cigarettes I've ever smoked—Old Golds—moist, full-bodied, satisfying. They must have been packed sometime before, when cigarettes were still being made of tobacco without additives. I gave one to Roper, with my strongest endorsement. He took it without enthusiasm.

"You'd enjoy smoking shit after the blitz we been through."

But he took the cigarette and lit up, dragging deep. "Jesus, this is good. Where'd you get it?"

I showed him the package. He nodded and then lost interest, but he smoked the cigarette down until he couldn't hold it anymore.

I was thinking, "Roper never calls me by my name. Neither does Clewes. Too hard. But they could call me Harry. What the hell difference does it make? What difference?"

Something in the air made us guess we'd be attacking again the next day, probably the attitude of the officers. We hoped another platoon would be taking the lead. We didn't like the idea of repeating the suicide mission, and it was reasonable to believe we would not have to go in first twice in a row. Even so, unless Headquarters realized the enemy's strength, we'd all be in trouble. It would take many times what we had to cope with the Germans. Why couldn't we just keep them occupied? Why did we have to try to take them out, a clear impossibility? But maybe we were wrong. Lynch had withdrawn us without wasting a second. Surely he'd reported to Troop the resistance we met, and surely the word had been sent up the line. Maybe from here on in, we'd just keep the Germans busy, without risking an all-out attack.

Shortly after Roper and I finished our cigarettes, our assault guns began to fire. Our artillery wasn't nearly powerful enough to overcome the German advantage, but it could keep them busy for a while. Maybe Headquarters had seen the light. Maybe we wouldn't be ordered to attack again. I looked behind me, into the perimeter, where our two guns were blasting away, and I saw a major I'd never seen before commanding the fire. I suppose he'd just been driven to our position, probably from Group Head-quarters. He was a short, round man, at least fifty-five years old. I'd never seen anyone nearly so old in the field. He wore neither helmet nor hat, so I could see his white curly hair. Between rounds, he bounced on his toes, his belly shook, his head jerked, and his arms flailed passionately. He was scolding the lieutenant in charge of the guns. I could imagine him saying, "Goddammit, Son, what the hell's wrong with you? You gotta keep them fuckin' guns firing until they're red hot. Let's blast the hell out of the fuckin' Krauts. Let's flatten them before the next attack. Watch me. See what I mean?"

Whatever the major said, he disapproved of the lieutenant and he kept the guns firing, obviously enjoying himself. He just knew our two guns could blow the Germans away. But after all that show, he didn't stay long, only fifteen minutes. The ridiculous old bastard just wanted to kibitz a little. Then he drove off like an impatient boy, looking for a war he liked better.

I kept expecting the Germans to answer our fire, but they sent in only one shell. They were mocking our puny assault guns. But that one shot turned out to be nasty. It came in at the tank flanking our left, a random shot fired in our general direction. It scored a near kill on the tank, which was positioned close to a tree at the edge of the woods. Our hole—Roper's and mine—was the nearest one to the tank, and I heard and saw what happened. A young member of the crew, only a year or two older than I, had been sitting on the edge of the turret, his body completely out of the tank. I heard the shell's scream and burst as one long, fierce, angry sound. At the same time, I saw the young tankman's body arch up several feet above the turret before he dropped on my side of the tank and landed neck first on the ground. He sprang up instantly, making a hideous noise—an aborted hoarse roar of fright and denial. It was a long grating sound that seemed to come up from his stomach. His legs did a weak, crazy dance, and he tried to return to a stable position, but the world wouldn't stand still for him. He kept gyrating and wobbling, frustrated. And then he extended his arms, with his palms facing the sky, as if begging for help. But he made no sound after that one hoarse roar. His face was dead white. He was still in one piece, but he'd been torn apart forever. I felt for him, shaken as I'd been by the explosion of the big shell so near our hole, and so did Roper.

"Jesus Christ," he said compassionately as he watched the reeling man. Nothing else. There was nothing else to say.

Sound and concussion left me trembling, with its roaring aftermath reverberating in my ears and brain. I was just gathering myself to help when an officer and a noncom from the far side of the perimeter grabbed the young tankman and tried to calm him as they moved him to the rear to be evacuated. Later, we heard from the jeep driver who took him to the medics that he wasn't hit, but he had internal injuries. We could see from the scarred bark that the shell had hit the tree near his tank a deep glancing blow. It was a miracle that no fragment got him. In fact the whole shell itself must have missed him only by inches. It was the sound and concussion that had sent him flying into a terrible state of mind, and maybe tore up his insides. Artillery is cruel.

The night was quiet. We kept expecting an attack or at least a probing patrol, but there was nothing, and no mortars or 88s either. The silence itself was deadly. I don't know how we managed to sleep, but when it wasn't our turn to watch, we went under. It was a dark escape. I slept lightly, but I slept, my mind half free of the dangerous place, and yet wondering in a dream-trance how we'd get out of this one. Even though I was outside the armored car all alone, the night on the bald hill seemed less risky. Tomorrow we were going into the woods again, toward Erckartswiller, the mysterious place we couldn't get close enough to see. No, the higher-ups would call off the attack. But that round major who took over our assault guns, the old guy with the white curly hair and the hostile, flailing arms, was just the kind of nut who'd tell the colonel we could take Erckartswiller without infantry or armor.

The morning dawned clear. We were tense as hell, waiting to hear some definite word. We didn't wait long. The lieutenant stood next to his tree stump, looking around for our attention. Why didn't he stand on it, the way he did yesterday? We watched and listened.

"Men, we go in ten minutes. The light'll be good then. Third platoon will lead. But the whole troop goes today. Okay."

Our first attack should have told Headquarters that the Germans would cut us to pieces, but they didn't get the message. They were in love with Erckartswiller, and they wanted us to give it to them. Crazy. Where was the infantry? Where was the armor? Where was the white-haired major? We knew the big boys were sending us in to do an impossible job. We'd be chewed up.

Again the sky seemed too tranquil for war. And again, the woods were silent and dark. The lead platoon penetrated beyond the point to which we'd gone the day before, and it drew no fire. Our platoon was right behind them, walking through the underbrush, looking for big old trees to fall behind when the firing began. It would have been better yet if we could have found a clearing with a natural declivity in it. That would've helped to keep us clear of shell bursts from trees above, and it would have protected us from small arms fire at the same time. But there were few such places in the forest. We kept walking, but the Germans still didn't fire. We knew they weren't asleep. They were waiting to get us far into the woods, where retreat would be costly. But they began to fire a little sooner than they should have to cut us off.

As soon as they opened up, we were pinned, just like the day before. But we were farther into the woods, so the way back was longer. And we did not get the order to withdraw, at least not right away. The Germans threw even more stuff at us than they had in the first attack. They added heavy artillery and depressed flak guns to the mortars and 88s, and the small arms fire was murderous, this time coming at us from the right flank as well as from the obliques and the center. We could pretty well stay under the rifle and machine-gun fire. But the tree bursts of artillery shells sent screaming hot steel fragments down on us. We were badly exposed. There was no real cover to protect us from this fire from above, except for branches that might deflect the flying steel—deflect it for better or for worse.

Our position was impossible. Tactically speaking, no act of courage by us would have made the least difference in the outcome. The German small arms fire alone was many times the strength of ours, and in fact we didn't even shoot back at them. They had obviously cleared fields of fire on their side of the woods, in anticipation of our advance, and though most of their bullets must have been stopped by trees more or less near us, many others flew clear paths to our positions. By contrast our fire would have been stopped by the forest before penetrating very far. Unless we got a lot closer to them, we'd have only trees to shoot at, and getting closer meant taking more and more artillery fire. Things were bad. We were all scared, hoping to hear the command to pull back and thinking we'd get it before the order was given. But after about twenty minutes, Troop ordered us to withdraw. Our penetration into the woods, though somewhat deeper than it had been on the first try, was negligible. We turned around for the second time and crawled back as fast as we could. Crawling a couple of hundred yards under heavy small arms fire, with artillery bursting around and overhead, is a scary, painful business, but we had the incentive of escape. We got out fast. And we were lucky two days in a row. Even the lead platoon lost only six men.

We went back to our holes depressed, but with the beginnings of a real hope that our situation might now be reappraised. It was obvious that we needed more power than we had to overcome the enemy, entrenched and equipped as he was. Maybe Group Headquarters would call Corps for help. If there was ever a time when we needed to know what was happening, this was it. It is beyond reason to order men into the face of impenetrable fire without telling them why the action is necessary. We didn't know anything. What the hell was Erckartswiller? Why were they sending a thinned-out cavalry troop to do the work of a regiment supported by armor? The men were saying top brass was on a glory trip with our bodies, especially the group commander, Colonel Nelson, the guy with the hand grenades strapped to his chest. But we didn't know anything and no one explained.

Soon after we got back from the second attack, the Germans began sending in the heavy artillery they'd begun to use against us in the woods. As soon as the first shells landed, we jumped into our holes.

"Where are you all running?" Lynch shouted. I peeped out at him in disbelief. He was wearing that goddam dumb grin.

And he was sitting straight-backed, on his tree stump, his legs crossed. He grinned and grinned. The shells kept coming in, and they landed close. But he sat and grinned. After a long minute or two, he rose and walked slowly, ramrod-erect, to his foxhole. For the first time, I began to wonder about his sanity, though not very clearly. There was danger enough. He didn't have to take crazy chances. We weren't impressed. I can't believe he meant to show us there was nothing to worry about or to give us a model of courage. If that was his aim, he failed. The lieutenant thought he was invulnerable. That's what his smart-ass grin said. "Death can't touch me."

I hated his guts then, and I wasn't alone.

Roper spoke for me when he said, "The goddam dumb son of a bitch."

The heavy stuff kept coming in. Some shells landed so close that we were badly shaken. Earth fell into the hole. I found myself nibbling mud. They had so much stuff it seemed they could score direct hits on every one of us. As usual when the going was bad, my breath drew shallow. I don't think I'd have broken down, but I was glad Roper was with me. As usual in a time of danger, he was worried, but in good control. I took advantage of his strong presence.

"I can't take much more of this shit," I told him.

He looked at me sternly, dug long fingers into my shoulder, and said, "Course you can. You have to."

That was all there was to it, but I needed his comforting command. It also helped that the bombardment soon ended. As usual, I filled the sudden quiet with imagined sounds. My mind's ear heard echoes of the recent shattering. And yet I quickly put the terrible barrage out of my mind. But the tranquil sky gave no comfort. I waited numb for the next mad act.

In midafternoon, a noncom told me to report to the lieutenant. I walked over to him right away, having seen him reclaim his seat on the tree stump he'd left so slowly when the barrage began. What could he want? I walked up to him and stood at attention. He looked past me, focusing his eyes on something to my right and well behind me. And his face was a blank. Even after he began to speak to me, his eyes looked elsewhere.

"Pag-lee-Arrow, we need a prisoner. I want you to go into the woods, as far as you have to, to get one. We're counting on you. Bring him back."

I said, "Yes, Sir. Is that all, Sir?"

He didn't answer. Instead he ended the exchange between us by saluting. That was a surprise. It's not usual to salute in the field because it may identify an officer to an enemy observer, making him a prime target. But of course I returned the salute and left.

When I got back to the hole, Roper asked, "What'd he want?"

I told him. Roper was shocked. "Jesus! What's he up to? What the hell does he want from you? We don't need no prisoner." Then he paused and said, "Now don't you do anything crazy."

I hated Lynch's guts for sitting on the stump when the rest of us jumped into our holes. I was scared of going into the woods to get a prisoner, but at first I didn't resent the assignment. I only slowly began to realize I'd been singled out to do a couple of very dangerous things over the past ten days—swim a freezing canal, miles from Squadron, to reconnoiter a village on the far side; stand guard all night, exposed to heavy fire, outside an armored car on a bald hill in German territory; and, now, go alone into a forest we all knew was dominated by the enemy, to get a prisoner. I accepted the jobs as the luck of the draw—I was a private, and I was among the last to join the outfit. It was natural that I drew tough details. Others did dangerous things, too.

But Roper's questions, "What's he up to? What the hell does he want from you?" got to me. Then there was the lieutenant's accusation, "By God, I'm an AMERICAN! What are YOU?" And the expression on his face—aloof, impersonal, detached—when he ordered me into the forest to get a prisoner. He was on the edge of madness, and responsible for at least some of my troubles. He hated my guts. He wasn't brave, he was deluded. And he wasn't a southern gentleman, which he wanted very much to be, he was a piddling sadist. I saw through him and he knew it. My kid's face told him. I was so immature I let him see what I thought of him.

I was of two minds about the order to capture a prisoner. I was worried that when I went into the forest, I'd be stretching my slim connection with safety to the breaking point. Our light perimeter was already miles from any unit strong enough to give us real protection. Leaving our circle of holes to try to get a German by myself meant giving up any chance of being helped by others. What with the stark failure of our second attack, the artillery bombardment that followed our retreat, and Lynch's strangely delivered orders to me, I wasn't exactly happy. I felt dread, heavy dread, but no panic.

Crazy as it sounds, one part of me saw the assignment as a mission that would leave me to myself. I didn't like leaving the perimeter, but with luck and care, I had a chance to make it. Bad as Lynch's assignment was, it gave me to some kind of control over my own actions. If I could take a prisoner without great risk, I'd do it. But if I couldn't, I'd just wait things out. As I thought over what lay ahead, I realized that dusk would bring my mission to a reasonable conclusion in the absence of an explicit order to the contrary. Meanwhile, I'd move carefully enough so the Germans didn't see me. I knew I might be taken by surprise, but I had more than a bare chance to make it out and back without being caught.

I moved into the woods very close to where the young soldier had been blown off the tank. That seemed better than the route we took during the two failed attacks. I didn't want to arouse the interest of the enemy's forward observers. But even in following this roundabout course into the forest, I was worried about stumbling into a German patrol. Though there'd been no signs of such activity, we knew they must have been keeping an eye on us. So I penetrated the woods slowly, choosing a path that would offer no long views of me from any direction. There was so much low growth between the trees that it wasn't hard to do. I was also careful to make as little noise as possible. Twice I came up to a small clearing, in which three or four stumps would have provided the only concealment. I skirted them, walking through the surrounding forest. By the time I came to a third cleared space, I must have been fifty yards to the left of our perimeter and as far toward Erckartswiller as our first attack had penetrated. After that I moved in slow stages about seventy-five yards to my right so that the perimeter was almost directly behind me. That seemed far enough.

There was a small clearing just ahead, roughly thirty yards in diameter, filled only with brush and tree stumps. I decided to take up a position on its near side, behind a huge, gnarled tree, with roots so massive above the ground that, between two of them, I was able to find a snug lodging that gave me cover as well as concealment. In the late afternoon light, the forest was a gloomy green, with only an occasional brightness.

From my position under the old tree, I waited and watched. The clearing ahead of me was all I could see well, but I never considered moving farther forward. I would just wait to see what I could see. Though I knew that at a certain point I'd have to return to the perimeter, I was not conscious of passing time. I looked ahead and around me, but above all, I listened. In that tangled obscurity, I knew the chances were that I'd hear anyone coming toward me before I saw him. My rifle butt was under my right pectoral, with the lower part of the barrel resting on one of the giant roots behind which I waited, hardly thinking. I looked at my right hand, over and over. Sometimes it was on the rifle stock and sometimes on the twisted old roots. Both hands were gnarled and chapped by war, as rough as the tree itself.

Alone in the forest I waited until I felt an hour had passed. Nothing happened. By then it must have been after four o'clock. The shadows of late autumn deepened. I waited. I was beginning to think it might be time to go back to the perimeter. But unable to decide that it was quite late enough, I waited some more. I listened and I watched. Nothing.

I was about to withdraw when I heard slight sounds on the far side of the clearing. Before I could decide what made the sounds—an animal, a man, a whole patrol—I saw a German soldier take a single step into the brightness of the clearing and then stop, not forty yards away. He was young, maybe twenty-one or twenty-two, and he wore a field cap instead of a helmet. I had him in my sights instantly—an easy shot. What I wanted was a target if he should be one of several on patrol. They might turn out to be too close and too spread out for me to back away slowly. If so, I could get him, empty my clip at the others, and run back to the perimeter before they flanked me. But he seemed to be alone. Like me, he chose not to cross the clearing. But he climbed onto a stump very near his side and looked around. I knew he couldn't see anything that might interest him from there. Had he been sent out like me, alone, to get a prisoner?

His next gesture saved him from any move I might have made against him. He pushed back his cap and scratched his hair, as if uncertain what to do. It was blond and curly. I thought about wounding him in the shoulder, and prodding him back to Lynch. Trying to take him without winging him first would have been very risky at that distance in the woods. But he seemed too much like me—a young man alone, at risk. I couldn't fire. He turned around, stepped off the stump, and walked directly away. I could make him out only as he covered the first five or ten yards on the far side of the clearing, but I was just about certain he would continue to move away from me. I wanted to be sure, so I lay still in the deep canal between the roots, looking and listening—listening hard—for signs of his return or the presence of other German soldiers. After fifteen minutes had passed, I cautiously went back to the perimeter the way I'd come from it, moving left and then flanking our position before I came out of the forest. I could have moved straight back through the woods to the perimeter, but for some reason I wanted to retrace my steps.

I was in no mood to tell anyone what had happened, not even Roper.

"Sir," I reported to Lynch, "I moved out to our left and penetrated the woods to where we were on the first attack, straight ahead from the middle of our perimeter. I stayed until it started to get dark. I didn't see anything."

Lynch nodded, but said nothing. And he didn't salute. His face was a blank. I hesitated, not sure I was dismissed. Then he turned away, and I went back to the hole.

I had no idea what he might be thinking, just as I had no idea why he'd sent me on the mission in the first place. One man, alone, to get a prisoner in that situation? I was glad I got back to the perimeter. But I also felt guilty for not having wounded the German.

"My compassion was a mask for my fear," I thought.

Then I thought about Lynch. "He's a lousy commanding officer. Why should I do something for him?" I was unsure about my trip to the woods. I had to keep the story to myself.

When I dropped into the hole, Roper said, "So you made it. That prick is after your ass."

I didn't answer at first. I just lay back in the hole and lit up. Then I said, "Yeah, maybe. I guess so."

"How'd it go?" Roper asked.

"It was okay. I'm glad I made it. But it's as bad here as in the woods."

He didn't say anything. He knew I didn't want to talk. We were in the same tough spot we'd been in for two days. But I was glad to be with Roper again.

The night was uneventful—no artillery and no attack, not even a probe of the perimeter. The Germans knew everything they needed to know about us, so they waited things out. Unless we got heavy reinforcements, we couldn't do a thing with them. In the perimeter, everyone knew this obvious fact. We knew and we didn't know what to expect when morning came. We hoped we'd be told to withdraw, but expected the order to attack again.

Dawn came, and we heard nothing. The sun rose higher, and still we got no word. We weren't eager to go in, but the waiting made us nervous. Maybe Headquarters really was deciding against a third attack. At about ten o'clock, after our hopes had risen, we had a strong clue that we'd be going in for the third day in a row. Our four pieces of artillery, one on each tank and the two assault guns, began bombarding the woods between us and Erckartswiller and, it seemed to us, the invisible village itself. After about ten minutes of this minor attempt at softening the Germans, we were told to get ready to move. Our platoon was leading again. Our perfunctory artillery preparation had drawn no return fire. We all understood the reason, and it made us grim. They'd rather catch us out of our holes and in the woods, where we stood a good chance of being wounded in the head and shoulders by tree-bursts from above. We'd learned the lesson during the second attack, and so had the Germans. Knowing how much stuff they had to throw at us and how their tree-bursts would hit us made our destruction seem inevitable. And you didn't have to be clairvoyant to know it wouldn't take them long to do it.

Lynch led the way, walking forward deliberately, straight into the brush and trees, and we spread out and caught up, flanking his advance. Roper was next to me, no more than twenty feet away. Lynch began to turn slightly to his right, straight toward Erckartswiller, and we adjusted our positions accordingly. The never-sighted village, our maddening objective, had taken on a life of its own. The brush grew thicker as we moved forward, and we were soon to lose clear sight of each other. But I knew roughly where Roper was until the action got very hot. I could see him, at least a part of him, lying or moving in the forest, even though I made no effort to keep him in view. I also knew where Lynch was, beyond Edwards, to my right. Once I was surprised to see how close T-5 Lane was to the lieutenant when they came into view for an instant, too close—one shell could get both. And I knew where Clewes was, beyond Roper, to my left. But I didn't really care where they were. Being closer to Lynch, or to Roper, for that matter, wouldn't have made me feel one bit better then, even though just the afternoon before I was relieved to return from the forest to the hole where my giant companion was waiting. We'd had our last conversation.

We were all together in our advance toward Erckartswiller, but in fact we were each of us all alone. I didn't want to move forward, but I did. We all did, reluctant men in a dream, horrified by the action we were committed to, and yet unable to alter it.

Along with my fear and reluctance to advance, I felt the unnatural silence of our early penetration into the woods. We were trying not to make noise. The sooner the Germans found out we were coming in, the sooner they could start firing. If we moved quietly, we might delay that terrible beginning. We slipped slowly past hanging branches so they wouldn't spring back noisily or snap, and we stepped on earth or leaf or root, not on dead twigs. But the silence I remember was not the result of this caution. It was an ambient silence, a palpable element that informed the dreamworld of the shadowed forest. I moved through it carefully—the dead heavy quiet. But however carefully I moved to save it, my loud shallow breath and fiercely beating heart threatened to destroy it.

The silent dream was abruptly shattered by a thousand sounds—explosions, screams of flying steel, uneven whirls fracturing the air, groaning tree limbs twisting off the bole, thuds, the splatter of bullet-torn leaves, long-arriving whistles, cutting chatters, all echoing and reechoing through the woods. Noises shook the world and kept shaking it with unending violence. Only the men were silent. Even the wounded made no noise. By some prearranged signal, the Germans had begun to fire everything they had at once—heavy guns, 88s, depressed antiaircraft guns, mortars, and a murderous cross fire of machine guns and rifles—and they continued to fire remorselessly. Like everyone else, I dropped to the ground as soon as they opened up. Rifle and machine gun fire kept us pretty much pinned down, but we had not yet given up the idea of moving forward. So we kept low and crawled against our strong desire to turn around and get back to our holes. From time to time we got up and ran a few yards, more to escape the hot place we occupied than to advance. The din was penetrant.

Despite the terrible noise, I could sometimes hear the movements of men to my right and left, and I could sometimes see parts of their bodies, Roper's to my left and Edwards'—sometimes Lane's and Lynch's—to my right. Like me, they seemed desperate and afraid. In the absence of the order to withdraw—we heard no such order that day—we could do nothing but wait to be hit.

In one of my short forward lurches, I broke through the edge of some scrubby growth between trees and startled three plump little deer, spotted babies no more than two feet high. Their eyes looked huge. For seconds, they and I were frozen in amazement. Then, with their rumps and rear legs trembling, they sprang electric into the air and darted to the rear, where I longed to follow. Instead, I hit the ground again to avoid being cut down. But there was no real safety anywhere because of the tree-bursting shells.

I looked around for a safer part of the forest. No place looked safe. But there seemed to be a partial opening in the woods ahead. I thought I might be a little better off if I could get there, where shell bursts from above might be less dense. The edge of the partial clearing was no more than fifteen yards from me. I really didn't want to move forward anymore, and even though my head told me a clearing would be safer than the woods, I didn't like the feeling of exposure I anticipated there. Besides, I couldn't stay there long before I'd have to move forward again. But I got up in a crouch and ran towards the clearing, through the noise and dense fire.

I was almost there when I got hit. A hot shell fragment cut the left side of my upper lip, right under my left nostril. The contact with steel was fleeting. My flesh seemed to melt. I think my head turned a little to the right. I put my tongue on the wound and licked the blood. For a minute I panicked, and instead of moving to the clearing I'd almost reached, I turned and ran back to where I'd been, and I hit the ground again.

It was a close call. But that day the forest was full of close calls. I had no idea how big the piece of flying steel had been, but I realized—no, I didn't realize, I felt in my bowels—that an inch or two of difference, and it might have gone through my face, taking my upper lip and front teeth with it, or it might have cut my nose away. I wiped my mouth again, this time with the upper side of my left index finger, and then I licked it. The wound was a deep nick, no more than I might have done with a mad stroke of a new razor blade. But I was shaken.

Still, it wasn't much. I began to think again and to look around. There seemed to be movement just to the right of the clearing I'd never reached. That would be Edwards. I looked to the left. Though I saw no movement, I knew Roper might be there. I decided to try for the clearing again. I didn't want to go forward, but I got up and ran anyhow.

At that moment I cared about nothing and no one. I thought I wouldn't survive the next five minutes. I needed a way out of the hell I was in, but there was none. Our situation was hopeless. I moved forward. Maybe because I still thought the clearing was a safer place than the woods. I didn't know. I didn't know anything. I just ran ahead.

As soon as I got to the middle of the clearing—even before I hit the ground—a shell passed through the trees and exploded with a loud snap and crack on the forest floor, spreading its fragments low. I recorded what happened like a camera. I was floating on air when I saw the explosion. I know I was. I felt, heard, and saw the burst as my right leg was rammed up from under me, and I was lofted high and turned around before landing on my right shoulder. I heard myself whisper, "I'm hit." By then I was already on my feet.

It all happened in a split second. I was in shock. When I stood up, I felt some distance away from myself, watching what I did with great interest. I grabbed my rifle by its loosened sling, and I twirled it around my head, and then threw it as far as I could into the brush. It turned out I hated the thing I'd been holding onto for dear life.

The cross fire and shell bursts continued dense, but apart from my vague sense that our attack was now stalled, men to my left and right hopelessly pinned down, I felt isolated from the battle. I was still curious about it, but I no longer felt that it was my concern. I must have crawled or hobbled a short distance to the rear. When I sat down to look at my wound, I was out of the cross fire of rifles and machine guns, though the action still sounded hot and close, and shells were still bursting around me. But I was acting like a man exempt from danger.

I unlaced my mutilated boot. I looked at the leg and saw a big hole where my calf used to be. Then I stuffed some remnants of my long woolen underwear into the wound, and retied the boot as well as I could. The opening in my leg was wide, a very deep irregular gash that left my calf looking like a piece of untrimmed red meat. I remembered the sulphur powder in my first aid kit. I was supposed to sprinkle the wound with it to prevent infection. So I untied my boot again, withdrew the underwear, and poured the powder into the wound. I marveled that there was so little blood. I felt no pain at all. I stuffed the torn underwear back in the hole, and then rewrapped the undone laces around my leg and knotted them firmly. It was sad to look at my beautiful boots, ruined, the right one mutilated beyond repair.

After the rough bandaging was finished, I ate my twenty-four-hour supply of sulphur tablets all at once, washing them down with four or five ounces of calvados. The alcohol made my stomach feel nice and warm. I stood up again, never doubting that I could walk. It didn't cross my mind to call and wait for a medic. I wanted to get out of there right away. The troop was pinned down. There was nothing for me to do where they were. I wanted to leave. But while I took care of my leg and drank the calvados, I somehow knew what was happening to the left and to the right of the clearing where I was wounded. Roper is stretched out long on the ground, pinned down by small arms. There's a giant pine just behind him. A big shell detonates against it, and Roper is jerked forward hard by a fragment that hits him in the back. Farther to the left, Clewes is moving forward a few feet to get away from the hottest cross fire, and he gets knocked down by many small fragments from a tree-burst. They hit him all over his back. It was a mortar shell. Edwards gets it in the back. To his right, Lynch and Lane are lying side by side, facing forward. A shell comes in, clearing the trees and bursting on the ground right in front of them. Lynch's face is skinned real bad and his eyes are burned. He goes mad for a time, but he makes it. I don't know how bad Lane is hurt.

With my leg tied up and the calvados warming me, I was ready to leave the battle for the rear. I stepped out to walk, but I fell down. I couldn't put any weight on my right foot. Some instinct told me to lock my knee and ankle, and using the heel of my foot as if it were the bottom of a crutch—my wounded leg—thrust forward without putting weight on the foot itself, only the heel. It worked fine, and I walked the three-quarters of a mile back to the troop's motor pool, oblivious to the enemy's fire, which was by then concentrated on the right side of our stalled advance. As I walked, I kept our former defense perimeter and the fairly clear land to its rear on my right, between me and the woods I had gone into for a prisoner. Most of the firing was directly behind me, but nothing landed close while I walked, just as nothing had come really close while I foolishly attended my wound in an exposed position. I should have crawled farther back, but I was intoxicated with the illusion of deliverance, and nothing but death or another wound could have changed my mood. I didn't think of the men I'd left behind, not even Roper or Clewes. The thought of deliverance controlled everything. I wanted only to escape from the chaos in the woods near Erk-kartswiller. I had served as a stranger, and I left as a stranger.

When I got to the motor pool, two men I didn't know were there guarding the vehicles. They ran toward me as soon as they saw me limping along, and they carried me to a jeep. Though it would have made sense for one to remain behind while the other drove me to the nearest medics, they decided they'd both go. I was impatient with myself for thinking they wanted to get away from the vicinity of Erckartswiller as much as I did, especially because I knew they'd be coming back for others as soon as they'd dropped me off, but I didn't stop thinking about them until the jeep got under way and I heard the machine gun vibrating on its mount.

"Stop!" I shouted.

The driver pulled up right away, asking, "Is the pain bad?"

I said, "No, I just want to unload the machine gun." He smiled as if what I said made sense.

I did the job quickly, and he started up again. They got me to an aid station within fifteen minutes.

The medics there reached for me, intending to carry me to a stretcher, but I waved them off.

"I can walk," I said, ready to show them.

Stiffening my wounded leg into a crutch, I stepped on my heel and fell over. I laughed, full of fun—I was off my rocker—and everybody laughed with me. My jeep companions left for the return trip even before I was given a shot of morphine and placed on a stretcher. I waved my thanks. After a few minutes, I was moved to a warm building to await evacuation by ambulance to a field hospital.

Not thirty minutes later, other wounded men from our troop began to appear. They were all hit in the head, neck, back, or shoulders. I was groggy with morphine, off my crazy high, when I saw Clewes later that afternoon, in the field hospital. He had very large bandages covering his neck, back, and shoulders. He was subdued, very sad. He told me Roper had been hit. He'd seen him thrust forward on the ground, but he didn't know how bad the wound was. I never saw Roper again, and that afternoon was the last time I saw Clewes. There were dozens wounded that day, and it turned out we never even got close to our objective. After the platoon was almost wiped out, the rest of A Troop was pinned down and mauled. Lynch and T-5 Lane were wounded— the crazy brave lieutenant—and Trenard, one of the Cajuns who'd carried me partway to church in Raville, was also hit.

The troop included about eighty-five men when we attacked on the third day. With the help of the medics we did some adding that afternoon in the field hospital. Our conservative estimate of the total of dead, wounded, and traumatized was seventy-six. Seven had gone off the deep end, suffering "battle fatigue," an unusually high proportion of the men in the action. No, it wasn't an action, it was a massacre. Eleven were dead or dying, and the remaining fifty-eight were wounded, like Clewes, mostly in the head, back, and shoulders. We never found out whether the others, nine or ten, were alive or missing, but the last we heard, nobody in our outfit ever got close to Erckartswiller.

The medical unit that first took care of my wound was efficient and considerate. Soon after I spoke to Clewes, heavily bandaged and subdued, I was taken to a field hospital farther to the rear. And the next day, I was taken into their surgery for X-rays and an eyeball examination of my wound, for which I was anesthetized. They didn't put me under until they explained that they would knock me out with an intravenous injection of Pentothal. I'd been anesthetized with gas and ether twice before—tonsils and a bad appendix—so I had doubts that a needle could do the job. The nurse told me to count backwards from one hundred, and I was asleep before I reached ninety-five. After they'd looked at the wound and cleaned it up, they left it open, the usual practice in World War II. They closed it up about ten days later, thus lowering the chances of infection. From the time I reached the field hospital and until the wound was thoroughly healed, I was injected with large doses of penicillin in the rump every few hours.

The morning after this first operation, I woke up at dawn in a warm cot, having slept like a rock through the night. For the first time in weeks I was free of the anxiety that I would die. I wanted to write home right away, in hopes of getting word about my wound to my family before they got the formulaic telegram from Washington. I was already beginning to think of other people again. I needed pencil and paper.

But before I could do anything about getting the writing materials, a full colonel came up to my cot, put his hand on my head, and said, "Don't worry about your wound, son. You're going to be all right, though it'll take a while to heal."

I was deeply moved by his kindness. What a contrast to the treatment I'd been getting. Of course the colonel could afford to be kind. Still, he didn't have to be. For no reason at all, it seemed, my mind flashed back to the explosion of the shell that got me. I saw it land very slightly behind me, and to my right. The fragment that got me must have passed between my legs after hitting the outer rear of my right calf muscle—twisting and tearing through. It missed the bone or barely touched it. Then my mind shifted to another scene, to the wound on my mouth, but the picture faded out as I began to see my face with missing pieces of jaw and teeth.

The colonel's message registered only superficially. It was several weeks before I understood he was saying my leg would not have to be amputated. I didn't know then that legs are complicated things, and that losing muscle, nerve strands, and blood vessels may leave the part of the leg below the wound a dying member. He was also saying that I had a bad wound, which wouldn't heal quickly. But the light dawned slowly, despite the colonel's clear message. Later that same day I learned the colonel was in charge of the entire medical unit. That made his taking the time to be considerate all the more unusual.

Soon after he left, I was served a huge breakfast. I ate it quickly and asked whether I could have more. My appetite had returned. The ward boy, a cheerful private, got me seconds. When he came for my tray, I asked for paper and pencil to write a letter home. He got me a piece of graph paper—it was all he could find—a pencil, and an envelope. I wrote a brief letter home. Just as I finished, a nurse came by. She looked at me with soft brown eyes. Then she pulled the big toe of my good leg, and said, "Cheer up. You're going to be fine."

It was the first clue I had that the subdued expression I'd seen on Clewes' face might be showing itself on mine. Even so, I began only slowly to realize that my euphoria at having escaped from the front with a leg wound was the manic surface of a dark mood. I was never bitter about my exposure at the front, but it left me feeling life is a risky business. Fortunately, it also helped me to value and cherish ordinary things.

Early on the morning of December 4, the colonel paid me another visit. He said in a kind, formal voice, "Son, it's my duty to present you with the Purple Heart."

"Thank you, Sir," I answered.

Both his tone and face told me he was embarrassed by the obligatory gesture, but then with his left hand he simply handed me the box that held the medal and offered his right to be shaken. We shook hands briefly, and he left. Both visits—the only times I ever saw him—surprised me. He seemed to have Siebold's sense of responsibility to those in his charge, and I think his way of doing his job was reflected in his entire staff—physicians, nurses, medical technicians, and ward boys. With few exceptions, all the people in the hospitals I was sent to over the next nine months afforded us privates more dignity than we'd known elsewhere in the Army, but the colonel and the staff of his field hospital were especially kind.

A few days after I received the Purple Heart, I was sent by hospital train to a station hospital in Dijon. During my first days there, the Germans began their push into Belgium. For days, we heard hour-by-hour accounts of the Nazi offensive, which at first seemed overpowering. One problem was the weather. It was so murky we were unable to make air strikes against them. As the days of German success became a week and more, our doctors began looking grim as they made their rounds. We soon realized they were being pressured to decide which men could be returned to the fighting. I had one more anxious time, not quite irrationally concerned that I might be returned to the front despite my wound. I learned for the first time that having been wounded did not exempt a man from further frontline duty. It seemed too cruel to think about. Most of the patients in my ward had suffered leg or arm wounds. They kept the orthopedics cases together. I knew that several had calf wounds, and I naturally wondered most about them. As it turned out, two of the first four men to be returned to the front had received machine gun wounds through the calf. At the time I didn't realize that their wounds, made by bullets, were likely to have been relatively smooth holes, rather than deep, jagged tears. Still, it was an awful thing for them to be sent back, and so soon after they'd been wounded. They could walk only stiffly. But it was their faces that got to us, tight-lipped and deathly gray. I saw their halting motion, their legs still bandaged, and in one case, still draining.

My mind had been recovering from the stresses of the battlefield. But I began to feel a new anxiety. If two men with calf wounds could be sent back to the lines, so could I. The good colonel's message had not sunk in. I only slowly realized that I had a bad wound that brought me close to losing my leg. When I was wheeled into the operating room in Dijon, lying on the butcher wagon, waiting to be prepped for the closure of my wound, a nurse who had just come from the States walked up to take care of me. When she removed the bandages to shave and clean the leg around the wound, she made a face that included surprise, pity, and discomfort. I thought she reacted that way because she had not seen battle-wounded men before, and that may well have been true. But instead of connecting her disturbed face with the gentle colonel's reassurance that I would not lose the leg, and his saying it would take a while to heal—instead of recognizing that I had a bad wound—I decided to play Humphrey Bogart.

"Pretty, huh?" I said to her, smiling slightly, as if I were in charge of the Universe.

She said, "You'll soon be all right," and she smiled back.

Though I'm not squeamish, I never looked at my wound, from the time I stuffed the shredded leg of my long underwear into it for the second time, minutes after I was hit, until a medical orderly removed the small stitches from the healed lips, leaving in place three long sutures that passed under the deepest part of the wound and spanned a distance of five inches. Under these three long lines that seemed to be holding my leg together, I saw a scarred trench where muscle had been. Laid open and trimmed before it was closed, the calf must have been quite a spread of raw meat.

After the operation on my leg, it was put in a cast. That should have made it obvious that I wouldn't be ready for combat duty soon. But I continued to worry. As the friendly colonel had predicted, the leg took a while to heal. The short stitches closing the surface of the wound were taken out in about two weeks. But they taped the neatly divided cast back on, and the three long sutures were not removed until well into January. And even then they put the cast back on until the end of the month. By that time my atrophied leg looked like a gnarled stick.

For the American forces in northern France, the two weeks just before Christmas were bad ones—at least until the weather cleared on December 24 and our air strikes began. After that, we more or less contained the last German offensive of the war. By the New Year, our troops were stalling the German advance, though it was to be mid-January before it became clear that their offensive had failed badly, resulting in great losses for them. We lost great numbers too, probably forty thousand dead and wounded. For as long as their attack threatened to cut our armies off from the supply centers in Liège and Antwerp, the wounded were being hurried back to the front.

It was only after this dangerous time was ended that I began to understand that my wound was bad enough to keep me in the hospital for a long time. Maybe if one physician had been in charge of the case, he might have made me realize sooner. But things weren't handled that way in the Army, so it was only after my medical chart had accumulated a record of slow progress that I began to see that I had a way to go. I also began to anticipate the reassuring pattern of my movement to the rear, which turned out to be a step-by-step return home—Paris, Le Havre, Cheltenham near Gloucester, and finally the States.

A lot of men sweated out the bad time with me in Dijon. We talked about the odds of our returning to the front, but we also talked about going home. From the safety of the hospital, temporary or not, we looked in both directions. We all enjoyed shooting the bull again, for hours, even while we were worried. I also spent a lot of time reading. The Red Cross had hundreds of paperbacks, mostly by nineteenth-century novelists. I couldn't get enough of Thackeray, Dickens, Trollope, and Wells. During these weeks, I wrote to my family almost every day as the best way of reassuring them I was okay. But only occasionally did I say what was really on my mind. Meanwhile I received almost no mail from home, and until mid-February only one letter written after they'd heard

I was wounded. I was alive to the particulars of family life as I hadn't been for months, especially for news about Robert, who was fast coming of age. I was also eager to hear from friends back home. But I hadn't yet begun to reexperience the kind of fantasy life that would have a Helen King at its center. And Abby Wofford was pretty much a distant memory, though we wrote to each other some.

From Dijon, I took with me a few strong memories besides my sense for the novels, the food, and the bed rest. The surgeon who closed my wound, a major, visited me three times in addition to his usual rounds. He was the closest thing to a regular physician I had. Once, right after the small stitches had come out, he stopped by, removed the split cast that was only taped together by then, and looked at the wound.

"What do you think?" he asked in a nice way.

Maybe I should have said, "Great job, Major, thanks."

Instead he heard me at my most naive. "It's a pretty big hole."

"I've seen worse," he said.

Then I made a smart-assed comment, which he didn't deserve. "Not in me, you haven't."

But he let me have the last word. He was kind then, and he was kind on his two other special visits.

On Christmas Eve a beautiful girl, dressed in a simple green gown and gold slippers, walked into our ward beside a white mule that carried two baskets filled with small gifts. An old man dressed like a clown led the docile animal. The Faery's child was about sixteen, trim and graceful—a miracle. Her pale skin was lovely, and she wore her straight blond hair long. Shy dignity intensified her good looks as she walked from bed to bed, distributing the presents. All of us just looked, taking in the scene. We couldn't believe she was real. A French orderly told us proudly that she was the daughter of the local count. When she reached my bed and handed me a gift, I barely heard her sweet voice, "Joyeux Noël, Monsieur."

Then she handed me a little red box tied with white ribbon. I said, "Merry Christmas. Thank you very much." I smiled with pleasure. She made Christmas magic.

Then there was Willie Becker, a seventeen-year-old German prisoner who took a shine to me. Willie didn't look at all like Robert, but he reminded me of my brother some. It was he who wheeled me into the operating room for the closure, promising to save my breakfast, which was yet to be served. Several men on the ward won bets (and several lost) when I woke up shortly before noon and ate the cold food. I heard that Willie had taken a lot of ribbing for protecting my tray and that it was his unequivocal refusal to believe that I wouldn't want to eat after the anesthesia that led to the betting.

One afternoon in the Dijon hospital, shortly after I was operated on and the cast put on my leg, a group of six officers— not medical officers—stopped at my bed. I was reading when they came up, so I don't know whether they had stopped at other beds before they came to mine. Their senior officer was the spokesman.

He came right to the point: "Soldier, how were you wounded?" he asked.

"I was hit by shrapnel."

"There's no shrapnel in this war. You mean shell fragment."

He was right. I'd been hit by a shell fragment and not canister shot. I didn't argue with his generalization. His demeanor didn't invite discussion. So I said, "Yes, Sir."

"How do you know?"

That question threw the switch to my impatience. "How do I know? I saw the shell explode," I said with fervor.

"What do you think it was?"

"Probably an 88, but I'm not sure. It might have been a big mortar shell. It wasn't a really big artillery round. I think it was an 88."

As soon as I answered, three of the other officers looked at each other and spoke in a whisper for a few seconds. They seem to have had enough. In fact, as I watched their faces while they spoke, I had the impression they hadn't wanted to question me in the first place. The senior officer, having heard their discussion, nodded.

Then he said, "Okay, soldier, that's all," and they walked away.

And that's all there was to it. I never heard from them again. But I thought the visit was strange until it crossed my mind they were checking to be sure my wound wasn't self-inflicted. But it was a jagged hole that almost tore the calf in two. It couldn't have come from a rifle bullet. I would have had to do the job with several blows of a dull axe. They wouldn't have questioned me at all unless someone had accused me. The obvious candidate was Lynch. Impossible! But maybe he tried to do me in one last time.

Shortly after this visit, several of us in the ward were told to pack our gear and be ready for shipment further to the rear. We were driven to a nearby railroad station, where we joined a hospital train that slowly made its way to Paris. With each mile of travel through the countryside, we felt a new liberty. We smiled at each other, for no reason we understood, as the distance between us and the place of war increased. I'm not sure who did it first, but within thirty minutes of our departure from Dijon, almost every one of us had taken off his hospital shirt. It was cold, but that didn't matter. We enjoyed our new sense of freedom through this pleasant narcissism—exposing our torsos proudly for all the world to see, as if all the world cared. The nurses, who included Madeleine Carroll, the movie actress, were understanding. They smiled as if they knew our nakedness confirmed our return to the rear.

"Who are you? Tarzan?"

It was only after a couple of hours of the self-display that they said we'd have to put our shirts back on, by which time we were cold enough to be grateful for the order.

When we got to Paris, we were taken to a huge hospital, a multistoried brick building which was an American installation from some time well before World War II. During the week that I was there, I was assigned to a room with only three beds, to which was attached a private bathroom finished in tile. The two men with whom I spent my time there before being shipped to England were pleasant, and so were the nurses who took up the job of injecting us with penicillin every four hours.

By this time, I was brimming with energy and in need of exercise. I was without crutches, which I'd had to leave behind, so for the first two days in the Paris hospital I hopped around on one foot, from bed to bathroom, and I even took a short trip across the corridor just for something to do. The cast on my leg was removed only when I reached England in early February, but even then I needed crutches because my leg could bear no weight. On the third day of my Paris stay, a Red Cross woman stopped by and agreed to get me a pair of crutches right away. Having measured me, she returned in about ten minutes with the best fit she could find, but in fact they were about an inch and a half too long, and they were not adjustable. She promised to come back with a pair the right size as soon as possible, but when she hadn't shown up by the third day, I decided to do the best I could with the ill-fitting pair.

Just for something to do, I took a walk through the corridors of the hospital, going farther than I had before. Moving along without an objective, I traveled quite a distance and came to a ward I thought I'd enter. As soon as I crossed the threshold, I was sorry I'd done so. All the patients were amputees. Trying not to call attention to myself by hurrying away, I turned around and started to leave. But I was stopped by the sound of the nickname I'd been given by O'Brien at Fort Benning—"CHUNKY!"

The voice that called me made a desperate noise—a mixed shriek and roar so loud the vocal chords seemed to rupture in the sounding. I turned around and saw Marlowe, O'Brien's reclusive sheep rancher friend from Wyoming. He was tense and red-faced, standing by the side of his bed, showing pleasure and doubt, starting toward me and yet not moving. I swung myself to his side and gave him a strong hug, which he returned with broken laughter.

"Oh, it's good to see you. I haven't seen anyone I know since my hand was blown off. Oh, it's good to see you. It's good to see you. My hand was blown off."

We sat on his bed, and I told him I had a leg wound that was just about healed, and then, in a general way, I asked him about himself.

"How has it been?"

"You know, I stayed behind at Benning when you guys shipped out. But I never made it to West Point. Somebody beat my father to the senator. I was sent over as a replacement. I just got to my new outfit when I was hit. The stump. I never saw action."

But then he dropped that part of the story and picked up a pad and pen he'd been using when he spotted me. "See," he said, waving the half-filled page, "left-handed. I'm learning to write with my left hand, and it's real easy. I think I'll be a sheep rancher after all. That's what the family has done for a long time, and that's what I'll do, too. It's a good life. I know the business already, and when I get back my father'll leave me alone. I have to get myself all healed up before they fit me with an artificial hand, but then I get a discharge. Won't that be great! I can't wait to get out of the Army. I'm tired of taking orders and being somebody else's body. I can't wait to get out."

He went on for another five minutes without stopping. I had accidentally opened the floodgate, and I felt the torrent of his relief. It was good to see someone I'd known in the States, but the pain apparent in his mania was hard to take. He seemed to have a good chance of making a life for himself, but I wondered whether the lost hand wouldn't intensify his old reclusiveness.

Seeing Marlowe did not make me think of Roper, Clewes, O'Brien, Oliver, or anyone else I'd known in the Army. Neither my mind nor the mind of any soldier I know worked that way. It may have been different for men who went overseas with the outfits they'd trained with in the States. But not for replacements. I wanted to put my GI days behind me. I'd never be able to forget them, but I wanted my memory to stop gathering painful material.

Shortly after I saw Marlowe, I left Paris. What little I saw of the city, I saw through the back windows of an ambulance as we rode along to the train station. We arrived in Le Havre at night. The harbor was lighted, and I was carried aboard the hospital ship on a stretcher by two German prisoners, men in their forties. They looked tired and defeated as they worked silently, walking smoothly to give me a good ride. The westbound crossing took longer than the trip from England to France, but we were light-hearted and didn't mind at all. Besides, the food was good. Within a few days, I was in an American hospital, set up in Quonset huts, just outside of Cheltenham, a town about thirty-five miles west and slightly north of Oxford. It was there that I had the first of several postclosure operations on my leg.

The man in the bed next to mine was named Ludinsky. He had fought in the Spanish Civil War before he enlisted in the United States Army to "fight the Nazis again," as he put it. "The only good German is a dead one," he used to say over and over.

He told me he was a member of the Communist Party and insisted that I tell him where I stood in politics. I was unsure how to explain that I thought Hitler and Mussolini and their followers had to be destroyed, and at the same time that I could not agree with him that the only good German is a dead one. (Ludinsky was considerate in the tacit exemption of Italians from his fiat.) He surprised me by recounting incidents of his killing particular German soldiers, individualizing them in various ways. He could not have thought much about death, not even his own.

His faith in materialism seemed simple. He was intelligent and yet ridiculously single-minded, inspired by hatred and the need to destroy opposition rather than by an ideal. He was also remorseless in citing Party-approved views, and impatient with me for questioning them. Once we read the Old Testament together over several days. Like him I saw that passages in Leviticus and Deuteronomy could make the Old Testament voice sound ignorant and punitive, but I also saw there much more sensitivity and intelligence than Ludinsky acknowledged. When he left for a convalescent hospital, I was relieved to be free of his persistent, uninquiring mind, but I also missed the give-and-take of our endless talk.

A few days after my arrival at the Cheltenham hospital, while I was reading in bed, with my head at its foot for better light, two hands were placed gently over my eyes, and I heard a man's voice.

"I say paahk and daahk. Where do I come from?"

"Boston!" I said.

I heard laughter as the hands were removed. My visitor was an Army chaplain, a Roman Catholic priest, about thirty-five years old. He had a nice full, cheerful face.

He asked me how I felt, and having heard that my wound was healed, he asked, "Would you like to attend Mass on Sunday?"

"I think I'd rather not," I said.

Then he asked, "Do you believe in God?"

I said, "I'm not sure, but the God I might believe in wouldn't expect me to belong to a church."

"Are you bitter?" he wanted to know.

"Not at all. I love life," I told him.

He smiled and said, "There's a blessing," and he left.

*

My five or six weeks at Cheltenham were pleasant, and despite the operations on my leg, I think of them as the beginning of my exit from the Army. There I began to walk again, though I did so with a limp that lasted more than a year. I was never able to leave the hospital grounds, but I could move around well enough outdoors to see the countryside—the beautiful Cotswold Hills, green even in February. They made the War seem far away. So did the visitors to the hospital, local matrons who came to see us once a week or so. I was taken up by one of them, a woman of about fifty, always dressed in the same heather tweeds, or so it seemed to my young eyes. Her name was Edith E. Martin. She came into the ward on a sunny day and walked up one side and down the other, as if doing medical rounds.

When she finished, she came back to my bed and said, "Yes, you'll do."

I felt like laughing, but I smiled instead. She asked, "Have you written to your mother?"

I told her, "Yes, the day after I was wounded and many times since."

She said, "You probably got it wrong. Men always do. I'll write to her to explain that you're well."

She sounded a little mad, but I liked her.

40 Prestbury Road
Cheltenham
Gloucestershire
England
Feb: 14th 1945

Dear Mrs. Pagliaro

I am sure you would like to get news from your son
Harold, whom I see at the Hospital every Wednesday. I go to
see the boys on Wednesdays.

Harold is getting on nicely & is always very cheerful.
You musn't worry about him, for he is well looked after. He
always has a nice smile for us, showing his lovely teeth. I
have a son, & two daughters, so I know how you feel with
your son so far away from you. Please try & not worry too
much. We Mothers must just bear it as bravely as we can.

I love going to see the Americans, they are so brave.

This is just to let you know that your son is getting on
nicely & very cheerful.

With kind regards,
Yours sincerely,

Edith E. Martin

When Mrs. Martin came to see me over the following weeks,
she brought homemade cake, and she was always in the company
of a young woman—never the same one on consecutive visits—
who would sit and chat, and later, walk the hospital grounds with
me.

During my last weeks in England, my mother wrote that
Robert would be taking a leave from Virginia Military Institute
after his first semester to enlist in the Merchant Marine. The news
relieved me. Though German U-Boats were still operating, they
weren't doing much against our shipping, and I thought he had a
better chance of surviving if he could avoid ground warfare. In

40, Prestbury Road
Chelltenham
Gloucestershire
England
Feb: 14ᵗʰ 1945.

Dear Mr Pagliaro

I am sure you would like to get news of your son Harold, who I see at the Hospital every Wednesday. I go to see the boys on Wednesdays. Harold is getting on nicely & is always very cheerful. You mustn't worry about him, for he is well looked after. He always has a nice smile for us, showing is lovely teeth. I have a son, & two daughters, so I know how you feel with your son so far away from you. Please try & not worry too much, we Mothers must just bear it as bravely as we can.
I love going to see the Americans they are so brave.
This is just to let you know that your son is getting on nicely & very cheerful
With kind regards,
Yours sincerely
Edith G. Martin—

Letter from Edith Martin to author's parents, during his recovery the Army, he might miss the European War, which was coming to a close, but I was afraid he would be sent to the Pacific, an assignment I still feared for myself, now that I was recovering steadily. But better things were in store. Early in March, I learned from a formal Board of Review, made up of medical officers, that I was being returned to the Zone of the Interior—to the United States. The combination of good news about Robert and my going home left me elated. Though it was against regulations to tell my folks I'd be returning, I tried to give them a broad hint by saying I felt sure everything was going to be "ship shape" before long.

Five days later, I left the hospital for the return voyage. We boarded a train and headed north to Scotland, where an American ship awaited us. On March 15, 1945, I left the Firth of Clyde, on the west coast of Scotland, and headed for home on the *U.S.S. America*, a hospital ship—at least part of it was. Like the *Mauretania* it was crowded, but not so crowded that anyone had to sleep on the decks. I had a bunk in a tier of three—white canvas laced to a steel frame—very comfortable. Officers were assigned staterooms, but we didn't mind the difference because our quarters were adequate—bright and spacious. And the food was exceptional—good ingredients in abundance, freshly prepared for each meal. I stopped smoking again, having lost my appetite for tobacco, but I wasn't really seasick, though the sea ran high. One day I saw a beautiful nurse with bright auburn hair at the rail of the deck above ours. We smiled and looked at each other for a minute, and then went in different directions. The passage was easy and relaxing. It was easy to get into the slow rhythm of life on board, with no danger ahead. The days passed, one running into the other. Everything was relaxed. At dusk on the tenth day, just before we pulled into Newport News, Virginia, I went up to look around. At the gang-board, I saw the loneliest seven men I have ever seen. They had come onto the main deck for the first time during the crossing, with all their gear, ready to disembark before the rest of us. I saw them moving feebly, like wraiths in a dark, silent cluster, near the ship's rail, breeding sorrow. They weren't really alike, but that's the way they looked. They all had a flat place in the middle of their faces, covered by a 4" by 4" bandage, where their noses should have been.

We came off the ship greeted by Red Skelton, of all people. He was friendly and amusing, but he interested us only for a moment, just an unexpected curiosity. He was irrelevant to our emotions just then. We were self-absorbed with feelings of homecoming, safety, the end of Army service. We were in the States again—the Zone of the Interior. Red Skelton was some Special Service officer's dumb idea of the part of America we'd want to experience first on our return. As we got into buses to be driven to the reception depot (which turned out also to be a port of embarkation for men and women being sent overseas), a newspaper reporter came by, asking if any of us were from Newport News or nearby places. When no one talked up, I told him I'd graduated from Woodrow Wilson High School in Portsmouth, which is just across the wide mouth of the Elizabeth River, but he was looking for native sons. I wasn't surprised, just a little disappointed. We drove off to the nearby Army post, where a nasty reception was waiting for us.

As soon as the buses emptied us near our barracks, where we stayed for only a day or two before being shipped to hospitals, a bunch of soldiers who were about to be sent to Europe began shouting at us.

"You guys think you're goddam hot shit just because the war is over for you. Smart-assed fuckheads. You think the goddam Purple Heart is everything. Up yours!"

I thought they were drunk, but they weren't. Some wounded men who'd arrived two days before us said they'd been getting the same abuse every time they left their barracks. I couldn't believe it. But even this foulmouthed insanity didn't interest us long. We were home. I was going to see my family, and soon I'd be discharged from the Army and belong to myself again.

Of course things happened to me during my remaining months in the Army, but only one or two of them belong in this book. For the short time that I was in Virginia, just a few miles from Portsmouth, I felt a strong pull towards Helen—felt it for the last time. I telephoned her to say hello, and got her mother instead. Though Mrs. King was genuinely kind, asking whether she could help me, the fact that Helen wasn't there gave me a comic sense of the futility of trying to reach her. Even if we'd spoken, we'd have spoken grotesquely different languages. Helen was not where I wanted to start my new life. There would be other women and marriage and children, but just then I wanted to renew my life at home, with my mother and father and brothers. I wanted to see them, and I wanted them to see me, happy and whole. And above all, I wanted to believe that Robert would be safe.

One week later, four days after I arrived at the Army orthopedics hospital in Longview, Texas, about to be operated on for the last time, I had a note from Father Timothy Rathbone, an Army chaplain. He ordered me to report to his office the next morning at eight o'clock.

When I arrived, he asked accusingly, "Why didn't I see you at Mass last Sunday?"

"I'm not a practicing Catholic," I told him.

He turned red with anger. "I've seen your record. I know you were a student at Columbia. It's a hotbed of Communism."

Then he looked at me hard and shouted in a fierce voice, "You're in peril of eternal damnation! Get out of my sight."

My visit to Father Rathbone's office was a late reminder that the Army, which had been good to me since I was wounded, still controlled me in ways I could never forget. Since 1945, I've dreamt hundreds of times that I've been drafted again. In the dreams I'm sent up to the front, and I'm given orders to do things against my will by a Stafford, a Henderson, or a Lynch. The threat of the front and death is always strong, but the anguish of having to submit to someone else's arbitrary power is even stronger. I'd kill or die before allowing that to happen to me again.

The Army's heavy grip on my imagination is somehow connected with my unwillingness to find out what happened to the guys I knew. As it was I learned more than I wanted to. About a year after I was discharged, I met Oliver by chance at the 42nd Street Station of the IRT. He had been shot through the chest by a sniper, and for a time they thought he was done for. He pulled through, but over the next twenty years he was in and out of mental hospitals, where I visited him every week. He died of a heart attack before he was forty-five.

One day while I was riding home from Columbia College, where I was a day student after the war, I ran into Marciano, the platoon sergeant during basic training. He was hit by a .50 caliber slug in a Luftwaffe strafing. He lost nine feet of his small intestine, and for the rest of his life he had to eliminate in a bag strapped to his side. He'd become a watch repairman in Brooklyn, where he and his wife still lived.

"Will you come to visit us, Chunky?" he asked, smiling.

I could see the wound in his eyes. "Sure I will," I said, and I meant it. But I could never bring myself to go.

There were many others. Albert Gunther, a slightly older neighbor in New York, was shot down in a B-25. Seymour Greenberg, who was in the first grade with me, was killed at Tarawa, his head half blown off. Frank Torlini, another schoolmate, lost his right kneecap. Word got back to me that Sergeant Raymond had been killed in the Battle of the Bulge, when the 87th was brought up to the lines. I also heard that Corporal Peschak, one of the few to survive Erckartswiller, was killed after crossing the Rhine in the early spring of 1945. There were many others. When I knew so much already, why would I want to find out more?

My advancing age has not helped at all. In fact, the war dream has kept itself up-to-date by incorporating my move through time to its advantage. After I'm redrafted, I try to explain that I am sixty-nine years old—as I did last night—but my plea is rejected as untrue. My good health makes it ridiculous that I should be excused. And when I tell the Army authorities that I'm a disabled veteran, the papers that would prove my claim are unavailable, and my scar is discounted as evidence.

Father Rathbone was a priest without charity. But the priest from Boston who visited me in Cheltenham had no trouble imagining I might not want to go to Mass. He just wanted to be sure I wasn't bitter, and when I said, "I love life," he answered, "There's a blessing." What a difference. Rathbone bothered me, but not for long. Good things were ahead of me. I was operated on in a few days. This one was a simple excision of scar tissue. I was up and around in no time, working the calf muscle to get it loose. From that point on, I'd be responsible for bringing the leg as close to normal as possible.

Ten days after the operation, I was given a month's furlough, beginning immediately. It took me no time to get ready and on the move. The cross-country bus ride from Longview to Mobile took fifteen hours, but I didn't mind the long trip. I was going home, and the bright sense of returning filled my mind during every mile. Along with my mother, father, and Edward, Robert was there, home from VMI to welcome me with the rest of the family. He would begin his tour in the Merchant Marine as soon as the spring term ended.

I have never known a more relaxing time than the month I spent in Mobile. My leg was coming along fine, and I was cheerful about it, even though it still needed some building up, and I was to limp for many months to come. Step by step the surgeons had made it look like a leg again. I was well enough to enjoy myself completely. The family meals, going to the movies with Robert, playing catch with Edward, swimming and fishing for speckled trout in the Gulf with my father and brothers, reading, telling my parents about the slow but steady progress of the wound, catching up on news from my father about his shipbuilding job (soon to end), and hearing about books and family from my mother— such things filled my days.

My last weeks in the Army were spent at Camp Upton, in Yaphank, New York, the same post to which the Long Island Railroad had taken me as a recruit almost two years before, when I had turned away from the noisy men around me and heard "I Walk Alone" with my mind's ear. By then, Upton was no longer an induction center, but a convalescent hospital. After the orthopedics people in Longview had finished their work, I was sent there to complete my recovery. The days were easy. Following a few morning chores, I'd spend my time in the Upton theater program, which was run by a bit-part character actor, Art Smith, who was a nice man and a good director. He was a good actor, too. We put on a musical, written by a couple of soldiers who planned a career in show business—*Show Time in New York* was the name of it. I had a small part in just one simple number, so I didn't develop my usual performance anxiety.

My only line was "Pleeza, no squeeza da banana," which I enjoyed saying.

During one of our rehearsals, Melvin Douglas visited us. He looked pouchy-eyed and indifferent, but it was fun to see him there as a colonel.

A few days before *Show Time* began its three-night run, the Japanese surrendered—on August 14—and within a short time, the Army began discharging us, first following a point system that took into account length of service, combat time, and other factors. But soon they were sending us home as fast as they could process our papers. I was called in and told formally that I was to be discharged on September 1, 1945. Though I expected the good news, hearing it filled me with a rush of pleasure. I laughed out loud. My life would obviously not be free of all constraints, but I was delivered from the Army's moment-by-moment control, with all that implied. Quickly packing a single duffle bag, I headed for the brick house in the Bronx to which my family had returned from Mobile some weeks before. But not Robert. By that time he had sailed the Atlantic, his ship had picked up a French infantry unit, and they traveled east through the Suez and beyond. The French troops were headed for Dien Bien Phu, in North Vietnam. My journey to the Bronx was quick. I was home within three hours, in time for dinner with my mother and father. At last the War had let me go. The family seemed safe again.

Epilogue

Late in the night a piercing phone call ripped
Me out of sleep. I heard a formal voice
Pronounce my brother Robert dead. It gripped
My soul, checking my breath, left me no choice
Except to hear—transfixed. Death's penetrant
Alarm rang shrill that night, and still alive
Tears through my head—I hear a permanent
Last cry. No known economy could thrive
Like Death's to stay time's power to repair,
Compel the wasting spirit to retreat,
Renew the wearing echoes of despair,
Sound and resound the ultimate defeat.
Though Death's song rends, I nourish his bequest,
Fiercely unwilling to accept his rest.

ON THE MORNING OF November 28, 1946, the *New York Times* printed the story of an accident on page 20. Inaccurate in its particulars, it is nevertheless correct in the main point. My brother Robert had been killed.

Lexington, Va. Nov 27 (AP)—

Cadet Robert X. Pagliaro of the Bronx, N.Y., 19-year-old third classman at Virginia Military Institute, was accidentally killed late last night when he stuck a lighted stick into a Civil War cannon, igniting some powder.

Maj. Gen. Richard J. Marshall, superintendent, said today that Cadet Pagliaro was one of several who had left the barracks without permission to investigate a report that a

225

delegation of students from another school were coming to "paint V.M.I."

The story goes on to say something about an Honor Guard of four cadets who were sent to accompany the body to New York, where funeral services were to be held, and it says something about Robert's service in the Merchant Marine, but it says nothing about why there was powder in a Civil War cannon. When later we spoke to the four young men who brought my brother's body home, we were told that there had been a customary torchlight parade in anticipation of the Thanksgiving Day football game, in which the cheerleaders, Robert among them, carried the torches. It was also the custom, they said, for the torchbearers to snuff out the lighted sticks by thrusting them into the nearest cannon muzzle, of which there were several along the route of the march. Robert chose a cannon in which an explosive had been placed by three cadets, who made themselves known right after the accident. They had manufactured the gunpowder themselves, in the chemistry lab. Though they had intended to set off the charge during the parade, they found themselves afraid to do so. General Marshall's story to the *New York Times* was obviously intended to protect the Institute against possible suit, but of course we never sued. It would have been too much like making money from Robert's death.

Telling you about Robert's death this way—telling the "facts"—gives me control of the terrible event by keeping me outside it. There are other insulating facts. My mother and father wanted Robert to have a Roman Catholic burial, but they didn't like the idea of his body's going into the reclaimed land of Saint Raymond's Cemetery, made up of incinerated garbage, the designated site for burial of the dead in the parish we lived in. The pastor would not hear of an alternative, Woodlawn Cemetery, because it included no consecrated ground. Impatient with technicalities, my parents bought a plot on a pleasant hill in Woodlawn, turning away from the Church. Another fact: Burt Lancaster's brother died within a day of Robert's death, and the two were laid out in the same funeral home near Fordham Heights. I had never seen or heard of Lancaster, who was just then making his reputation, but I felt sympathy for his handsome face in sorrow. Another fact: Robert died at night between Tuesday and Wednesday of one week, and I returned to classes at Columbia on Tuesday of the week following, trying to get back into a rhythm of life in some ways hopelessly broken.

By November of 1946, I had decided finally against engineering, and I was groping my way towards an academic career in literature. Things were not quite settled for me, but I was beginning to make choices that reflected my deepest interests, and I was beginning to feel that I could be both useful and involved in my work. Robert telephoned a couple of days before he died, and we talked about the future. He enjoyed hearing my new plans, and then he talked about himself. He told me that his second tour at VMI was not going well. After his service in the Merchant Marine, he could no longer take the discipline of the military academy. It seemed to him childish and mindless, calling not for strength of character, but for a willingness to be absorbed into a system of endless coercion. Unfortunately, it was not easy to get into college then, with the GI Bill supporting many thousands of former service men and women who had filled the classrooms of the Academy. So Robert would have to stay where he was until a transfer was possible. I hung up thinking of him as ready to make a change that would bring him, like me, close to a choice of career.

During the night of November 26–27, I was awakened by the telephone. Jarred into alertness, I ran down the steps from my bedroom to the landing just above the dining room, and picked up the receiver. An official sounding voice said, "This is the

Commandant of Virginia Military Institute. Are you a relative of Cadet Pagliaro?"

"Yes," I told him, "I'm his brother."

He then said, "I have very bad news. Cadet Pagliaro has been mortally wounded in a cannon explosion."

I stood still, choking, with my mouth open, while the message ran deeper and deeper into me. Then I must have groaned. By that time my father was by my side. He took the phone, and I was close enough to hear the same message repeated.

"I have very bad news. Cadet Pagliaro has been mortally wounded in a cannon explosion."

It was pathetic that my father asked, "How bad is it?"

"Mortally" is Italian and English at the same time. He knew what "mortally" means in both languages. He probably knew it in Latin from his days as an altar boy. He just couldn't know it then. It was too much to ask of him. And my mother. And Edward. Robert can't be dead. He can't be dead. That's the idea that went through our heads for days. He can't be dead. But he was.

I was on the ropes for months, going through the motions of living, feeling down and empty. Nothing made me happy, not food or people or work. The war had already left its mark on me, but Robert's death burned the memories deep—one of my worst fears realized. How could this have happened? I kept asking the question, compulsively, as if some answer could wipe away the grim truth. Nothing was right, and it seemed to me then that nothing could ever be right again. Robert was dead, and I felt dead, too.

Gradually, though, I began to look around. The world was full of life. I was young and had a life of my own to build. My old energy started to return. I began to enjoy my food. And I started to think about women again. It didn't happen fast, but my life began to take on a rhythm I looked forward to. Though nothing would ever blot out the war, I realized I had a lot to be grateful for—health and a vitality no defeat short of death could take away. What I had told the good priest from Boston was true—I love life. I stopped using my energy in gloom. Instead, I began to use my mind the way Oliver and I used to do—looking at things, feeling, and thinking about what I felt.

I wanted to give a real shape to my life—to commit myself to a profession that would quicken the best part of me in useful work. Now, I think I might have been an engineer or a teacher or anything that would have consumed my energy and made me feel useful. But at the time the choice seemed crucial. By then I knew my mother wanted me to teach literature, and of course my father wanted me to be an engineer. I thought about both possibilities, and others besides. When I finally decided to work towards a Ph.D. in English, I was sure I'd made a rational decision. But later I realized my mother had influenced me so deeply toward literature that my choice was preordained. And so was my satisfaction, especially during the early years of my career. I've never regretted the choice. It's only that in later years I began to understand that all work done in the right spirit pleases God.

My life has been rich—my wife, my children, my work, and my private thoughts. I know I'll never forget my terror at the front and its awful fulfillment in Robert's death. But somehow, being lowered to the depths of fear and sorrow makes me cherish life all the more, and in some unexplainable way it makes me understand it better, too. My fascination with the past sometimes pulls me back, but much more often it gives texture to the moment, making life more abundant than it would otherwise have been. My experience of war has been a fountainhead of life, a terrible baptism I would not trade for anything, even if I could—though neither would I repeat it for anything.

Sometimes I've tried to put its worst memories to rest, but I've never had much luck. Thinking about the nightmares that see me drafted gets me nowhere. In fact, it may help the dream to keep itself up-to-date, having me age in good health and in good enough condition for Army life. Talking about it to other people in real terms never appealed to me until I began to talk about it in this book. Maybe that will help.

Once, only three years ago, my wife thought I might like to follow the route my outfit had taken in the autumn of 1944. We gave it a try, revisiting all the places from Raville to Erckartswiller. Raville was the only one of the dozens of villages we visited that hadn't changed at all. The others were all modernized—renovated houses, new houses, new hotels. But not Raville, probably because it was poor and out of the way of tourists. For whatever reason, time had stopped there. The place seemed dead. The buildings were all the same. You could spot the patched-up artillery holes in stone walls. I showed my wife the barn where I'd eaten and slept, where the great old sow had been slaughtered, where I was dragged to church by the Cajuns, and where Roper and the schoolmistress had their love affair. But I didn't like being there, and we left after ten minutes.

On the same trip, we rented a house in Uberach, about twenty minutes by car from Erckartswiller. We drove to the old battleground, moving slowly down the mountain road where T-5 Lane kept us in touch with Headquarters as he nervously handled his radio. I looked over the flat clearing where we had dug holes in a circle before attacking the village we never saw. I guessed where Roper and I had dug in, and I looked for the place where the young tank man was blasted, and for the stump Lynch sat on. But things had changed. The woods where I'd gone for a prisoner were thinned out, and Erckartswiller turned out to be the smallest village I'd ever seen in the Vosges—nothing mysterious about it. The whole experience revived dark feelings, but it did nothing to help me.

But something good happened the next morning. I met a man, an old soldier, who confirmed my double sense that the war would always be with me and that it made me richer, even though it held me in its grip. I was on the train platform at Obermodern, headed for a day in Strasbourg. Not two minutes after I got there, a neatly dressed man, at least eighty, came up and spoke in rapid French. I had a hard time following, but I got most of what he said. After wishing me a good morning, he told me he'd served with the Free French in several battles nearby. He had wounds from two different battles. The second, a head wound, was serious. To show me where he'd been hurt, he placed his left index and middle fingers in the sizeable scarred dent in his forehead. The memory of the wound still gave him pain. His eyes were a lively blue, but the left one, directly under the scar, was less expressive than the right. The nerves there were dead. He was a slight, intense man, with fine features, no more than five feet seven. I could tell his skin, weathered tan and dry, had been fair, and his white hair, cut short, had been blond. There was something about him outside the run of time. He had a mission—to recite his remembrance of the War. Though he was compelled to talk, he was not otherwise irrational. The past worked through him, and he spoke it as it came.

He mentioned Sarrebourg, and I remembered that I'd seen a large Free French unit there about a week before we went to Erckartswiller. A few days later, they'd cut behind us to take the Saverne Gap before going on to Strasbourg, while we protected their flank. That's when he got the head wound. So he and I had been hit at close to the same time, in nearby battlefields.

"Were you in the war?" he asked, abruptly. I was surprised. He'd seemed completely self-absorbed. But then I realized he wasn't changing the subject at all.

"Yes, I was wounded at Erckartswiller, in early December."

"Aaah! Erckartsville!" He pronounced the name slowly in French, raising his right hand gently, his good eye wide open. He conferred a blessing on me. We were part of the same brotherhood. The old man lived inside the War, without a letup. He made me see I was outside. But I knew where he was coming from.

Index

(*continued*)

Colophon

Design and typography by Tim Rolands
Cover and title page by Teresa Wheeler

Text and display set in Adobe Minion,
designed by Robert Slimbach

Printed and bound by Edwards Brothers,
Ann Arbor, Michigan